"Cool Deliberate Courage"

"Cool Deliberate Courage"

JOHN EAGER HOWARD

IN THE

AMERICAN REVOLUTION

By
Jim Piecuch and
John H. Beakes, Jr.

HERITAGE BOOKS
2020

HERITAGE BOOKS
AN IMPRINT OF HERITAGE BOOKS, INC.

Books, CDs, and more—Worldwide

For our listing of thousands of titles see our website at
www.HeritageBooks.com

Published 2020 by
HERITAGE BOOKS, INC.
Publishing Division
5810 Ruatan Street
Berwyn Heights, Md. 20740

Copyright © 2009 Jim Piecuch and John H. Beakes, Jr.

Heritage Books by Jim Piecuch and John H. Beakes, Jr.:
"Cool Deliberate Courage" John Eager Howard in the American Revolution
"Light Horse Harry" Lee in the War for Independence:
A Military Biography of Robert E. Lee's Father

Heritage Books by John H. Beakes, Jr.:
De Kalb: One of the Revolutionary War's Bravest Generals
The European Diaries of Kendall Douglas Beakes, 1944–1951
Kendall Douglas Beakes. Re-transcribed and Edited by John H. Beakes, Jr.
A History of One Branch of The Beakes Family in America, 1682–1996
Otho Holland Williams in the American Revolution

Library of Congress Control Number: 2009937045

The portrait of John Eager Howard on the cover is courtesy of the
Cowpens National Battlefield of the National Park Service.
The Battle of Hobkirk's Hill painting on the cover is courtesy of Pamela Patrick White.
The portraits in this book are reproduced courtesy of Independence National Historic Park.

All rights reserved. No part of this book may be reproduced or transmitted in any form or by any means, electronic or mechanical, including photocopying, recording or by any information storage and retrieval system without written permission from the author, except for the inclusion of brief quotations in a review.

International Standard Book Number
Paperbound: 978-0-7884-5893-4

DEDICATIONS

To Rosemary Beakes, my wife of forty-three years, whose love and support make everything possible.

John H. Beakes, Jr.

In memory of my late grandmother, Elsie Collins Martineau, a great storyteller.

Jim Piecuch

ACKNOWLEDGMENTS

Several librarians and archivists have provided invaluable assistance with the research on John Eager Howard. Francis P. O'Neill, Reference Librarian, and Elizabeth Proffen, Curator of Special Collections at the Maryland Historical Society handled my many requests for information with patience and professional excellence. Bonnie Coles of the Library of Congress is a splendid public servant, respectful of our nation's heritage and extremely effective in supporting those who study it.

The illustration of a part of The Battle of Hobkirk's Hill was painted and reproduced with the permission of Pamela Patrick White, 1330 Bunker Hill Road, Everett, PA 15537.

CONTENTS

Introduction 1

Chapter One
Baltimore's Farewell to a Revolutionary War Hero 7

Chapter Two
Campaigning in the North 11

Chapter Three
Battling for South Carolina 31

Chapter Four
Triumph at the Cowpens 47

Chapter Five
The Race to the Dan 69

Chapter Six
Guilford Courthouse 81

Chapter Seven
The Second Fight for Camden – Hobkirk's Hill 99

Chapter Eight
The Final Campaign 113

Chapter Nine
Politician and Businessman 133

Illustrations .... between 46 and 47

Epilogue 147

Bibliography 149

Index 161

INTRODUCTION

When General George Washington reviewed the strategic situation in September 1779, it seemed likely to him that the British high command would soon make a major effort in the southern colonies. The commander-in-chief of the Continental Army confided to Major General Benjamin Lincoln, who commanded Continental forces in the South, that "Southern operations appear to have been for some-time past a favourite object in the British cabinet. The weakness of the Southern states affords a strong temptation; the advantages are important and inviting." [1]

Realizing that the British might be committed to a major effort in the South was one thing, but responding to such a move in an effective manner was something else. When the British began to send sizable forces to the South by sea a few months later, Washington wanted to send a strong reinforcement to Lincoln, but he found that he could not provide anything close to the numbers that the British were able to send southward from New York. Writing to Congress on April 2, 1780, Washington described how thinly his troops were stretched in the northern theater, but recommended that "notwithstanding these Objections perhaps something should be hazarded" to support the American Army in the South. He then reported that "I shall therefore put the Maryland line and the Delaware Regiment under marching Orders immediately," and asked Congress's concurrence with his decision. [2]

Congress gave its assent, and on April 16, 1780, the Continental infantry units from Maryland and Delaware, about 1,400 infantrymen plus officers and support, marched out of their camps around Morristown, New Jersey, and headed toward the southern theater. They were commanded by Major General Baron Johann De Kalb, an experienced French officer who had accompanied the Marquis De Lafayette on his trip from France to America in 1777. [3]

Among the field officers with these units was twenty-seven-year-old Lieutenant Colonel John Eager Howard, whose battlefield prowess over the coming year-and-a-half would raise his name from relative obscurity to wide recognition across the length and breadth of the country. Currently serving as the deputy commander of the 2nd Maryland Regiment, Howard had been on active service since the summer of 1776, and in those four years he had performed capably, earning the respect and confidence of those who knew him. There was little flash or sparkle about him. He did his job, did it well, and didn't make much fuss about it. [4]

Although it was not yet obvious to most of the men around him, the heart of a formidable warrior beat within the breast of this quiet soldier. There had been one brief instant in Pennsylvania, at the Battle of Germantown in October 1777, when a discerning observer might have realized that there was something special about this man's performance in combat, but the instant where he led a surge past the Chew

House was so brief, and so obscured by other events, that most people missed it. On that day, Howard had taken over regimental command when his colonel was injured, and had led his troops in an aggressive assault that penetrated deep into the British position. That brief moment at Germantown had been the harbinger of how this fine combat soldier would perform in the months ahead, when he would time and again stand with his steady troops at the point of greatest danger, and would unfailingly meet the challenge with steadfast valor, unflappable calm, and unerring decision-making. [5]

DeKalb and his command reached Petersburg, Virginia in early June, where they received the bitter news that the city of Charleston, South Carolina, and with it the entire Continental Army in the South, had surrendered to the British in May. Recognizing that their objective had now changed from helping defend Charleston to resisting British efforts to dominate the South, De Kalb led his little force into North Carolina. Here he encountered two problems that would continually plague the Continental troops for the remainder of the southern campaign—the difficulty of achieving coordinated operations between the Continental units and state militias, and the constant shortage of provisions. The southern terrain and climate also introduced new elements into strategic considerations, particularly the importance of the great rivers of Virginia and the Carolinas to movement in the region.[6]

As he surveyed the Southern theater from his post in New Jersey, Washington understood instinctively that the rivers of the South were important keys to victory. Four years earlier, when his army had lost the campaign for New York City and been chased in full retreat across New Jersey, Washington had been saved by his foresight in understanding how to use the Delaware River as part of his defensive strategy. Long before his men reached this river, he had sent parties ahead to capture all the boats for miles around, and they were ready to carry his exhausted army to the safety of Pennsylvania when they arrived at the river. With all the boats in the hands of the Americans, the British pursuers had no way to get across, and therefore had no choice but to allow Washington and his tiny force the chance to lick their wounds and prepare to fight another day. After his men had spent a few days resting and regrouping, Washington used that same river as part of his offensive strategy, when it served as a highway to carry his army to the lightning surprise attacks on Trenton and Princeton in December 1776 and January 1777. [7]

This eminently practical Virginian had traveled up the Potomac River into the backcountry many times in his youth, and his great Mount Vernon estate looked down over a wide expanse of that mighty waterway. He knew from personal experience how vital the fording places, the ferries, and the boats that plied the rivers could be to controlling an area, and he understood how any rainstorm in the mountains or the melting snow in the spring could create a raging torrent as water rushed from the mountains to the sea. From his own experience, Washington had a deep appreciation of how to plan military maneuvers that used the ever-changing dynamics of the large rivers to advantage, as he shared in one of his letters to his subordinate, Major General Nathanael Greene, just after Greene had been ordered to take command of the Southern Army in late 1780:

> *"(if the Enemy should continue to harrass those parts of Virginia which are intersected with large navigable Rivers) I would recommend the Building a number of flat bottomed Boats of as large a construction as can be conveniently transported on Carriages; this I conceive might be of great utility, by furnishing the means to take advantage of the Enemys situation by crossing those Rivers which would otherwise be impassable."* [8]

Greene had been with Washington during the New York-Trenton-Princeton campaigns, and had personally witnessed the success that came from his commander's astute use of the Delaware River. Greene's own experience was undoubtedly reinforced by Washington's advice to pay heed to the rivers and control of the boats, and he demonstrated a voracious appetite for information about the rivers from the moment that he first learned he would be in command in the South. As a result, the coming southern campaign would reveal a number of instances where a retreating American army would be shielded by a river and have a monopolized use of all the boats, while a pursuing British force would have to break off the chase while their prey rested safely on the other side. [9]

While grand strategy was the purview of senior commanders like Washington and Greene, regimental commanders like John Eager Howard were charged with the day-to-day operations that kept the men ready to fight, moved them quickly to where they needed to be, and managed their actions when they were in actual combat. In the seventeen months between April 1780 and September 1781, John Eager Howard would compile an exceptional record as a combat infantry commander and day-in, day-out regimental leader. George Washington had laid out the standard for regimental commanders early in the war:

> *"It will not do for the Commanding Officer of a Regiment to content himself, with barely giving Orders, he should see (at least know) they are executed. He should call his men out frequently and endeavour to impress them with a Just and true sense of their duty, and how much depends upon subordination and discipline."*

Howard continually met this demanding standard, and the troops under his command demonstrated their discipline and grit on many occasions. When his troops needed to be trained in the techniques devised by Baron Friedrich von Steuben for maneuvering and fighting, Howard insured that his men developed the requisite skills, which led one historian to observe that "No officer of this hard fighting army used the bayonet so freely as he." When his men were overwhelmed by a victorious British army, Howard remained calm and determined, and began immediately to collect and organize his remaining troops to prepare for the next round of combat. In short, whether he was in camp, on the march, or leading his proven troops on the battlefield, John Eager Howard could always be counted upon to employ his men to the best possible advantage, no matter how dire the situation. One historian who carefully studied the southern campaign called him "one of the finest regimental commanders in American history," and another has referred to him as "the outstanding American infantry commander of the war." Nathanael Greene's grandson, George Washington Greene, described Howard as "a man of excellent parts, sound judgment, a bearing in which equanimity bordered close upon reserve, and a cool deliberate courage which made him particularly useful in the decisive moment of battle."[10]

Essentially, regimental commanders of Continental troops made the difference between victory and defeat in the set-piece infantry battles of the eighteenth century. There are many romantic stories associated with the Revolutionary War in the South, such as the partisan forays of Francis Marion and Thomas Sumter, and the nattily clad cavalry of "Light Horse Harry" Lee galloping across the countryside creating havoc wherever they could. However, while these contributions were important to the ultimate American victory, none of them, together or separately, was enough to win the War for Independence. Unless the long lines of tough, red-coated British soldiers could be dealt with on the formal field of battle, the colonies would never triumph. The British army, despite the best efforts of militia commanders such as Marion, Pickens, Clarke, and Davie, had the strength to control an area they occupied until they were challenged by a comparable fighting force. To win this war, the American army would have to show that it could stand toe-to-toe with their British foes and prevail in straight-ahead infantry combat.[11]

A hard-fighting American brigadier general named Daniel Morgan devised an ingenious battle plan at the Cowpens, South Carolina, that made the strength and resilience of the Continental Line even more vital. In Morgan's arrangement (which was copied in several subsequent battles in the South,) militia units and lightly equipped riflemen were positioned in the front lines and ordered to fire a few volleys and then retreat, all for the purpose of slowing down and weakening a strong British infantry attack. After the British troops had suffered casualties and tired themselves fighting through these initial lines of defense, they would come face-to-face with a line of sturdy Continental infantry, whose purpose was to meet the full brunt of the British attack, and smash the assaulting ranks. The performance of the Continental infantry in these few crucial minutes of the battle would determine victory or defeat, and it was here that the performance of John Eager Howard was unparalleled in the history of the war.[12]

Morgan's design depended ultimately on the Continental infantry and regimental commanders like Howard. The leaders had to keep troops steady and alert in the nervous moments while they waited in battle formation for the fighting up ahead to be completed, and for the enemy to appear in their front. They had to maintain strict discipline and issue clear, crisp orders for the men to maintain their formation and fire coordinated, concentrated musket volleys. In the critical moments of a battle, even when there were surrounded by ghastly scenes of blood, gore, death and destruction, they had to be able to think clearly and seize the precise moment to launch a deadly bayonet attack that would lead to victory. Howard's fame as a combat infantry commander came from his superb performance in these situations.

This is the first book devoted to the military contributions made to the American Revolution by John Eager Howard. The narrative can only be pieced together from a small number of documents that have lain largely unexplored for over two hundred years. Constructing the story from these snippets of history is something like stitching together the remnants of an old battle flag—the pieces are fragile and there are missing details where a segment has been lost and there are sections that bear the scars of enemy musket balls and artillery rounds. Accordingly, there will be parts of the story where Howard is lost to sight for a time, as the historical record does not provide detailed descriptions of his specific actions within the larger sweep of the narrative. Still, just as with the old battle flag, the broad outlines can be seen very clearly, and the story can be told from the parts that remain.

Any story written about the American Revolution inevitably shows the overriding influence of George Washington. One largely unstudied matter is how he guided the transition from the largely unorganized force that he inherited around Boston in 1775 to the tough, highly professional army that prevailed at Yorktown six years later. John Eager Howard received his military education while serving in this Army, and the commander-in-chief had made clear his expectations in his General Orders of May 8, 1777:

> *"Officers, attentive to their duty, will find abundant employment, in training and disciplining their men—providing for them—and seeing that they appear neat, clean and soldier-like—Nor will any thing redound more to their honor—afford them more solid amusement—or better answer the end of their appointment, than to devote the vacant moments, they may have, to the study of Military authors."* [13]

Accomplished professional officers like John Eager Howard did not spring to full maturity just by donning a uniform. They worked hard, and studied military subjects diligently throughout their service. Most importantly, they learned from experience. Washington understood what it took to learn the art and science of soldiering, and he steered his young officers along that path throughout the war.

In addition to insuring that young officers worked diligently at developing their military skills, Washington's leadership methods helped him to find and promote able young men like Nathanael Greene, Henry Knox, and the Marquis de Lafayette, and to weed out officers who were unlikely to contribute to the success of American arms. Washington did all he could to foster an environment where professional competence and battlefield performance were the primary paths to advancement, and it was in such an atmosphere that a man like John Eager Howard would rise to prominence.

The publisher and authors of this book believe that further study of many of the men who served under Washington will provide valuable insights into the Revolution, particularly in the South, which has not been studied as extensively as the war in the North. Accordingly, our work on John Eager Howard is intended to be the first in a series on individuals who made significant contributions to the success of George Washington's army. For the first hundred years after the Revolution, the deeds of men like Howard were well known and taught throughout the land, but these stories are now largely forgotten. These men deserve to be remembered. They persevered for years, in perilous times, with scant resources and in the face of bitter discouragement and loss. Yet they prevailed against overwhelming odds, and left succeeding generations the priceless heritage of a nation of free people.

---

1 George Washington to Benjamin Lincoln, September 28, 1779, George Washington Papers, Library of Congress (hereafter LOC), Washington, DC (quotation).
2 Washington to Continental Congress, April 2 1780, Washington Papers, LOC, (quotations).
3 Washington to Robert Howe, April 13, 1780, Washington Papers, LOC; Otho Holland Williams, "A Narrative of the Campaign of 1780," in William Johnson, *Sketches of the Life and Correspondence of Nathanael Greene, Major General of the Armies of the United States in the War of the Revolution*, (Charleston: A. E. Miller, 1822), 1:485.
4 Rieman Steuart, *A History of the Maryland Line in the Revolutionary War 1775-1783* (Baltimore: The Society of the Cincinnati of Maryland, 1969), 98.
5 John Eager Howard to Timothy Pickering, Jan. 29, 1827, in "Colonel John Eager Howard's Account of the Battle of Germantown," *Maryland Historical Magazine*, Vol. 4 (December 1909), 314-320.
6 Williams, *Narrative*. 485.
7 David Hackett Fisher. *Washington's Crossing*. (New York: Oxford University Press, 2004), 134, 214, 267-68.
8 Washington to Nathanael Greene, November 8, 1780, Washington Papers, LOC, (quotation).
9 John Buchanan, *The Road to Guilford Courthouse: The American Revolution in the Carolinas* (New York: John Wiley & Sons, 1997),288-289.
10 Washington to Fisher Gay, September 4, 1776, Washington Papers, LOC; George Washington Greene, *The Life of Nathanael Greene, Major-General in the Army of the Revolution* (New York: Hurd and Houghton, 1871), Vol. 3, 114 (quotation); Buchanan, *Road to Guilford Courthouse*, 162 (quotation); Hugh Bicheno, *Rebels & Redcoats: The American Revolutionary War* (London: HarperCollins, 2003), 202 (quotation).
11 John S. Pancake. *This Destructive War: The British Campaign in the Carolinas, 1780-1782*. (Tuscaloosa: University of Alabama Press, 2003), 49, 117-118, 125-126.
12 Craig L. Symonds. *A Battlefield Atlas of the American Revolution*. (Baltimore, Nautical and Aviation Publishing Company of America, 1986). 90-91.
13 General Orders, May 8, 1777, Washington Papers, LOC.

CHAPTER ONE

BALTIMORE'S FAREWELL TO A REVOLUTIONARY WAR HERO

The steamboat *United States* arrived in Baltimore harbor at two o'clock on Sunday morning, October 14, 1827, carrying the President of the United States, John Quincy Adams. He was returning to Washington after a visit to his home state of Massachusetts. When the President awoke at Barnum's Hotel on Sunday morning, he was looking forward to a relaxing Sabbath before diving into his packed schedule of political meetings and public appearances the next day. However, these plans changed abruptly when he received word from John Eager Howard's family that the old soldier had died just a few days before, on Friday, October 12, at the age of seventy-five. Colonel Howard's brother-in-law, Benjamin Chew, called on the President on Sunday evening to discuss the funeral services, which were to begin on Monday morning at 10 o'clock.[1]

Then, as now, it was very difficult to rearrange the President's schedule, as there were literally hundreds of people expecting to see him at scheduled appointments and events. Yet President Adams instantly recognized that paying tribute to an important member of the Revolutionary generation should take precedence over anything else on his schedule. He immediately ordered that all other events on his calendar be deferred so that he could pay his respects to the nationally esteemed veteran. The Chief Executive then composed a gracious note to the Howard family, writing that the entire nation would learn with universal regret of the death of one so "eminently adorned with the honours of the cause of Independence."[2]

The next morning, Monday, October 15, dawned crisp and clear, and the President rode in his carriage to Belvidere, Colonel Howard's home north of the city, where the body lay in state. President Adams somberly paid his last respects, and then stepped out onto the well manicured grounds of the Howard estate, where he joined "great multitudes of the citizens" who had gathered to form the funeral procession. Leaders of the city and state took their places in the long line, as did military units from Fort McHenry and elements of the Maryland militia. Once underway, the mourners moved from Belvidere to Old St. Paul's Cemetery, making "a circuit thorough the principal streets of the City." The crowd was so large that President Adams thought that the entire population of Baltimore must have either been in the procession or watching from the curb or windows along the route.[3]

This ceremony was the city's farewell to a revered Revolutionary warrior, whose battlefield exploits were still remembered, even though they had occurred almost fifty years earlier. John Eager Howard had faced the gravest dangers on many a battlefield with steely determination, practiced military skill, and an exceptional ability to remain calm, grasp the moment, and deliver the decisive blow with devastating effectiveness. It was written of this funeral procession that the "military appeared in fine order," and that "the hollow beat of their muffled drums told that a soldier had gone to his rest."[4]

While Howard's name had first risen to prominence when he was an infantry commander during the Revolutionary War, he had been a citizen-soldier in the finest sense of the word. Born on the Howard farm about ten miles northwest of Baltimore Harbor on June 4, 1752, he had not grown up with dreams of martial glory, nor had he viewed the military as a path to fame or advancement. Instead, when the War started in 1775, he had been a typical twenty-two-year-old son of an upper middle class Maryland family, preparing for a life of planting, harvesting, and discharging the social and civic responsibilities of his class. Young Howard did not particularly stand out from the crowd—he had neither the obvious brilliance of an Alexander Hamilton, the swashbuckling derring-do of an Aaron Burr, nor the eloquence and martial flamboyance of "Light Horse Harry" Lee. Howard's abilities were less obvious than those of his gifted contemporaries, and his modest, reserved deportment tended to downplay even further his rock-ribbed sense of determination, an attribute that would rise to full flower in the moments of greatest peril on future battlefields. While Hamilton, Burr and Lee all received university educations, Howard's schooling, like that of George Washington, was an entirely local affair, although he benefited from the teaching and ministry of a formidable Episcopal priest from his region, the Oxford-educated Reverend Thomas Cradock.[5]

Howard and his family were members of St. Thomas Episcopal Church in the Garrison Forest, near Howard's home, where Dr. Cradock was the rector from 1745 until his death in May 1770. In the formative period of his youth, Howard had been taught an ethic of duty and service from Dr. Cradock's pulpit, and these principles helped to establish the foundation on which he built a successful military career.[6]

Cradock believed ardently in the rights of Englishmen, which undoubtedly helped fire the sympathies of young John Eager Howard and many of his contemporaries for the Revolutionary cause. Speaking almost three decades before the official break with England, Cradock had admonished his listeners to remember "that we are Britons; that we are the sons of those who valued life less than liberty, and readily gave their blood to leave that liberty to posterity." Cradock spoke these words in 1747 to commemorate the British victory over the Scots at the Battle of Culloden, but they fit perfectly with the sentiments expressed by the firebrands who led the American drive for independence from Great Britain in the 1760s and 1770s.[7]

John Eager Howard was only twelve years old in 1765 when the British Parliament sowed the first seeds of the Revolutionary War by passing the Stamp Act, the first of many attempts to impose taxes on America to help pay the enormous debt that had accumulated during the French and Indian War. While Howard was growing to adulthood over the next ten years, the American colonies and the government of Great Britain were continually wrangling over taxes, and with increasing acrimony. While he was in his late teens and early twenties, the disagreements moved steadily toward a crescendo. At first, Parliament sought workable ways to collect taxes from the colonies with legislation such as the 1767 Townshend Acts, but the slide toward open warfare became virtually irreversible with events such as the Boston Tea Party in 1773 and Britain's decision to close the port of Boston in 1774. [8]

Young Howard's official involvement with revolutionary activities began when he accepted an appointment to Baltimore County's Committee of Observation in 1774, a duty he shared with his friends John and Thomas Cradock (sons of the rector) and his cousin Mordecai Gist. The organization's primary responsibilities were to insure that people did not violate the embargo on trade with Britain and that merchants did not unfairly raise their prices to take advantage of the situation.[9]

Marylanders also began to prepare for possible war with Britain. In December 1774, the colony's Provincial Convention ordered citizens of the colony to prepare for armed resistance, urging all of the province's male inhabitants between the ages of sixteen and fifty to organize themselves into companies of sixty-eight men, choose commissioned and noncommissioned officers, "and use their utmost endeavors to make themselves masters of the military exercise." It recommended that each volunteer be equipped "with a good firelock [musket] and bayonet ... half a pound of powder, two pounds of lead ... and be in readiness to act on any emergency."[10]

While Marylanders prepared themselves for military service, fighting broke out between British troops and American militia at Lexington and Concord, Massachusetts, on April 19, 1775, and news of these events reached Maryland nine days later. On July 26th, the Provincial Convention issued the "Association of the Freemen of Maryland" and directed the county committees of observation to circulate the Association for people's signatures. By signing, an individual pledged "to repel force by force" if the British took further military action against the colonies. Those who refused to sign the Association, labeled "Non-Associators," were required to pay increased taxes and surrender their firearms. While John Eager Howard's own commitment to the revolutionary cause never wavered, his family came to represent the divided nature of the population when his younger brother Cornelius refused to sign the Association, stating that he would not sign because he did not support mob actions such as destroying tea.[11]

In spite of family differences, Howard continued to work actively in support of the Revolutionary movement and to impress others with his leadership ability. He had joined the militia by December 1775 and was elected second lieutenant in the 5th Company of Baltimore County. His duties with the committee expanded to include gathering arms and ammunition to prepare for military operations. In March 1776 he and John McLure procured wagons to carry "eight Boxes arms & ten reems cartridge paper," and the two men took steps to obtain "a ton of lead." Howard's increasing prominence in Maryland caused confusion between himself and another prominent Marylander, John Beale Howard, so about this time Howard began to use his middle initial or full middle name in his correspondence, a practice which he maintained for the rest of his life.[12]

By May 1776 it had become clear that the British government intended to subdue the colonists by force, so Howard and the Baltimore committee began to take additional steps to defend the colony. On May 13 the committee urged the Council of Safety to allow eight companies of Baltimore militia to form a battalion and asked the Council "to appoint field officers for them."[13]

Just a few weeks later, on July 2nd, 1776, the Continental Congress resolved that the United States were henceforth independent of Great Britain, and two days later, the delegates signed the Declaration of Independence. The events of the past decade, from the Stamp Act protests to the creation of a new provincial government, had gradually drawn John Eager Howard and many of his fellow Marylanders on the long journey from being loyal servants of the British crown to becoming men who had forsaken all allegiance to Great Britain. Americans had joined together in open rebellion, and Howard had been actively involved in the revolutionary movement for over a year-and-a-half. Now it was time to take the final step—to don a uniform, leave behind the comforts of home, and march northward to join the fight.

---

1 John Quincy Adams, *The Diary of John Quincy Adams, 1794-1845* (New York: Longmans, Green & Co., 1929), 309.
2 John Quincy Adams to Howard Family, Oct. [14], 1827, Bayard Papers, Maryland Historical Society, Baltimore (hereafter MHS).
3 Thomas J. Scharf, *The Chronicles of Baltimore, Being a Complete History of Baltimore Town and Baltimore City from the Earliest Time to the Present Day* (Baltimore: Turnbull Brothers, 1874), 424; John Quincy Adams, *Diary*, Oct. 15, 1827, 309-10 (quotations).
4 Scharf, *Chronicles of Baltimore*, 424 (quotation); "Sketch of Colonel Howard," [c. 1833], Bayard Papers, MHS (quotation).
5 "Papers used in preparing the Biography of J. E. Howard. October 1833," Bayard Papers, MS 109, Box 2, MHS; Rev. Ethan Allen, *The Garrison Church. Sketches of the History of St. Thomas Parish, Garrison Forest, Baltimore County, Md.* Rev. Hobart Smith, ed., (New York: J. Pott & Co., 1898), 8.
6 Allen, *Garrison Church*, 347; Donald Enholm, David Skaggs, and W. Jeffrey Welsh, "Origins of the Southern Mind: The Parochial Sermons of Thomas Cradock of Maryland, 1744-1770," *Quarterly Journal of Speech*, Vol. 73 (1987), 212.
7 Allen, *Garrison Church*, 23-24 (quotation).
8 Aubrey C. Land, *Colonial Maryland: A History* (Millwood, NY: KTO Press, 1981), 246-248, 259, 296, 298, 300-01, 303; "Proceedings of the Conventions of the Province of Maryland, Held at the City of Annapolis in 1774, 1775, & 1776," *Archives of Maryland*, Vol. 78 (Baltimore: James Lucas & E. K. Deaver, 1836), 4.
9 Dawn F. Thomas, *The Greenspring Valley: Its History and Heritage. Vol. 1: A History* (Baltimore: Maryland Historical Society, 1978), 126-127.
10 *Proceedings of the Conventions of the Province of Maryland, held at the City of Annapolis, in 1774, 1775 & 1776.* (Baltimore: James Lucas & E. K. Deaver and Annapolis: Jonas Green, 1836). *Archives of Maryland*, Volume 78, 8-9 (quotations).
11 Land, *Colonial Maryland*, 304-05, 306 (quotation); "Journal of the Maryland Convention July 26 to August 14, 1775," in William Browne, ed., *Archives of Maryland*, Vol. 11 (Baltimore: Maryland Historical Society, 1892), 4, 15-16; Henry C. Peden, *Revolutionary War Patriots of Baltimore Town and Baltimore County, 1775-1783* (Silver Spring, MD: Family Line Publications, 1988, v; McHenry Howard, "Joshua Howard and his Children."
12 Peden, *Revolutionary War Patriots*, 304; John McLure and John Eager Howard to the Maryland Committee of Safety, March 12, 1776, in "Journal of the Maryland Convention," 240 (quotation).
13 "Journal of the Maryland Convention," 422 (quotation), 448, 496 (quotation).

CHAPTER TWO

CAMPAIGNING IN THE NORTH

Earlier, June of 1775, the Second Continental Congress had assumed control of the thousands of American volunteers who had mustered outside of Boston in the wake of the April battles at Lexington and Concord, Massachusetts. Designating this force the "Continental Army," Congress appointed George Washington of Virginia its commander-in-chief on June 15. Maryland contributed its first troops—two companies of riflemen—to the Continental Army in the summer of 1775. A year later, as it became clear that a major British offensive loomed, Maryland sent more soldiers to assist Washington. On July 10, 1776, six Maryland companies under the command of Colonel William Smallwood marched from Annapolis. They were joined at Head of Elk, the northernmost reaches of Chesapeake Bay, by three additional companies from Baltimore. The combined force arrived in New York on August 8 and reported to General Washington for assignment.[1]

Washington welcomed the reinforcement, since he was facing a very serious threat. He forced the British to evacuate Boston in March 1776; the garrison sailed to Halifax, Nova Scotia to await the arrival of a fleet and army from Britain. By mid-August 370 British transports, supported by 73 warships of the Royal Navy, had carried 32,000 troops to the New York area. Their commander, General Sir William Howe, established his initial base of operations on Staten Island. He intended to seize New York and operate from there to drive a wedge between New England, which British leaders considered the heart of the rebellion, and the colonies west and south of the Hudson River. Washington anticipated Howe's plans and began shifting troops from Massachusetts to New York even before the British left Boston. However, he faced a dilemma. If he deployed his whole army on Manhattan Island, the British could occupy Long Island unopposed and threaten New York City from Brooklyn Heights, while if Washington placed his entire force on Long Island, the British could use their naval superiority to cut off the Continental Army. Washington decided to compromise, sending about half of his army to Long Island and keeping the remainder on Manhattan.[2]

The Continental Congress reacted to the emergency at New York by ordering the creation of a "flying camp" of 10,000 men. A flying camp was a force designed to move quickly where needed, unencumbered by heavy equipment. Congress recommended that Pennsylvania furnish 6,000 men for this unit, Delaware, 600, and Maryland, 3,400.[3]

In response to Congress's request, the Maryland Convention resolved on June 25 that "this province will furnish 3405 of its militia, to form a flying camp, and to act with the militia of Pennsylvania and the Delaware government … from this province to New York inclusive." The act thus restricted the troops from going into New England and also stipulated that the troops' term of service would expire on December 1, 1776, unless Congress discharged the men earlier. Like many Americans in the early days of the war, the members of the Maryland Convention hoped that it might all be over in a few months.[4]

John Eager Howard's service with the Continental Army began with the formation of the flying camp. The Convention appointed Brigadier General Rezin Beall to be commander of the unit, which was organized into four battalions and one additional company. On July 16, the twenty-four-year-old Howard was commissioned a captain in the Second Battalion, commanded by Colonel Josias Carvil Hall, who would serve with Howard for much of the war. Lieutenant Colonel William Hyde was the battalion's second-in-command, and the major was Howard's boyhood friend, John Cradock. Company officers were responsible for enlisting the men they would command, and on July 17 at Baltimore Hyde accepted the thirty volunteers that Howard recruited. Howard's popularity in Baltimore was such that he was able to recruit his entire company in a single day.[5]

According to his sister, Howard could have been commissioned at a higher rank, but refused the offer to serve as a colonel or major because he realized that he did not yet have the knowledge or experience to hold such a position. Howard, in a display of modesty and common sense rarely seen among officers in the War for Independence, declared that "he thought he could do very well" as a captain "but did not know that he could do as well in a higher [rank]."[6]

Before setting out for New York, Howard had to arrange for his own financial support while on active service. He sold a parcel of land in Baltimore, received payment in gold, and turned the money over to his younger sister, Violetta, so that he could draw upon the funds "as he wanted it for his expense in the army."[7]

The Maryland flying camp reached New York City in August, 1776, at about the same time that Smallwood's troops arrived. Beall and Smallwood immediately engaged in a dispute over rank, with Beall rejecting the Convention's suggestion that he act under Smallwood. The contentious commanders, however, were soon distracted from their quarrel when British forces began landing on Long Island on August 22. Washington rushed ten more regiments from Manhattan to reinforce the defenders under Major General Israel Putnam, bringing the Continental force there to about 9,000 men.[8]

Putnam left about half of his men on Brooklyn Heights and advanced the others to the Heights of Guan. This forward position was vulnerable to a flanking attack, and Howe quickly took advantage, sending 10,000 men on a night march to strike the exposed American left. The next morning, August 27th, the British assault overwhelmed the Americans. Smallwood's Marylanders performed heroically (although Smallwood himself was away on other duty), making a determined stand at Gowanus Creek despite being heavily outnumbered. Howe rejected his generals' advice to continue the attack and did not assault the second American line on Brooklyn Heights.

Washington withdrew his army from Long Island on the night of August 29.[9]

Howard and his unit were posted away from the fighting and did not see action in the Battle of Long Island or the subsequent combat at Kip's Bay on September 15 or at Harlem Heights the following day. These defeats forced Washington to abandon New York City and retreat north to White Plains. He occupied three hills overlooking the town, deploying his 14,500 men in a line three miles long. Howe approached the position early on October 28 after a leisurely march of seventeen miles in ten days. Washington decided to force an action and sent 1,500 New England soldiers forward to engage Howe's troops. The British advance guard, composed mainly of German troops hired by the British government to augment its manpower, commonly known as Hessians, soon drove the Americans back.

The New Englanders retreated to Chatterton's Hill, a commanding position a half mile west of Washington's line. Realizing that he would have to retreat if the British seized the hill, Washington had already dispatched troops to fortify the summit. As more British troops reached the field, he ordered an additional brigade that included William Smallwood's Marylanders to reinforce the position. When the British launched their attack, Smallwood's troops and a New York regiment moved downhill and assailed a Hessian unit struggling to cross the Bronx River. This maneuver checked the British assault, but another Hessian unit supported by cavalry drove off the American regiments on the extreme right of Washington's line. The American forces had no choice but to retreat. At this moment Captain John Eager Howard led his company into what was very likely his and its first taste of combat. Howard and his company covered Smallwood's retreat as he and his men abandoned Chatterton's Hill and returned to the main American line. They probably suffered few losses since Howe did not mount an aggressive pursuit. Washington abandoned his position at White Plains during the night of October 31.[10]

The Continental Army now began to melt away as demoralized soldiers returned to their homes. Washington lamented on November 3 "that there are some Soldiers, so lost to all Sense of Honor, and Honesty, as to leave the Army, when there is the greatest necessity for their services." He asked for his officers' assistance in putting an end to desertion and forbade the granting of leave, but to little avail. Leaving part of his army farther up the Hudson River under Charles Lee, who had returned from his service in the South, Washington crossed the Hudson into New Jersey with the remaining troops. Against his better judgment, Washington deferred to the advice of subordinates, particularly General Nathanael Greene, and left a strong garrison at Fort Washington isolated on the New York side of the River. Howe stormed the post on November 16 and captured its 3,000 defenders along with a large quantity of supplies. Washington, with few options remaining, had to abandon Fort Lee on the western bank of the Hudson and began a withdrawal across New Jersey. Pursuing British troops captured between 90 and 100 Americans, mostly from Howard's flying camp. General Greene attributed their capture to the "irregular and undisciplined" nature of the flying camp's men.[11]

The Continental Army continued to dwindle in size, and the Maryland flying camp departed for home the day that their enlistments expired, December 1. This was a deep disappointment to Washington, who wrote to Lee that day that "the Enemy are advancing, and have got as far as Woodbridge and Amboy [New Jersey] .... The force I have with me, is infinitely inferior in Number and such as cannot give or promise the least successful Opposition. It is greatly reduced by the departure of the Maryland flying Camp men." Three days later, Greene criticized the Marylanders for leaving the army at such an important juncture, noting that they "left us at Brunswick, notwithstanding the enemy were within two hours' march and coming on. The loss of these troops at this critical time reduced his Excellency to the necessity to order a retreat again." Greene, noting that the Army could muster no more than 3,000 men, declared that the loss of the flying camp troops provided "convincing proof of the folly of short enlistments." To Washington and Greene, the Marylanders' departure showed a lack of commitment to the Revolutionary cause, but the soldiers believed that they had served their time and were entitled to return home.[12]

Having lost the Maryland flying camp, and with the militia refusing to turn out in a situation they considered hopeless, Washington ordered Lee to join him with the 5,000 troops under his command. Lee dawdled, finally began the movement, and riding well ahead of his men, was captured by British cavalry on December 13 at a tavern where he had stopped for the night. With his army dwindling daily, no prospect of reinforcement, and the pursuing British at his heels, Washington crossed the Delaware River into Pennsylvania. He wisely gathered up all the boats for miles along the eastern bank to prevent the British from following him across. Howe, satisfied with his victories, followed tradition and called an end to the campaign for the winter. He dispersed many of his British and Hessian troops in garrisons across New Jersey.[13]

The British—and many Americans—believed that the struggle was all but over. John Eager Howard may have harbored similar feelings. The New York campaign had been frustrating; relegated too often to inactive sectors, Howard could do little more than carry out his routine duties and await news of the Army's battles, news that was invariably bad. The only combat he had seen was while covering a retreat after one of the army's many defeats. Under these circumstances, and given the Revolution's bleak prospects, it would have been understandable if Howard had chosen to end his military service. But his sense of duty would not allow it.

Upon returning home with the Maryland flying camp, Howard learned that the Continental Congress had asked Maryland to furnish seven regiments for the next year's campaign. On December 10th, 1776, Howard accepted a commission as major in one of these units, the 4th Maryland Continentals. His former commander in the flying camp, Josias Hall, was the regiment's colonel. Howard must have been reluctant to return to military service, because his colleague and postwar correspondent, Lieutenant Colonel Henry "Light Horse Harry" Lee, wrote in his memoirs that Howard acted "in obedience rather to the wishes of the State Commissioners, than to his own inclination."[14]

General George Washington remained determined to continue the struggle. He concluded that only a victory could revive the revolutionaries' flagging spirits, so he undertook a daring operation to achieve it. On the night of December 25, Washington ferried most of his remaining troops across the Delaware River in a cold, biting wind, and then divided them into two columns to approach the town of Trenton, New Jersey, from different directions. The 1,600 Hessian soldiers posted at Trenton were caught by surprise. American artillery swept the streets, preventing the Hessians from forming their battle line. About 500 escaped; over 900 were captured and the rest were killed. The Americans suffered only a handful of casualties. Washington withdrew back across the Delaware with his prisoners and a large quantity of captured supplies.[15]

Inspired by the victory, the state militias began to turn out again, and Washington decided that he was strong enough to continue the offensive. He crossed the Delaware a second time on December 30th with his strengthened force and marched to Trenton, where he learned that Howe had dispatched 6,000 British troops to drive the American troops from New Jersey. The British thought that they had trapped Washington with his back to the Delaware late in the day on January 2nd, 1777, but the American commander found an escape route and made a night march along the frozen New Jersey roads to strike the British garrison at Princeton. Two British regiments advancing from Princeton encountered Washington's attacking force on the morning of January 3rd. They managed to fight their way through the American lines and meet other British units advancing from Trenton; Washington captured most of a third British regiment that had been left at Princeton. As a result of these defeats, Howe decided to abandon most of New Jersey and concentrate his forces closer to New York. Washington marched north to Morristown, New Jersey, and established his winter camp there. In just ten days, his victories had turned the American situation from defeat and despair to victory and optimism.[16]

Washington's success eased Howard's task of recruiting volunteers for the 4th Maryland. Howard and the regiment's other officers filled the ranks, organized the recruits, and trained them for the coming campaign. In early April, Howard marched part of the regiment northward and joined Washington's army at Rocky Hill, New Jersey, near Princeton. Washington had decided to await General Howe's move, so the Continentals did little other than maneuver. On June 30th, Howard received news that his father, Cornelius Howard, had died on June 14th. Colonel Hall, "supposing I might have business of my own that required my attention, sent me down to superintend the recruiting service," Howard later recalled. He reached Baltimore on July 9th or 10.[17]

John Eager Howard, as the oldest surviving son, had to attend to his father's estate as well as handle recruiting duty. Although it was common practice in the eighteenth century for a man to leave the bulk of his property to his oldest male heir, Cornelius Howard provided generously for his wife and all of his surviving children. John inherited ten lots in Baltimore and three slaves: Jason, Dinah, and Nat. Three Baltimore lots that Cornelius left to his wife, Ruth Eager Howard, would revert to John upon Ruth's death.[18]

While Howard was home in Baltimore, the British army finally moved. General Howe had told officials in London that he would open the 1777 campaign with a march overland to attack Philadelphia. Instead, he spent June and half of July maneuvering in northern New Jersey in an effort to bring Washington to battle on favorable terms. When it became clear that Washington would not expose his army in a manner that would make a British victory certain, Howe withdrew to New York and decided to move his forces to Philadelphia by sea. The British army of 13,000 men sailed from New York on July 23. Howe first sailed into Delaware Bay, concluded that a landing there was too risky because Washington had anticipated him and deployed his army in the vicinity, then turned back to make his approach via the Chesapeake Bay.[19]

With the British fleet approaching the mouth of the Patapsco River, residents of Baltimore became alarmed that their city might be Howe's target. Local officials turned to twenty-five-year-old Major Howard to deal with the emergency. Howard calmly assessed the situation and recognized that a lack of troops made Baltimore indefensible. On August 21, he informed John Hancock, president of the Continental Congress that the British fleet was visible from Baltimore's court house, and that observers had counted from 60 to 200 vessels (Howe's fleet actually numbered 260 ships). Howard reported that he was "employed with what officers are in Town in providing waggons to remove the Treasury—This appears to me to be an object of great importance .... If it is possible, I shall endeavor to remove the [military] stores from this place."[20]

Brandywine

Howard's precautions proved unnecessary, as Howe ignored Baltimore and landed without opposition at Head of Elk at the northern end of Chesapeake Bay. Washington placed his army south of Philadelphia, blocking the main road to the American capital with 8,000 Continentals and 3,000 militia. The American forces were deployed behind Brandywine Creek, where there was no bridge; the road crossed a shallow portion of the stream at Chadd's Ford.[21]

Employing the tactics he had used on Long Island, on September 11th Howe left the Hessians to demonstrate on Washington's front while 8,000 British veterans under Major General Charles, Earl Cornwallis, marched northwesterly to an upper ford. The forest screened Cornwallis's movement, so that the British were across the Brandywine and preparing to attack when Washington learned of their presence. The

American general hastily repositioned his troops, but it was too late. The British triumphed after a hard fight that cost Howe five hundred casualties. Washington's losses were more than twice as high.[22]

Major Howard rejoined Washington's army a few days after the Battle of Brandywine. As General Howe was advancing to secure the Lancaster Road near Goshen, Pennsylvania, Washington put his troops on the same road, trying to menace the British left. On the morning of September 16, learning that Howe was approaching, Washington put his whole army "in motion for the purpose of meeting and engaging them in front." Howard and his troops were present, but the engagement did not last long. The advanced guards of both armies met and opened fire. Howe extended his line and attacked both American flanks and a British victory appeared to be unfolding when a torrential rainstorm brought the fighting to a halt. The Americans withdrew.[23]

Howard later attributed the Americans' difficulties in what was often referred to as the "Battle of the Clouds" to the poor quality of their weapons. "The ... inferiority of their arms ... never brought them into such imminent peril as on this occasion," he wrote. "Their gun locks not being well secured, many of their muskets were soon unfit for use," while their badly constructed cartridge boxes did not keep their ammunition dry, and the army was "rendered thus totally unfit for action."[24]

After ten days of further maneuvering, Howe forced Washington to abandon Philadelphia. The Continental Congress fled to York, Pennsylvania, and British troops marched into Philadelphia on September 26.[25]

Germantown

The commander-in-chief, having been reinforced by 1,000 Continentals and 2,000 militia, was contemplating an offensive. Howe, apparently having learned little from the disasters at Trenton and Princeton, had again divided his army. One detachment was operating south of Philadelphia, clearing American defenses along the Delaware River that blocked the Royal Navy's access to the city. A second group occupied Philadelphia, while the third and largest, about 8,000 men, had taken up a position at Germantown, about seven miles north of Philadelphia. The countryside was open, but Howe did not order the troops to entrench, although a few units constructed light earthworks. Washington, being well-acquainted with the area, considered the position vulnerable and determined to attack.[26]

The British line extended for about five miles, from the Schuylkill River on the left or southwestern flank to the Old York Road on the right, northeastern flank. Germantown lay approximately at the center of the line. Washington intended to take advantage of the road network to strike the British from four points. General John Armstrong would lead 1,500 Pennsylvania militia down the Manatawney or Ridge Road, along the Schuylkill, to keep the British units there occupied, while General William Smallwood would lead a similar number of Maryland and New

Jersey militia on the Old York Road to tie down the British right. Two divisions of Continentals commanded by General John Sullivan of New Hampshire, consisting of Sullivan's own brigades of Maryland, Delaware, and Pennsylvania troops, and General Anthony Wayne's two brigades of Pennsylvanians, were to advance down the Philadelphia Road toward Germantown and strike the British there. The main blow, however, would be struck by General Nathanael Greene's divisions, composed mostly of Virginia Continentals. Greene's orders were to advance down the Lime Kiln Road and attack the British forces east of Germantown. If the plan worked, Greene's blow would shatter the British line and force it back so that he could swing to the west and, said Sullivan, the enemy "must have been pushed into the Sculkill or have been compelled to Surrender."[27]

Washington began forming his troops at seven o'clock on the evening of October 3. From their camp at Methacton Hill, the various units would have to march between 14 and 25 miles in the cloudy darkness of the new moon to reach their designated attack positions by the appointed time of 5 a.m. on October 4. The complex plan and confusing tangle of roads, complicated by poor visibility, slowed the march of all of the columns, and both of the Continental detachments found themselves on the wrong routes, resulting in further delays. Meanwhile, the British received intelligence of the impending attack. Howe alerted his subordinates and shifted the position of a few units, but did little else to prepare for battle. Some British officers took the warnings more seriously and dispatched patrols to watch for the approach of Washington's army.[28]

John Eager Howard and the 4th Maryland Regiment formed part of Sullivan's division. Two of Sullivan's brigade commanders, Smallwood and Mordecai Gist, had been assigned to the Maryland militia for the operation, so Colonel John Hawkins Stone acted as commander of the 1st Maryland Brigade and Colonel Moses Hazen assumed command of the 2nd Maryland Brigade, which included the 4th Maryland Regiment. Along the route of march, Sullivan allowed his tired men a brief halt to rest and avoid any British patrols that might be lurking in the thick fog. At that time he also distributed the rum ration, the traditional eighteenth-century method of fortifying troops for battle.[29]

Having gotten his division on the proper road, Sullivan approached Mount Airy, where the British 2nd Light Infantry Battalion had an outpost. The column was well behind schedule; Howard noted that the sun had already risen, "but was soon obscured" by a thickening fog. British pickets spotted the Continentals advancing through the mist and sounded the alarm. Two pieces of artillery posted near the Allen family's house east of the road opened fire on the Americans, bombarding them with six-pound shot as Sullivan's forward units shifted from column to line of battle. The artillery fire "killed several persons," Howard noted, and also signaled both armies that the fight had begun.[30]

The British fell back while Sullivan formed his division. Stone's brigade moved down a lane to the far right, and Hazen's took position on their left, with Colonel Josias Hall's 4th Maryland situated at the eastern end of the line about two hundred yards from the Allen house. "Soon after being formed," Sullivan sent orders for the division to advance. Moving across an open field, the Continentals approached "the encampment of the British Light Infantry in an orchard, where we found them formed to receive us," Howard explained. "A close and sharp action commenced." General Wayne's troops were supposed to advance alongside the Marylanders and cover their left, but had not yet arrived, enabling the British to send troops east of the road to outflank Hall's regiment. Seeing this maneuver, Sullivan rushed the 6th Maryland to his left to check the attack. With their flank secure, the Continentals exchanged volleys with the 2nd Light Infantry for at least fifteen minutes, at which point "the British broke and retreated." Howard reported that the 4th Maryland had several men killed, and four officers and more than thirty privates wounded, in this action.[31]

When the British troops east of the road fled, most of their comrades on the left also pulled back, and the 6th Maryland returned to its position farther to the right. This put the 4th Maryland on the left flank once again. During their advance, Hall's regiment angled to the left. The company on the extreme flank, commanded by Captain Daniel Dorsey, crossed the road and engaged some British troops who remained behind and had taken refuge behind houses. Hall wanted to recall Dorsey's company, and sent Howard, his second-in-command, because Lieutenant Colonel Samuel Smith was on detached duty. Howard rode to the scene, and after assessing the situation, "judged it not proper to call them off, as it would expose our flank." Howard returned to Hall with his report. The colonel, who was on foot, demanded to borrow Howard's horse and declared that he would fetch Dorsey's troops himself. Hall dashed off, and because he was "riding one way and looking another, the horse run him under a cider-press, and he was so hurt that he was taken from the field." Howard assumed command of the regiment.[32]

Wayne's troops finally came into action on Sullivan's left, their commander, according to historian Thomas J. McGuire, having apparently "decided to act independently on this morning." The Pennsylvanians launched a furious assault, driving back the British light infantry and 5th Regiment. Howe rushed the 40th Regiment forward to strengthen the line, but Wayne's Continentals overwhelmed them.[33]

With his left flank covered at last, Sullivan ordered his men to resume the advance. The British had partially recovered from their earlier reverse, and Sullivan observed they "made a Stand at Every Fence wall & Ditch" as they fell back. The Continentals dismantled the fences as they moved forward, but were delayed by the need to remove these obstacles. Eventually they reached the abandoned British camp and pushed through it, capturing the two six-pounder cannon that the British had hauled back from Mount Airy.[34]

Howard led his men past "Cliveden," the stone country house of Pennsylvania's royal chief justice, Benjamin Chew. "We were fired at from the upper windows but received no injury," Howard wrote. The Marylanders continued to advance for another four or five hundred yards "to an orchard, where we were halted by Colonel Hazen.[35]

Thus far Sullivan's and Wayne's troops had performed splendidly, driving the enemy and inflicting considerable losses, but now Washington's plan began to unravel. When Wayne's Pennsylvanians shattered the 40th Regiment, its commander, Colonel Thomas Musgrave, rounded up about a hundred men and took refuge in the Chew house. These were the troops who had fired ineffectively on Howard's regiment. Musgrave posted men at all the windows on the first and second floor and in the basement, with orders to fire on the Americans and bayonet any enemy soldier who tried to enter the building.[36]

Not long after Musgrave occupied the Chew house, Washington and his staff reached the field in the rear of Sullivan's and Wayne's troops. Halting about two hundred yards north of the house to observe the fighting, Washington could see Sullivan's troops firing volleys into the fog, but could not discern their British opponents. "I am afraid General Sullivan is throwing away his ammunition," Washington told his aide Timothy Pickering. The commander-in-chief sent Pickering forward to tell Sullivan to cease firing. Pickering did so, and it was probably this command that resulted in Hazen ordering his brigade to halt.[37]

Riding back to Washington, Pickering came under fire from the Chew house and noticed American artillery beginning to fire on the building. Pickering found Washington in the middle of a debate over how to handle the British forces in the house. Several officers urged Washington to bypass the structure and press the attack, but Brigadier General Henry Knox, the army's chief of artillery, argued that it was too dangerous to leave a fortified position in the rear of the army. Washington deferred to Knox, and more artillery was ordered up to bombard the house. The cannonade tore through doors and windows without seriously damaging the thick stone walls. Musgrave's troops remained concealed until the American artillery ceased fire to allow the infantry to attack; the British then rushed to the windows and shot down the Continentals of the 1st and 3rd New Jersey Regiments. A desperate attempt to set the Chew house on fire also failed.[38]

The delay at the Chew house might not have been consequential if Greene had been on the scene to deliver the main attack. However, the Rhode Island general's misdirected march did not bring his forward units to the field until the battle was raging around the house. Howard's regiment and the rest of Sullivan's division remained idle, and unopposed by the British. "We were halted so long that our men sat down some time, being greatly fatigued by having been on their feet from seven o'clock the preceding evening," Howard wrote. Wayne's division, meanwhile, having heard the roar of cannon and musketry in their rear, believed that the British were counterattacking from that direction and withdrew. As they traversed the ground toward the Chew house, General Adam Stephen's brigade from Greene's detachment saw them moving through the fog and mistook them for British troops. Stephens's troops opened fire, Wayne's Pennsylvanians, similarly confused, responded with their own volley, and for several minutes Washington's troops fought one another while the British regrouped.[39]

On the far left of the American line, Smallwood and Gist with the New Jersey and Maryland militia encountered elite British troops: the loyalist Queen's Rangers and the light infantry and grenadier companies of the Guards Regiment. Some of the militiamen fought well, while others fled, and the British soon drove back the attackers. With reinforcements coming forward, Howe's counterattack pressed Greene's front and left flank. These Continentals held for a while, but the disarray on their right caused by Stephens's mistaken contest with Wayne allowed the British to move forward. With both flanks now threatened, Greene fell back. Sullivan's men, left as idle spectators, could not see the British forces gathering opposite their position until they emerged from the shroud of fog and attacked the division's right flank. Sullivan described the ensuing chaos: "Their Cartridges all Expended, the force of the Enemy on the Right Collecting to the Left to oppose them, being alarmed by the firing at Chews House so far in their Rear" and by shouts that the British had surrounded them, the division "retired with as much precipitation as they had before advanced" despite "Every effort of their Officers to Rally them."[40]

Only one of Sullivan's regiments retained its organization, Howard's 4th Maryland. Although he had never before exercised command on the battlefield, the twenty-five-year-old Howard kept his soldiers in position and under control until he received orders to retreat. The regiment then retired in good order. As they passed opposite the Chew house, "the enemy sallied out ... and fired on our rear." Unfazed, Howard ordered some of his troops to face about, "and gave them a fire, which killed the Officer in front, and checked them. We retreated at leisure."[41]

By ten o'clock that morning, the battle was over. The British pursued the Americans as far as Whitemarsh before halting. Washington had lost about 1,000 men at the Battle of Germantown, about twice as many as the British, but the army's morale actually improved afterwards. The soldiers knew that they had fought well, and many believed that only the fog and the British good luck in securing the Chew house had prevented Washington from achieving a victory.[42]

For John Eager Howard, the day's fighting must have inspired mixed feelings. Doubtless he was disappointed in the battle's outcome, yet he must have taken pride in his own performance. Thrust unexpectedly into regimental command, he had led his troops in a successful attack and kept them in order during the subsequent retreat. He had shown excellent judgment when he rejected the order to have Dorsey's company withdraw, because he clearly saw that this would endanger the 4th Regiment's flank. He had been cool in stopping the attack from the Chew house during the withdrawal of his unit. The Battle of Germantown gave Howard his first real chance to lead a sizable force in combat, and he demonstrated the self-possession, tactical skill, and clear judgment that became his hallmarks as an infantry commander on the battlefield.

Saratoga

The Continental Army's morale received another boost a few weeks later, when word arrived that their northern brethren had won a decisive victory over the British at Saratoga, New York. In June 1777, General John Burgoyne marched from Montreal, Canada, with 7,000 British and Hessian troops. Burgoyne planned to move down Lake Champlain, seize Fort Ticonderoga near the lake's southern end, and then advance down the Hudson River to Albany, New York. This accomplished, New England would be isolated at last and the rebellion brought closer to its end. Although Burgoyne did not expect assistance from Howe, his plan was predicated on Howe's keeping Washington fully occupied.[43]

Burgoyne's campaign began well. He moved rapidly on Ticonderoga, occupied Mount Defiance which commanded the fortress, and forced the Americans to evacuate the post on July 5. Then the situation changed. Moving at a pace of barely a mile a day through swamps and forest where the Americans had destroyed every bridge and felled trees to block the roads, Burgoyne's supplies began to run low. The Americans took advantage of Burgoyne's slow progress to assemble thousands of militiamen, while Howe's own dilatory maneuvers allowed Washington to reinforce the northern army with a unit of Virginia riflemen under Colonel Daniel Morgan. When Burgoyne dispatched some of his Hessians to gather supplies, the American militia soundly defeated them on August 14 at Bennington in present-day Vermont, a battle that cost Burgoyne 900 men.[44]

A month later, Burgoyne crossed to the west bank of the Hudson, but a few days later found his progress blocked by Major General Horatio Gates and 7,000 troops, most of them Continentals, occupying a strong position north of Saratoga. Burgoyne tried to fight his way through but was defeated on September 19. Burgoyne attacked again on October 7th, was repulsed, and the American counterattack captured some of the fortified British positions. With his effective force reduced to less than 5,000 men and Gates's army reinforced to nearly four times that number by thousands of militia, Burgoyne surrendered on October 17th. American confidence soared, as did hope that Britain's ancient enemy, France, might at last come to the aid of the revolutionaries.[45]

Washington encamped his army at Whitemarsh, Pennsylvania, to watch General Howe. The British commander, however, showed no inclination to undertake a major offensive. While the Continentals waited, John Eager Howard became involved in an altercation with Captain-lieutenant Patrick Duffey of the 4th Continental Artillery, and wound up facing a court-martial.

There is no record of what caused the dispute between Howard and Duffey, but the provocation must have been great for Howard to have responded in such an uncharacteristic manner. At the court-martial on December 3rd, 1777, Howard was charged "1st with wounding Capt. Lieut Duffy with his Sword; 2d Abetting a riot in Camp; and 3d in front of his Men at his request assembled attempting the life of Capt with a loaded firelock and fixed Bayonet being utterly subversive of Good Order and Discipline." After hearing the evidence, the court decided "that Major Howard did not intentionally wound Capt. Duffy, and therefore acquit him of the Charge." On the second charge, the court declared that "they are of Opinion however Justifiable the Motives were by which Major Howard was first actuated his Conduct in that End was such as tended rather to promote than suppress a riot they therefore Sentence him to be reprimanded in Genl. Orders." Howard was acquitted of the third charge, and the court's language in their ruling on the second charge clearly indicated that the officers believed Howard had a good reason to behave as he did toward Duffey.[46]

Duffey was brought before the same court-martial on charges of abetting a riot and assaulting and abusing Howard. The court found Duffey guilty of the first charge and sentenced him to a reprimand in general orders. On the second charge, Duffey was found not guilty on the grounds that Howard was "not in the execution of his office" when Duffey assaulted him. Duffey continued to cause problems, and was finally dismissed from the service in October 1781 for "Scandalous and Infamous behavior unbecoming the Character of an officer ... Being drunk; Rioting in the street; Abusing a French soldier; And acting in a seditious and disorderly manner."[47]

A few weeks after the incident with Duffey, Howard and the Marylanders separated from the main army when General Washington took most of his troops into winter quarters at Valley Forge, Pennsylvania. The commander-in-chief sent the Maryland troops to Wilmington, Delaware, where they were spared much of the suffering that their comrades experienced during the difficult winter of 1777-78. Still, it was not an easy time for the Maryland Continentals. Captain William Beatty wrote that in Wilmington the soldiers "fared very well as to the quarters but the duty Was very hard & the troops Very bare of Clothing." Fortunately, a few days after reaching Wilmington, a British vessel ran aground on the banks of the Delaware River and the men secured "a valuable Prize of cloathing &c."[48]

The troops also got the opportunity to receive needed training. In early 1778, self-styled "Baron" Friedrich von Steuben, a former Prussian officer with extensive knowledge of European infantry tactics, arrived at Valley Forge to teach the American soldiers a new system of drill that included battlefield maneuvers and the effective use of the bayonet. Commander-in-Chief George Washington enthusiastically supported these endeavors, urging Congress to appoint von Steuben inspector general of the Continental Army so that the Prussian could institute a "uniform system of manual and manoeuvres" for the Continental Army. Once von Steuben, who became the army's third and moste effective inspector general, had adapted the European techniques to suit the more individualistic Americans and conducted initial training with a small, hand-picked cadre of troops, the system was taught to the entire army, most of which was encamped at Valley Forge. However, Washington did not forget his Maryland troops in Wilmington, and he sent one of von Steuben's principal assistants, the Marquis de Fleury, there to train them. From Fleury the officers and men of the Maryland Line learned von Steuben's system for maneuvering and using the bayonet, skills that they would employ with deadly effectiveness for the remainder of the war.[49]

The winter provided time for training, but it also saw the troops afflicted with disease while squabbles broke out among the officers. George Lux of Baltimore informed General Nathanael Greene in April 1778 that "Our Division of Marylanders at Wilmington, from what I can learn, are declining fast, for their numbers are much reduced." Worst of all, Lux reported, "Genl Smallwood is very unpopular among them, owing to his Stateliness and excessive Slowness of Motion." Smallwood had recently issued orders that no officer should call on him for any reason except "between the Hours of 3 and 6 in the Afternoon—a pretty Condition he would be in, were the Enemy to attack him in the morning. I am pretty confident," Lux continued, "that he is not liked by a single Officer in the Division." Lux, who considered Smallwood a friend, was at a loss to explain the general's behavior, and thought it would be best if Smallwood resigned. Howard made no comments about Smallwood. In the wake of his confrontation with Duffey, he had probably reverted to his usual quiet, unassuming manner and preferred to avoid conflict whenever possible.[50]

When the Maryland Continentals rejoined Washington's army at Valley Forge in June 1778, many men had not yet recovered from their winter ailments. The 4th Maryland arrived with 455 men, but only 269 were fit for duty. The regiment did not remain long at Valley Forge; Washington had already dispatched troops to watch for enemy movements, and by June 18, the last of the Continental forces left the camp when the commander-in-chief learned that the British were evacuating Philadelphia.[51]

The Americans were reaping the fruits of the Saratoga victory. The French government, now convinced that the revolutionaries could succeed, saw an opportunity to strike a blow at their European rival. On February 6th, 1778, France signed a treaty recognizing the independence of the United States and entered the war as an American ally. Britain now had to prepare for a global war against the United States, France, and very possibly, France's ally Spain. General William Howe, stung by criticism of his slow pace of operations, resigned. He was replaced by General Sir Henry Clinton. Clinton, along with his appointment to command all British forces in North America, received orders to send 5,000 troops to Canada to replace Burgoyne's lost army, 5,000 to the West Indies to protect the valuable sugar islands, and 2,000 to Pensacola in West Florida to guard against possible Spanish intervention. Recognizing that he could not hold both New York and Philadelphia with his diminished force, the British government gave Clinton permission to evacuate the latter city and concentrate the army in New York.[52]

Washington hoped to attack the British army as it marched across New Jersey. Slowed by their long train of wagons and intensely hot weather, the British covered only five or six miles a day. They reached Monmouth Court House on June 27, with Washington only a few miles behind them. The American general decided to strike the British as they began their march the following morning.[53]

Charles Lee, who had returned from captivity after a prisoner exchange with the British a month earlier, took command of the Continental Army's advance units. His 5,400 men attacked the British on the morning of June 28th, but Clinton, who had guessed Washington's intentions, met the Americans with 6,000 of his own troops. Lee began to fall back, and when Washington reached the scene and found his troops retreating, the commanding general became enraged. He dismissed Lee (who was later tried by court-martial and cashiered from the service) and ordered a renewal of the assault. The fighting continued until late afternoon, with neither side able to gain an advantage. Each army suffered approximately four hundred casualties. The British continued their march the next day, satisfied that they had conducted a successful rear guard action. Washington's troops were equally proud of their achievement, having once again stood solidly against their opponents. John Eager Howard was a spectator at Monmouth. Washington had assigned the 4th Maryland to a defensive position at a streambed called the West Ravine, where the men witnessed the fighting but did not participate.[54]

The Battle of Monmouth was the last major engagement in the northern theater. Clinton would not jeopardize the British hold on New York by venturing far from the city with a large force and Washington kept a close watch on the city, hoping for, but never getting, an opportunity to come to grips with the enemy. The stalemate would last until the end of the war. Meanwhile, Clinton and his superiors in London devised a new strategy, one that would draw John Eager Howard and the Maryland Continentals into some of the most intense fighting of the war.

Not long after the Battle of Monmouth, Howard was ordered to Maryland "to take up the recruits," replacements to fill the ranks of the state's regiments. Howard must have spent a considerable time waiting for the new men to be assembled, and possibly in training them. During his stay in Maryland, Howard also reported that he "sold some valuable property to pay my expenses." Both the Continental and state paper currencies had depreciated significantly, and the Continental Congress found it difficult to raise money to pay its officers and men even with near-worthless paper notes.[55]

Maryland officials tried to remedy the deficiency in pay by providing special, additional compensation to the state's Continental officers. When Major Howard finally returned to Washington's army in New Jersey with the recruits in mid-February 1779, he brought along $66,366.66 "for the purpose of paying each officer in the

Maryland Line four hundred dollars being a present from the state of Maryland."[56]

While Howard was absent in Baltimore, Brigadier General William Smallwood's relations with his subordinate officers continued to deteriorate. Late in 1778, Smallwood had Captain Edward Norwood of the Maryland Line tried by a court-martial, whose members ordered that Norwood be discharged from service. Convinced that he had been mistreated, Norwood sought the support of his fellow officers. On December 28th, 1778, the officers signed a letter testifying "that Captain Norwood, (who is discharged the service by sentence of a court-martial on a disagreement with General Smallwood) during the campaigns in which he served with us, has ever conducted himself in such a manner as to command our warmest friendship and esteem, as an officer and a man of honor." The signers also noted that Norwood was "a warm friend and advocate for the liberties of his country." Howard felt strongly enough about the matter to sign the document, as did his two superiors in the 4th Maryland, Colonel Josias Hall and Lieutenant Colonel Samuel Smith. Many other officers from Howard's regiment and the 2nd and 6th Maryland signed the document as well.[57]

Howard probably signed Norwood's paper while he was still in Maryland, as Norwood submitted it, along with his own letter to the *Maryland Gazette*, which published both on January 5th, 1779. Norwood declared that he had been discharged "for only saying General Smallwood was a partial man and no gentleman .... I am sorry to say, such a system of despotism will appear to be springing up in our army, that an officer who does his duty ever so exactly, and has neglected to pay a servile court to a haughty superior, holds his commission by a very precarious tenure."[58]

Smallwood was infuriated by Norwood's criticism and the officers' support for Norwood. He apparently did not shy away from letting the officers know how he felt. The dispute festered for well over a year, and on March 1st, 1780, the Maryland officers became so incensed at Smallwood that they sent him a brief note, asserting that "your scurrilous observations on the testimony we gave of our favorable opinion of Capt. Norwood, discovers that malevolence of presumption, more than the probity and liberality of your mind." Howard signed the note, along with Otho Holland Williams, Benjamin Ford, and several other officers. They had clearly had their fill of Smallwood's pettiness in keeping the quarrel alive. Explaining why some officers had not signed the note, they referred to a missive Smallwood had written earlier: "The other gentlemen, whom you took occasion to abuse in your ungentlemanly performance of 105 pages, are out of camp." Norwood's dismissal had created a massive rift in the officer corps of the Maryland Line.[59]

Howard's involvement in the Norwood-Smallwood controversy did not directly harm his career, as he was promoted lieutenant colonel of the 2nd Maryland Regiment on March 11th, 1779. However, Smallwood may have orchestrated the filing of charges that led to Howard's trial by court-martial in March 1780. The timing indicates that this might well have been the case, since Howard was charged in March shortly after signing the note criticizing Smallwood, yet Howard's alleged offenses had occurred in January.[60]

The winter of 1779-80 was as severe as that experienced by the American army two years earlier at Valley Forge. The Continentals were encamped at Morristown, New Jersey, and suffered through brutally cold temperatures and frequent snowstorms. These conditions may have been responsible for the first charge against Howard, "Disobedience of orders of the 17th., 18th, and 24th. days of January in point of cantoning the battalion or detachment under his care and command and not parading the battalion and remaining with it, or otherwise having it in a state and condition fit for action, agreeable to the orders given him on the evening of the 30th. of January for that purpose." The second charge was that Howard neglected his duty "in not furnishing the morning reports and weekly returns of his battalion at the time ordered and in a correct military manner." The third change was that when Howard drew rum rations for his battalion, he had distributed them to officers' servants and unarmed officers in addition to the combat troops.[61]

The officers of the court heard the testimony, and found Howard guilty of several of the charges. Although he was acquitted of disobedience with regard to his actions on January 17th, 18th, and 24th, he was found guilty of "not remaining with the part that was paraded, and in not having it in a state and condition fit for action." On the second charge, the court found no problem with the timeliness of Howard's reports, but ruled "that in general the reports he furnished were incorrect and unmilitary." Howard was found guilty of the third charge respecting the distribution of rum. The court recommended that Howard be reprimanded in Washington's general orders.[62]

Earlier, George Washington had subtly tried to intervene in the proceedings by requesting that General Arthur St. Clair come to camp and testify at Howard's trial. Then, after the court reached its verdict, Washington took an even more remarkable and uncharacteristic step that further indicates there was something improper about the whole affair—the commander-in-chief overruled the court. Washington declared, he concurred with the court "in the instances in which they acquit Lieut. Colonel Howard, but painful as it is to him at all times to differ from a Court Martial in sentiment, he cannot concur with them in opinion where they find him guilty of disobedience of orders." Washington went on to provide a lengthy justification for Howard's conduct, although he did concede that Howard "was wrong" in regard to the rum rations and that Howard's reports "were incorrect."[63]

Whether Washington was simply trying to remedy a perceived injustice toward a valuable officer or suspected that the charges against Howard were inspired by Smallwood and wanted to send a message that such pettiness was unacceptable, Howard emerged from the incident relatively unscathed. He would soon be facing bigger problems. The British put their new strategy into operation in the autumn of 1778, and it had proven successful. The southern states and the revolutionary cause were facing a serious threat in the spring of 1780, and Washington decided to send the Maryland and Delaware troops to help retrieve the situation.

1   Rieman Steuart, A History of the Maryland Line in the Revolutionary War, 1775-1783 (Baltimore: Society of the Cincinnati of Maryland, 1969), 154.
2   Don Higginbotham, The War of American Independence: Military Attitudes, Policies, and Practice, 1763-1789 (New York: Macmillan Company, 1971), 151-53.
3   Steuart, History of the Maryland Line, 5. The Continental Congress lacked the legal authority to enforce its decisions in regard to raising troops and funds for the Continental Army. Congress could only request that the states furnish a specified number of men or amount of money; compliance was voluntary.
4   "Muster Rolls and Other Records of Maryland Troops in the American Revolution," Archives of Maryland, Vol. 18 (Baltimore: Maryland Historical Society, 1900), 29.
5   Thomas, Greenspring Valley, 1:128-29; Steuart, History of the Maryland Line, 7; "Muster Rolls and Other Records," 53.
6   McHenry Howard, "Joshua Howard and his Children."
7   McHenry Howard, "Joshua Howard and his Children."
8   Steuart, History of the Maryland Line, 154; Higginbotham, War of American Independence, 154-155.
9   Higginbotham, War of American Independence, 155, 158; Howard H. Peckham, The War for Independence: A Military History (Chicago: University of Chicago Press, 1958), 42-43.
10 Peckham, War for Independence, 45; Higginbotham, War of American Independence, 161; Benjamin Chew Howard, "Colonel John Eager Howard of Maryland," unpublished biography, 1870, Item 923.573H849ho1870, Society of the Cincinnati Library, Washington, DC.
11 George Washington, "General Orders, Nov. 3, 1776, George Washington Papers, Library of Congress (hereafter LOC), Washington, DC (quotation); Higginbotham, War of American Independence, 162; Peckham, War for Independence, 45; Nathanael Greene to Gov. Nicholas Cooke, Dec. 4, 1776, in Richard K. Showman, ed., The Papers of General Nathanael Greene, Vol. 1 (Chapel Hill: University of North Carolina Press, 1976), 362 (quotation).
12 George Washington to Charles Lee, Dec. 1, 1776, Washington Papers, LOC; Greene to Cooke, Dec. 4, 1776, in Showman, ed., Papers of Greene, 1:362.
13 Higginbotham, War of American Independence, 163-164.
14 Steuart, Maryland Line, 98; Henry Lee, Revolutionary War Memoirs, 591 (quotation).
15 Higginbotham, War of American Independence, 166-68.
16 Higginbotham, War of American Independence, 169-71; Peckham, War for Independence, 55-56.
17 John Eager Howard to the Executors of Stephen Sheldenmire, June 1, 1809, Bayard Papers, MS 109, MHS.
18 "Last Will and Testament of Cornelius Howard," May 18, 1777, Baltimore County Register of Wills.
19 Higginbotham, War of American Independence, 183-84.
20 John Eager Howard to John Hancock, Aug. 21, 1777, Papers of the Continental Congress, 1774-1789, National Archives Microfilm Publications, Roll 96, Item 78.
21 Higginbotham, War of American Independence, 184-85.
22 Higginbotham, War of American Independence, 185-86; Peckham, War for Independence, 69-71.
23 John Eager Howard to Col. Bentalou, March 4, 1826, Revolutionary War Collection, MHS, MS 1814, Box 11 (quotations); "Papers Used in Preparing the Biography of J. E. Howard, Bayard Papers, MHS.
24 Howard to Bentalou, March 4, 1826, Revolutionary War Collection, MHS (quotations); "Papers Used in Preparing the Biography of J. E. Howard, Bayard Papers, MHS.
25 Higginbotham, War of American Independence, 186.
26 Higginbotham, War of American Independence, 186; Peckham, War for Independence, 71.
27 Thomas J. McGuire, The Philadelphia Campaign: Germantown and the Roads to Valley Forge (Mechanicsburg, PA: Stackpole Books, 2007), 49-50.
28 McGuire, Philadelphia Campaign: Germantown, 46, 52, 53, 54-55, 56-57.
29 John Eager Howard to Timothy Pickering, Jan. 29, 1827, in "Colonel John Eager Howard's Account of the Battle of Germantown," Justin Windsor, ed., Maryland Historical Magazine, Vol. 4, No. 4 (Dec. 1909), 314; McGuire, Philadelphia Campaign: Germantown, 61, 69.
30 "Howard's Account," 314; McGuire, Philadelphia Campaign: Germantown, 65, 67.
31 "Howard's Account," 314; McGuire, Philadelphia Campaign: Germantown, 69.
32 "Howard's Account," 314-15.
33 McGuire, Philadelphia Campaign: Germantown, 69, 71-73, 80-81.

34 McGuire, Philadelphia Campaign: Germantown, 73 (quotation); "Howard's Account," 315.
35 McGuire, Philadelphia Campaign: Germantown, 81-82; "Howard's Account," 315.
36 McGuire, Philadelphia Campaign: Germantown, 82-83.
37 McGuire, Philadelphia Campaign: Germantown, 86.
38 McGuire, Philadelphia Campaign: Germantown, 86-92.
39 McGuire, Philadelphia Campaign: Germantown, 97-99; "Howard's Account," 319.
40 McGuire, Philadelphia Campaign: Germantown, 105-09, 111 (quotation).
41 "Howard's Account," 315.
42 McGuire, Philadelphia Campaign: Germantown, 123-24.
43 Peckham, War for Independence, 60-61.
44 Peckham, War for Independence, 62-65; Higginbotham, War of American Independence, 189-93.
45 Peckham, War for Independence, 66-68, 74-76; Higginbotham, War of American Independence, 194-97.
46 George Weedon, Valley Forge Orderly Book of General George Weedon (New York: The New York Times, 1972), 147-49.
47 Weedon, Valley Forge Orderly Book, 147-49; General Orders, Dec. 3, 1777, General Orders, Oct. 11, 1777, George Washington Papers, Library of Congress.
48 William Beatty, "Journal of Capt. William Beatty. 1776-1781," Maryland Historical Magazine, Vol. 3, No. 2 (June 1908), 119.
49 George Washington to Continental Congress Conference Committee, Jan. 29, 1778 (quotation); Washington to William Smallwood, May 1, 1778, Washington Papers, Library of Congress.
50 Showman, ed., Papers of Nathanael Greene, 2:366-67.
51 Valley Forge Muster Roll, http://valleyforgemusterroll.org/ContinentalArmy/TheRegiments/4thMd, accessed May 15, 2006.
52 Piers Mackesy, The War for America, 1775-1783 (Lincoln: University of Nebraska Press, 1993), 156-57.
53 Peckham, War for Independence, 95.
54 Peckham, War for Independence, 96-97; Higginbotham, War of American Independence, 246-47; Samuel S. Smith, The Battle of Monmouth (Trenton: New Jersey Historical Commission, 1975), 27-28.
55 John Eager Howard to the Heirs of Stephen Sheldenmire, May 26, 1809, Bayard Papers, MHS.
56 William Smallwood, receipt dated Feb. 14, 1779, William Smallwood Papers, MHS.
57 Testimony of the Officers of the 2nd Maryland Brigade, Dec. 28, 1778, Maryland Gazette, Jan. 5, 1779, in Thomas J. Scharf, The Chronicles of Baltimore. Being a Complete History of Baltimore Town and Baltimore City from the Earliest Time to the Present Day (Baltimore: Turnbull Brothers, 1874), 183-84.
58 Edward Norwood to the Printer, Maryland Gazette, Jan. 5, 1779, in Scharf, Chronicles of Baltimore, 183-84.
59 Maryland Officers to William Smallwood, March 1, 1780, in Scharf, Chronicles of Baltimore, 183-84.
60 Rieman, Maryland Line, 98.
61 George Washington, General Orders, March 22, 1780, George Washington Papers, Library of Congress.
62 George Washington, General Orders, March 22, 1780, George Washington Papers, Library of Congress.
63 George Washington to Arthur St. Clair, Feb. 24, 1780; George Washington, General Orders, March 22, 1780 (quotation), Washington Papers, Library of Congress.

CHAPTER THREE

BATTLING FOR SOUTH CAROLINA

Stalemate settled in around New York in the waning months of 1778. Both the American and British armies continually maneuvered and skirmished, looking for an edge. Despite the fact that his Continentals proved the value of Baron von Steuben's training by their performance at the Battle of Monmouth, George Washington remained reluctant to risk a pitched battle unless he had a clear advantage, and the British were equally wary.

Meanwhile, ominous developments for the Americans were taking shape in the South. French intervention meant that troops, ships, supplies, and money had begun flowing across the Atlantic Ocean to assist the Americans and to threaten Britain's valuable West Indies colonies. Although this danger had forced the British to curtail their operations, neither General Sir Henry Clinton nor his superior, Lord George Germain, was willing to relinquish offensive operations against the rebels. Germain, Secretary of State for the American Department and the official responsible for directing military operations in North America, believed that the British could still achieve success with their limited manpower by attacking the Southern colonies. The region was less populated than the North, and much of the population—more than half in South Carolina—consisted of African American slaves. The deposed royal governors reported that Loyalists constituted a large proportion of the white inhabitants, which simultaneously reduced the number of troops that the rebels could field while providing a pool of additional manpower for the British. The forces available to defend the region would be further reduced by the Americans' need to divert some of their troops to guard against possible slave uprisings and to protect the frontier from the powerful Creek and Cherokee Indian nations, both of whom generally supported the British. Thus the Americans would not have much strength available to oppose a British invasion. Germain expected that a small number of regular troops, aided by Loyalists, could subdue Georgia with ease, and once that task was accomplished, a larger force could conquer South Carolina.[1]

Clinton launched the first phase of the Southern operation in November 1778, dispatching 3,000 troops from New York to seize Savannah, Georgia. The British troops routed the defenders and captured the town on December 29th. Shortly afterward they were joined by a force that had marched overland from St. Augustine in East Florida. However, the British were too weak to hold the interior of Georgia against the American forces gathering to oppose them. In September 1779 a French fleet and army arrived and joined the Americans in besieging Savannah. The outnumbered British garrison managed to hold out and repel a Franco-American assault on October 9th. This victory convinced Clinton to undertake the second phase of his plan: an attack on Charleston, South Carolina.[2]

Clinton sailed from New York with 8,000 British troops in December 1779, and after a storm-wracked voyage of seven weeks began landing troops on February 11th, 1780, at a point thirty miles south of Charleston. The American commander in the South, Major General Benjamin Lincoln of Massachusetts, made no serious effort to oppose Clinton's advance. Instead he withdrew behind Charleston's fortifications. The British cut off the town's communications with the interior of South Carolina, began siege operations, and forced Lincoln to surrender on May 12th. American prisoners numbered about 6,000, including all of the South Carolina, North Carolina, and Virginia Continentals in the American army except a regiment of Virginia Continentals under Colonel Abraham Buford that had arrived too late to assist Charleston's defenders. Buford attempted to evade the British but was destroyed by their cavalry at the Waxhaws, just south of the North Carolina border, on May 29th.[3]

By this action, Clinton had eliminated all of the American forces in the South except for a few diehard militiamen who rallied to determined leaders such as Francis Marion and Thomas Sumter. Satisfied that both Georgia and South Carolina were now firmly under British control, Clinton returned to New York. He left Lieutenant General Charles, Earl Cornwallis, in command in the South.[4]

George Washington took steps to reinforce the southern army in an effort to hold Charleston. In mid-April 1780, he dispatched some of his best troops, the seven Maryland Continental regiments and one from Delaware, to aid Lincoln. Organized into two brigades under Generals William Smallwood and Mordecai Gist, the force numbered 1,400 rank-and-file infantrymen. Commissioned and non-commissioned officers, drummers, and others brought their total strength to more than 2,100 soldiers. Washington appointed Major General Baron Johann De Kalb to command the detachment.[5]

A large, physically powerful man, De Kalb was the son of Bavarian peasants. He had joined the French army and served with distinction in the European wars from the 1740s to 1760s, earning decorations, promotions, and the honorary title of "baron." In 1777 he had accompanied the Marquis de Lafayette to America and offered his services. Congress commissioned him a major general that September. Since then he had served under Washington in Pennsylvania and New Jersey, but had seen little action.[6]

Some of the Maryland and Delaware troops were not optimistic about their assignment and considered it a "forlorn hope," the military term for a mission from which the troops were not expected to return alive. As lieutenant colonel of the 2nd Maryland Regiment, twenty-seven-year-old John Eager Howard readied his men for the march southward into unknown territory. The small contingent of Continentals could hardly be expected to stem the British tide alone, yet Howard and his comrades were prepared to do their utmost to retrieve the situation.[7]

When their preparations were completed, the Maryland and Delaware regiments broke camp at Morristown, New Jersey on April 16th. Their initial destination was the Head of Elk in Maryland, where the Elk River flowed into Chesapeake Bay. The troops covered the 150-mile distance in three weeks. Howard took this opportunity to visit his family in Baltimore, where he also got ready for the ordeal ahead. He sold more property to obtain money for the expenses he would incur during the upcoming campaign. Howard was fortunate to receive payment in Portuguese gold coins rather than state or Continental paper currency that had depreciated rapidly and seemed to lose value by the day. Because captured officers were required to pay for their subsistence while in captivity, Howard left some of the proceeds with a friend "as a provision in case of my being taken prisoner," indicating that he was hardly optimistic about the army's prospects.[8]

The Continentals boarded boats at Head of Elk and sailed on the Chesapeake and its tributaries to Petersburg, Virginia. They arrived in late May and camped there for a week, resting and making further preparations for their journey. While at Petersburg they learned of Charleston's surrender, sparking a debate among the senior officers as to whether they should continue the march southward. After considerable discussion, they decided that it was important to keep an army in the field in the Carolinas. Accordingly, as the various regiments were ready they began leaving camp at the end of May, and by early June all units were on the road headed for North Carolina. They reached Hillsborough, North Carolina, 147 miles from Petersburg, on June 22nd.[9]

Howard and his fellow soldiers had entered a region that was different in many ways from their home states and from the northern territory in which they had campaigned for the previous four years. Their success now depended on their ability to understand the geography of the South, cope with the climate and topography, procuring enough food to sustain themselves, and deal with the partisan warfare that was now intensifying across Georgia and the Carolinas.[10]

These states had three distinct geographic regions. The low, flat coastal plain extending inland about one hundred miles from the Atlantic Ocean, commonly called the "Lowcountry," was home to the prosperous rice plantations and the majority of slaves. The piedmont area to the west consisted of rolling foothills that ascended gradually to the third region, the Appalachian Mountains. The settled areas of the piedmont and Appalachians, known together as the "Backcountry," were populated mainly by small farmers who raised corn and wheat and did not own many slaves. There were few towns, and most of these consisted of little more than a dozen or so dwellings clustered around a store or a courthouse. The Creek and Cherokee nations lived west of the settled areas.

Rivers offered the primary means of transportation in the South. Although some roads existed, they were usually little more than cart paths that turned rapidly to mud in wet weather. The rivers formed in the Appalachians grew in size as numerous tributaries joined together. The northernmost river, the Dan, flowed easterly until it joined the Roanoke River, which continued in an eastward direction to the Atlantic.

The other major rivers were: the Neuse, Haw, Deep, Yadkin, Catawba, Broad, and Savannah. All followed a generally southeastward course to the sea. Many of the rivers joined and took on new names at their confluence; the Haw and Deep Rivers flowed into the Cape Fear River, the Yadkin joined the Pee Dee, the Catawba flowed into the Wateree which was a tributary of the Santee River, while the Broad and Saluda Rivers united to form the Congaree River, which in turn flowed into the Santee. These rivers were often wide and relatively shallow, but could rise rapidly several feet in rainstorms. A few bridges spanned smaller streams but there were none on the large rivers. Crossing points were limited to fords where the water was shallow, or at locations where an enterprising settler had established a ferry. These rivers constituted significant obstacles to an army's movement while at the same time offering potentially strong defensive positions if an army occupied the bank across from an enemy. For both armies, but especially the British, the rivers were important routes for the shipment of supplies and troops. The British constructed a chain of forts in South Carolina to guard their shipping on the Santee River, however, vessels were vulnerable to attack from enemy forces that could take shelter in the heavy riverside brush at narrow points in the stream. Leaders of both sides had to consider the location of rivers as well as crossing points in all of their planning. American Lieutenant Colonel Henry Lee noted that "the settlements on the river are rich and populous .... Therefore the motions of the army must be from river to river, striking at the head of navigation and receiving by boats the produce."[11]

As Lee observed, food was more likely to be obtainable along the rivers, yet procuring sufficient provisions for the troops and forage for the horses was a problem that plagued both armies. Any time a force ventured into the areas between rivers for an extended period, the soldiers were likely to run short of food. Loyalists often drove their livestock into the woods and hid their grain to prevent American troops from seizing it, and pro-American settlers, known as Whigs, did likewise when the British approached. The British had one advantage: they could usually pay for provisions in gold and silver, a powerful incentive even for committed Whigs to sell them foodstuffs. American officers, who usually could only offer paper currency as payment, found few sellers. Even when the Americans did have gold or silver, such as Howard had procured in Baltimore, there was often no food to be had. Whigs and Loyalists frequently destroyed each other's crops and carried off livestock, while men summoned for militia duty were often away at planting time and could not put in a crop. Troops moving through an area stripped it bare of provisions, so that those who followed found little to eat. Thus Howard declared that money "became useless in procuring any thing whatever for the army," while his fellow Marylander, Otho Holland Williams, added that there were seldom any supplies to purchase in the vicinity of the army's camps. On several occasions, the troops subsisted on frogs caught in ponds near their encampment.[12]

Lack of food made soldiers more susceptible to illness, another common problem in the hot southern climate. Diseases such as malaria and yellow fever took a heavy toll of both armies, incapacitating large numbers of troops for weeks. Rum, the usual prescription for warding off disease in hot weather, actually exacerbated the problems. Other common illnesses, including smallpox and dysentery, increased the numbers of men unfit for duty. Insects such as mosquitoes and ticks were a constant nuisance, while soldiers on the march suffered from heat exhaustion and sometimes died of heat strokes. Sudden, violent thunderstorms soaked and chilled the men. A British soldier described the hardships he encountered on "forced marches, under the rage of a burning sun ... sinking under the most excessive fatigue, not only destitute of every comfort, but almost of every necessary which seems essential to his existence." During one expedition, he stated, more than fifty men died from the combination of heat, hunger, and fatigue. His American counterparts would have understood his complaints, as they suffered similarly.[13]

Howard and the Maryland and Delaware Continentals would have to learn from experience. They spent a week at Hillsborough before De Kalb ordered them to break camp on June 30 and continue their southward journey. On July 6 the troops reached Wilcox's Iron Works on North Carolina's Deep River. Colonel Otho Williams, commanding the 6th Maryland, reported that the men were in good spirits but had to halt their march "for want of provisions." The longer the Continentals stayed in one place, the more difficult it became to find food for the troops and fodder for the horses. If they pressured the local inhabitants to provide supplies to a point where a family would not have what it needed for its own survival, they alienated the populace and risked pushing them into the arms of the British. While De Kalb struggled to feed his army, he also encountered difficulties with the North Carolina militia. Major General Richard Caswell with 1,500 men was roaming near the South Carolina border, well within striking distance of the British garrison at Camden. De Kalb ordered Caswell to unite with the Continentals, but Caswell ignored him.[14]

Given the many problems he faced, De Kalb showed no hesitation in handing over command to his newly-appointed superior, Major General Horatio Gates. The English-born Gates looked much older than fifty-three. For that reason, and his parental concern for the welfare of the soldiers, his men in the North had affectionately nicknamed him "Granny" Gates. He had served in the British army and participated in the expedition that founded Halifax, Nova Scotia in 1749. Gates' abilities had impressed the expedition's commander and colonial governor, Colonel Edward Cornwallis, who had assisted Gates in obtaining promotion to captain. After serving in North America during the French and Indian War (1754-1763), Gates resigned from the army. He supported the American colonists in their opposition to British taxation, a stance that led him to move to Virginia in 1772. At the outbreak of the Revolution, Congress appointed him a brigadier general, and Gates helped George Washington organize the fledgling American army at Boston. In 1777 he had commanded the army that triumphed at Saratoga.[15]

Gates had aligned himself with a faction in Congress that feared that Washington, who strongly advocated a professional army, might establish a military dictatorship. These congressmen found Gates, with his favorable attitude toward the militia, a more trustworthy guardian of liberty and some delegates angled to replace Washington with Gates. Upon learning of Charleston's surrender and without consulting Washington, Congress appointed Gates to replace the captured Benjamin Lincoln as commander of the Southern Department.[16]

Lynches Creek, Rugeley's Mill, and Camden

General Gates joined the army at Wilcox's Iron Works on July 25th. He found his troops desperately short of supplies, making some type of movement imperative. Believing that it was essential to advance in order to bolster the South Carolinians' flagging morale, Gates had a choice of two routes. The shorter led directly to Camden, passing through pine forests where provisions were scarce and Loyalists were numerous. The longer ran through Salisbury and Charlotte, areas more abundant in supplies and whose inhabitants were mostly Whigs. The general had to consider other factors as well. A message from Thomas Sumter, who had organized several hundred South Carolinians into a partisan force and was operating north and west of Camden, indicated that British troops in the area were scattered and might be vulnerable if Gates acted quickly. In addition, Caswell ignored Gates' order to link up with the Continentals. By taking the shorter route, the army would move toward Caswell's militia and could unite with them, strengthening the American force while insuring that Caswell did not fall prey to a British attack. Therefore, Gates chose to march on the direct route to Camden.[17]

The troops set out on July 27th, stopping frequently to forage. Unfortunately, the first corn crop had already been harvested and the second was not yet ripe. The hungry soldiers ate the unripe corn anyway, supplementing it with green peaches. Occasionally they managed to find a few head of cattle. On August 3rd the exhausted and hungry troops reached the Pee Dee River in South Carolina. Howard, Williams, and the other Continental officers did their best to help keep up their men's morale. They went among the men offering encouragement, "appeased murmurs, for which, unhappily, there was too much cause. The officers, however, by appealing to their own empty canteens and mess cases, satisfied the privates that all suffered alike; and exhorting them to exercise the same fortitude of which the officers gave them the example." On one occasion when a sufficient supply of corn was obtained to provide a good meal, the officers waited until all the troops were served and then shared the small portion that remained.[18]

Gates' movements had not gone unnoticed. Loyalists rode to Camden to inform the British commander, Lieutenant Colonel Francis, Lord Rawdon, of the Americans' route and progress. Although he was only twenty-six-years-old, Rawdon so impressed Earl Cornwallis with his ability that Cornwallis had given Rawdon field command in South Carolina while the earl attended to administrative duties in Charleston. Having informed Cornwallis of Gates' approach, Rawdon ordered additional troops to Camden and then marched north to delay Gates. The British reached Lynches Creek on August 7, only thirteen miles from Caswell's position. Finally, conscious of his vulnerability, the North Carolinian hastened to join Gates, which he did later the same day.[19]

Gates resumed the advance with his reinforced army. Rawdon fell back behind the west branch of Lynches Creek (sometimes called Little Lynches Creek) and occupied a strong position. On August 12th Gates attempted to outflank the British, and Rawdon fell back to Camden. The Americans then pushed forward a few miles to Rugeley's Mill, the plantation of Loyalist Henry Rugeley, only thirteen miles north of Camden. There Gates received additional reinforcements: eight hundred Virginia militia under Brigadier General Edward Stevens. The Virginians had hurried to join Gates. Howard noted that "the heat was so oppressive they could not march in the day, and therefore they had for several nights made forced marches to come up with us, which broke the spirits of the men."[20]

General Gates now formulated his plans, although he shared them only with his aide, Major Thomas Pinckney, and his engineer officer, Colonel John Christian Senf. Gates sent Senf southward to find a strong defensive position closer to Camden, where his army would threaten the town. Having opened a regular correspondence with Thomas Sumter and conferred in person with Francis Marion, Gates intended to use Marion's partisans to harass the British line of communications between Charleston and Camden, while Sumter interdicted the routes leading from Camden to the British post at Ninety Six in western South Carolina. To reinforce Sumter, Gates detached 100 Marylanders and 300 North Carolina militia with two pieces of artillery on August 14th. Gates believed the partisan operations would either induce the British to abandon Camden, in which case he could pursue and attack them, or force Rawdon's smaller force to assault Gates in his strong position.[21]

Unfortunately, Gates did not inform any of his other subordinates of his intentions. He also overestimated the size of his own army, assuming he had 7,000 fighting men until a field return compiled on August 15 revealed that his rank and file soldiers amounted to less than half that number. He reassured Otho Williams that the smaller force was sufficient for his purpose, without bothering to enlighten Williams regarding his plan to take up a defensive position. When the army marched from Rugeley's Mill at ten o'clock that night, the officers and men believed that they were going into battle.[22]

The British did not intend to sit idly while Gates put his plans into effect. In response to Rawdon's message, Earl Cornwallis, who was the nephew of Gates's former patron, left Charleston on August 10th. He arrived at Camden late at night on August 13th. After Rawdon briefed him on the situation, Cornwallis declared "I resolved to take the first good opportunity to attack the rebel army." At ten p.m. on August

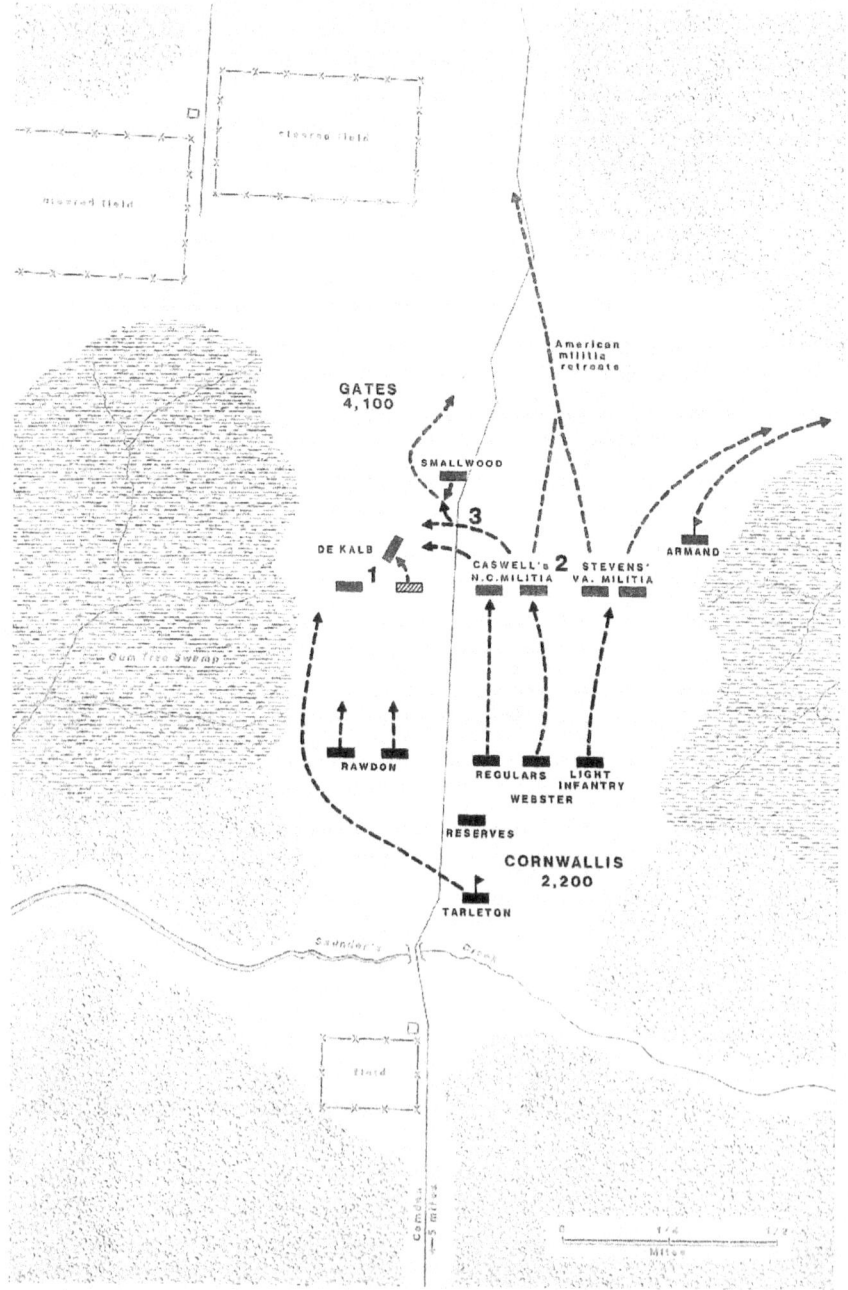

15th, the very same hour that Gates began his march, the British troops left Camden to strike the Americans in their camp at Rugeley's Mill.[23]

Neither side expected to encounter the other on the march, but both commanders took precautions. Gates placed the sixty mounted troopers of Colonel Charles Armand's Legion at the head of his column. These cavalrymen advanced on the road, while three hundred Virginia and North Carolina militia moved through the woods on either side to screen the flanks.

Cornwallis ordered the cavalry of Lieutenant Colonel Banastre Tarleton's British Legion to lead the British column. Tarleton and Armand's mounted troops encountered one another at about two o'clock on the morning of August 16th. The British had already passed the position that Gates hoped to occupy. Under a full moon, the British dragoons routed Armand's men before they were pushed back by the Americans on their flanks. Tarleton called up infantry support and drove off the American militia. The retreating soldiers ran headlong into the 1st Maryland Brigade, which was marching in column on the road and temporarily threw the American army into confusion.[24]

With his plans in disarray, Gates summoned his generals to a council of war. "Gentlemen, what is best to be done?" the commander asked. De Kalb had earlier told Colonel Williams that the army should retreat, although such a move in the presence of the British was fraught with risk. Now the Baron remained silent, as did the other officers. Finally, Stevens spoke up, answering Gates' question with one of his own. "Gentlemen, is it not too late now to do anything but fight?" The remark was met with silence. Gates, hearing no objections to Stevens's suggestion, ordered the officers to return to their respective commands without further comment.[25]

Both armies now prepared for battle. The field was bordered by swamps to the east and west, which prevented either opponent from attempting to outflank the other. However, if the units holding the extreme right or left of the line were overwhelmed or driven off, whichever army suffered such a reverse would be doomed. Gates did not have to worry about his own right flank, where he placed Mordecai Gist's 2nd Maryland Brigade. De Kalb, who commanded the American right and Gist posted Lieutenant Colonel John Eager Howard and his 2nd Maryland Regiment on the far right abutting the swamp. The two generals trusted Howard, as acting commander of the regiment, to hold his ground. The left of Gist's line extended to the Great Wagon Road that bisected the battlefield, where it connected with Caswell's North Carolina militia. Next to the North Carolinians, Stevens's Virginia militia continued the line to the swamp on the American left. Gates held Smallwood's 1st Maryland Brigade in reserve behind his center, and supported the infantry with seven pieces of artillery.[26]

Like Gates, Cornwallis followed eighteenth-century military practice by assigning his best troops to the right of the line. Three companies of British light infantry held the extreme right, followed by the 23rd and 33rd Regiments of British regulars. Lieutenant Colonel James Webster, a reliable veteran, commanded this wing. Left of the road, Cornwallis posted his provincial troops—American Loyalists. The Volunteers of Ireland held the line next to the 33rd Regiment, followed by the British Legion infantry and Royal North Carolina Regiment, the latter opposite Howard's 2nd Maryland. In reserve to the left and rear of the North Carolinians stood three hundred North Carolina Loyalist militia under Colonel Samuel Bryan. Lord Rawdon commanded the British left. Cornwallis kept control of his main reserve, two battalions of the 71st Regiment of Scottish Highlanders, and the British Legion cavalry. Two pieces of artillery supported the British left, two were assigned to the right, and another two remained in reserve. Altogether, Cornwallis fielded some 2,200 troops against Gates's 4,000.[27]

First light on August 16th found the armies arrayed in battle formation. Although less than a quarter-mile separated them, the morning fog obscured the ranks drawn up in the open pine forest. As the commanders made final adjustments to their lines, the artillery began blasting away at the shadowy figures moving in the distance; the smoke of cannon fire further clouded the field. Near Smallwood's brigade, Gates, Major Thomas Pinckney, and Otho Williams, who was serving as the army's adjutant general, conferred. Williams noticed that the British forces opposite the militia were still moving into position, and suggested that they were vulnerable to attack. Gates agreed and dispatched Williams to order Stevens to assault the British right. The commander-in-chief then sent instructions to Smallwood to advance and occupy the ground vacated by the militia, while Pinckney rode to De Kalb with orders for the right wing to join in the attack. Williams, after relaying Gates' order to Stevens, obtained the latter's permission to lead forty or fifty volunteers ahead of the main force "to extort the enemy's fire at some distance, in order to the rendering it less terrible to the militia."[28]

Through the fog, Cornwallis saw the American militia begin their forward movement and misinterpreted it as simply an attempt to alter their deployment. Hoping to take advantage of the temporary disarray, the earl ordered Webster to attack. At the same time, he sent a messenger instructing Rawdon to assail the troops in his front to prevent the Americans from reinforcing their left.[29]

Webster's veteran regulars lowered their bayonets and rushed forward with a cheer. The Virginia militiamen, many of whom had never before seen combat, panicked. Most threw away their muskets without firing a shot, turned, and fled, discarding anything else that might slow them down—cartridge boxes, canteens, blankets—as they ran. Their terror infected the North Carolinians, who joined in the flight. Only Colonel Henry Dixon's regiment, posted just east of the road next to the Continentals, stood firm. Gates and Caswell rode into the throng of fugitives, urging them to rally, but without success. "They ran like a Torrent, and bore all before them," Gates reported. He, Caswell, Stevens, Senf and other officers were swept along in the flood of frightened men. At various points Gates and his officers fruitlessly attempted to halt the militia and put them into a defensive line. Eventually the men scattered, some fleeing along various roads and others through the woods. Hearing no further sounds of battle from the south, Gates and Caswell concluded that the fighting was over and decided to ride to Charlotte, North Carolina, where they hoped to reassemble their forces.[30]

Webster ignored the fleeing militia and wheeled to his left, into Smallwood's advancing brigade. The Marylanders had been thrown into confusion when some of the frightened North Carolinians and Virginians literally forced their way through the lines of Continentals in their haste to escape the British. The Maryland officers quickly restored order, however, and met Webster's charging regulars. The Continentals' volley checked the British advance, and the two sides, fairly equally matched, held their ground and exchanged fire.[31]

On the American right, Rawdon and De Kalb carried out their orders to advance and moved forward almost simultaneously. Accounts of what followed are contradictory, but it appears the Maryland and Delaware Continentals halted first. Howard, on horseback behind his regiment, waited for the North Carolina provincials to come within musket range before he gave the order to fire. The Marylanders' muskets roared, halting the Loyalists' assault. Along the rest of the brigade's line, the veteran Continental soldiers likewise staggered the approaching provincials with their volley. Rawdon urged his men forward, but the heavy fire from the Maryland and Delaware troops sent the line reeling backwards. Again they came, and again the Continentals' musketry forced them to withdraw. Believing his soldiers had gained the advantage, De Kalb ordered a counterattack. Charging with fixed bayonets, the Continentals pressed Rawdon's troops back, taking several prisoners. "Howard ... drove the corps in [his] front out of line," thus threatening to outflank the British left. He exhorted his men to continue moving forward while musket balls whistled around him. Cornwallis, seeing his line falter, ordered the 71st Regiment to their support. The Highlanders stabilized the line, but the British could do no more than hold their ground. Even after Cornwallis committed Bryan's militia, the Continentals stood firm, proving their own mettle and the value of von Steuben's training. The outcome of the contest remained in doubt.[32]

The struggle between the British and the two Continental brigades raged for almost half an hour. Cornwallis, observing the action with a keen eye, noticed at last that Smallwood's brigade began to falter. The earl committed his last reserve, Tarleton's cavalry, ordering them to pass through the ranks of the 23rd and 33rd Regiments and charge the Continentals. The blow was too much for Smallwood's troops, already weakened by casualties and exhaustion. The American line broke, rallied briefly a short distance in the rear, and then gave way entirely. Cornwallis struck the left flank of Gist's brigade with Webster's infantry while Tarleton's horsemen circled to assault the American rear. De Kalb was mortally wounded, and Gist, Howard, and their troops were powerless to resist the British. All the Continentals could do was make their escape before they were encircled. Some fled northward into the woods, trying to stay parallel with the road, while others, including Howard and most of his remaining men, waded through the swamp on their right, where the mud and dense brambles kept the British from pursuing them. The Marylanders of the 2nd Brigade generally managed to avoid the British cavalry, which pursued the retreating Americans for twenty-two miles along the Great Wagon Road and intersecting routes, capturing many of the fleeing soldiers.[33]

The Battle of Camden was a devastating defeat for the Americans. At a cost of 324 killed, wounded, and captured, Cornwallis had destroyed Gates' army. Seven hundred men, 505 of them Continentals, had been taken prisoner; the number of American dead was never determined, but was probably around 250. The army also lost all of its artillery, wagons, and supplies. Most of the militia returned to their homes rather than attempt to reorganize and rejoin the surviving Continentals. The hapless citizen-soldiers were accused of cowardice by civilians and Continental soldiers alike; they bore much of the blame for the disaster. The rest of the blame fell upon Gates. Having gone to Charlotte after being swept from the field, Gates found neither troops nor supplies and decided to continue to Hillsborough, where the North Carolina legislature was meeting, to plead for assistance. The move was justifiable under the circumstances, but when it was learned that he had traveled 180 miles from the battlefield in just three days, Gates' political enemies added the charge of cowardice to that of incompetence. Even officers who supported Gates or took no side in the political disputes expressed dismay at their commander's actions, although Howard was one of the few who never criticized Gates, either publicly or in private. Gates' reputation was ruined, and Congress began pondering his removal from the southern command.[34]

The Maryland and Delaware Continentals were the only Americans to emerge from the Battle of Camden with their reputation enhanced, an achievement that they purchased at a high cost in blood. At that dark hour for their cause, Americans everywhere praised the fortitude of the Continentals who had stood and fought while their commander and the militia fled the contest. "Though overpowered by numbers their bravery is highly to be commended and honoured," Gates wrote. Even Cornwallis noted that the Continentals had made an "obstinate resistance." De Kalb, Gist, Williams, and Howard were singled out by many for their valor on the battlefield. None of the eyewitnesses recalled seeing Smallwood after he ordered his brigade into action; however, he apparently remained on the field until his troops were forced to retreat. John J. Jacob, a Maryland officer who fought at Camden, recalled in a postwar memoir, "I saw, in particular, such coolness and personal bravery in General Gist, Colonel Howard, and some others ... that I am confident upon equal ground we could have fought, and I think subdued an equal number of the British troops." Henry Lee, who was assigned to the southern department later in the war and learned the details of the battle from participants, wrote that "Lieutenant Colonel Howard demonstrated a solidity of character, which on every future occasion, he displayed honorably to himself, and advantageously to his country." In another account of the battle, George Washington Greene, grandson of General Nathanael Greene, declared that "no one fought longer or more gallantly than [Howard] on that fatal day, or was more prompt, when the fortune of the field was decided, in collecting and reorganizing the remnants of the shattered army."[35]

Jacob noted that at Camden, Howard "was among the last that left the field, collected also at first about 50 or 60 men, but which increased ... to 80 or 90." Jacob was part of this group. After clearing the swamp, Howard led them in a southerly direction for "five or six miles and then turned westward." At one o'clock in the afternoon, Howard halted the men in the woods for a rest. A straggler joined them and reported that a badly wounded officer remained on the battlefield, so Howard permitted a few men to return and carry him back. The officer survived, but one of his arms had to be amputated later. Howard then resumed the trek to Charlotte, North Carolina, which they reached three days later. Colonel John Gunby of Maryland and Captain Robert Kirkwood of Delaware were among the officers and men who had joined Howard's party. The troops subsisted on "watermelons, peaches, etc.," Jacob stated. Fortunately, they managed to avoid capture by Loyalists, a fate which befell several of their comrades. Some of these erstwhile British supporters had originally turned out to assist Gates but changed sides after learning of the American defeat.[36]

When Howard and his little band arrived at Charlotte, they concluded, as Gates had earlier, that little could be accomplished there. News soon arrived that Tarleton had surprised and routed Thomas Sumter's partisan corps at Fishing Creek, South Carolina on August 18th. This put an end to any hope of substantial reinforcement from that quarter. Other than a small unit of North Carolina mounted militia under Major William R. Davie, no new troops arrived in camp. A steady trickle of Continental survivors from the Battle of Camden did rejoin the army, however, including Brigadier Generals Smallwood and Gist. Smallwood, as the highest ranking officer on the scene, assumed command. He agreed with his subordinates that Charlotte could not be held if Cornwallis, as expected, made a determined push northward. By noon on August 19, the remnants of the army were on the road marching east to Salisbury, North Carolina.[37]

At Salisbury, Smallwood resumed the machinations that had characterized his career in the northern theater. Expecting that Gates would be removed, Smallwood began angling for the command. First he reorganized the remaining Continentals, whom "he officered according to his pleasure." Those officers without a place in the reconstituted units received his permission to go to Hillsborough; Howard and Williams, neither of them desiring a confrontation with their argumentative superior, did so without complaint. Then Smallwood opened a direct correspondence with Congress in violation of the chain of command, "in which, he intimated the great difficulties he had encountered and the exertions he had made to save a remnant of General Gates' army." He also wrote to those of his friends with political connections asking for their help in securing him promotion to major general. Congress soon elevated him to the rank he sought.[38]

Gates, Smallwood, and Gist consolidated the surviving Continentals into a single regiment that numbered between 700 and 800 men. The Delaware Regiment was reduced to two companies and the Maryland regiments were similarly restructured. Colonel Otho Williams received command of the unit, and Lieutenant Colonel John Eager Howard became his second-in-command. Gates clearly wanted the Continentals in the hands of his two best combat officers. The consolidation left several officers without commands appropriate for their ranks, so Gates dispatched them to their home states to recruit.[39]

Williams and Howard set to work restoring discipline so that the troops would regain their morale and fighting ability. Guards were posted about the camp, "parade duties were regularly attended ... and discipline, not only began to be perfectly restored, but even gave an air of stability and confidence to the regiment, which all their rags could not disguise," Williams observed. He noted that in their free time, the troops also engaged in "manly sports" that improved their physical conditioning along with their morale. Despite frequent food shortages and the lack of clothing, rum, and pay, the troops "saw their officers constantly occupied in procuring for them whatever was attainable," and did not complain.[40]

The Continentals might not have recovered from the shock of Camden had Cornwallis not given them sufficient time. He did not begin his invasion of North Carolina until September 8th, and he moved at such a languid pace that it took his army until September 26th to advance from Camden to Charlotte. Meanwhile, developments farther west threatened to undermine his plans.[41]

To cover his left flank on the march to North Carolina, Cornwallis assigned Major Patrick Ferguson, Inspector General of the Loyalist militia, to advance along a separate route to the west of the main army. Ferguson, with a handful of provincials and perhaps one thousand Loyalists, mostly South Carolinians, reached Gilbert Town, North Carolina, at about the same time Cornwallis set out from Camden. His movements, however, had stirred up the settlers living west of the Appalachians, the so-called "Overmountain Men." These people had purchased a vast tract of land from the Cherokees before the war in violation of the British government's Proclamation of 1763, which forbade settlers from acquiring Indian lands without the king's approval. The Cherokees insisted that they had been deceived in the transaction, and British Indian agents were sympathetic. Believing that Ferguson and the British threatened their possession of the disputed territory, the Overmountain Men mobilized to strike the Loyalists.[42]

Ferguson learned of the group's approach and fell back to Kings Mountain, South Carolina, just below the North Carolina border. He took a strong position, apparently inviting his enemies to attack so that they would be crushed between his force and the reinforcements he had requested from Cornwallis. But Cornwallis did not send reinforcements. On October 7th the "Overmountain Men" surrounded the Loyalists. Several assaults finally won a lodgment at one end of the Loyalists' position. Ferguson was killed leading a counterattack, and the remaining Loyalists surrendered.

When reports of the defeat reached Cornwallis, he abandoned his invasion plans. The British army withdrew from Charlotte, taking up winter quarters at Winnsboro, South Carolina. Gates' soldiers had gained a further reprieve. Howard and Williams welcomed the news of the victory at Kings Mountain and Cornwallis's retreat, and they felt more confident about the army's prospects. They had reinvigorated their men and prepared them for the battles that they knew lay ahead. Now it was up to their commander to take advantage of the additional time that the Kings Mountain victory had gained. Gates was preparing to do so, with the help of an old friend from Saratoga.[43]

---

1   Jim Piecuch, *Three Peoples, One King: Loyalists, Indians, and Slaves in the Revolutionary South, 1775-1782* (Columbia: University of South Carolina Press, 2008), 125-28.
2   Mackesy, *War for America*, 234; 277-78.
3   Higginbotham, *War of American Independence*, 356-57.
4   Piecuch, *Three Peoples, One King*, 184.
5   Jim Piecuch, *The Battle of Camden: A Documentary History* (Charleston, SC: The History Press, 2006), 13.
6   Piecuch, *Battle of Camden*, 13-14.
7   John Eager Howard to Sheldenmire Heirs, May 26, 1809, Bayard Papers, MHS.
8   Otho Holland Williams, "A Narrative of the Campaign of 1780," in William Johnson, *Sketches of the Life and Correspondence of Nathanael Greene, Major General of the Armies of the United States in the War of the Revolution*, Vol. 1, (Charleston, SC: A. E. Miller, 1822), 486-88; John Eager Howard to William Johnson, n.d., Bayard Papers, MHS; John Eager Howard to Sheldenmire Estate, May 26, 1809, Bayard Papers, MHS (quotation).
9   Williams, "Narrative," 488-89.
10 Henry Lee, *Revolutionary War Memoirs*, 171.
11 M. F. Treacy, *Prelude to Yorktown: The Southern Campaign of Nathanael Greene, 1780-1781* (Chapel Hill: University of North Carolina Press, 1963), 3-4, 58-59; Henry Lee, *Revolutionary War Memoirs*, 36 (quotation).
12 W. T. R. Saffell, ed., *Records of the Revolutionary War, containing the Military and Financial Correspondence of Distinguished Officers* (Philadelphia: G. G. Evans, 1858), 101 (quotation); 104; Treacy, *Prelude to Yorktown*, 4-9; Henry Lee, *Revolutionary War Memoirs*, 386.
13 Treacy, *Prelude to Yorktown*, 3-4; Dan L. Morrill, *Southern Campaigns of the American Revolution* (Baltimore: Nautical & Aviation Publishing, 1993), 85; Pancake, *This Destructive War*, 215-216.
14 Williams, "Narrative," 489.
15 Piecuch, *Battle of Camden*, 12-13
16 Piecuch, *Battle of Camden*, 13.
17 Pancake, *This Destructive War*, 100-101.
18 Pancake, *This Destructive War*, 101; Williams, "Narrative," 488-89 (quotation).
19 Josiah Martin to Lord George Germain, Aug. 18, 1780, in Piecuch, *Battle of Camden*, 67.
20 Martin to Germain, in Piecuch, *Battle of Camden*, 67-68; Henry Lee, *Revolutionary War Memoirs*, 191 (quotation).
21 Thomas Pinckney to William Johnson, July 27, 1822, in Piecuch, *Battle of Camden*, 36-43.
22 Otho Holland Williams, "Narrative of the Camden Campaign," c. 1780, in Piecuch, *Battle of Camden*, 28.
23 Lord Cornwallis to Lord George Germain, Aug. 21, 1780, in Piecuch, *Battle of Camden*, 53-54.
24 Buchanan, *Road to Guilford Courthouse*, 161-62.

25 Williams, "Narrative," 494-95.
26 Buchanan, *Road to Guilford Courthouse*, 162-63.
27 Buchanan, *Road to Guilford Courthouse*, 163-65.
28 Williams, "Narrative," 495 (quotation); Pinckney to Johnson, July 27, 1822, in Piecuch, *Battle of Camden*, 41; John Christian Senf, "Extract of a Journal concerning the Action of the 16th August, 1780," in Piecuch, *Battle of Camden*, 24.
29 Cornwallis to Germain, Aug. 21, 1780, in Piecuch, *Battle of Camden*, 54; Banastre Tarleton, "Account of the Battle of Camden," in Piecuch, *Battle of Camden*, 63.
30 Horatio Gates to Samuel Huntington, Aug. 20, 1780, in Piecuch, *Battle of Camden*, 20.
31 Buchanan, *Road to Guilford Courthouse*, 167-68.
32 Buchanan, *Road to Guilford Courthouse*, 167-68; Henry Lee, *Revolutionary War Memoirs*, 184 (quotation). The exact deployment of the 71st Regiment when it joined the battle is uncertain. The documentary evidence is not explicit, but implies that both battalions of the 71st were sent to support the British left. However, an archaeological study of the battlefield seems to indicate that one battalion of the 71st fought on the British right.
33 Pancake, *This Destructive War*, 106; Buchanan, *Road to Guilford Courthouse*, 168-69; Morrill, *Southern Campaigns*, 94.
34 "Return of the Killed, Wounded, and Missing ... in the Battle Fought near Camden," "Return of the Prisoners Taken ... at the Battle Fought near Camden," in Piecuch, *Battle of Camden*, 147, 148; Buchanan, *Road to Guilford Courthouse*, 171; Pancake, *This Destructive War*, 106-107.
35 Gates to Huntington, Aug. 20, 1780; Cornwallis to Germain, Aug. 21, 1780, in Piecuch, *Battle of Camden*, 20, 54; John J. Jacob, *A Biographical Sketch of the Life of the Late Captain Michael Cresap* (Cincinnati, OH: J. F. Uhlhorn, 1866), 24; Henry Lee, *Revolutionary War Memoirs*, 186; George Washington Greene, *The Life of Nathanael Greene, Major-General in the Army of the Revolution* (New York: G. P. Putnam, 1871), Vol. 3, 113-14.
36 Jacob, *Sketch of Cresap*, 25 (quotations); Williams, "Narrative," 497.
37 Williams, "Narrative," 499-501; William Smallwood to Horatio Gates, Aug. 22, 1780, in Piecuch, *Battle of Camden*, 46.
38 Williams, "Narrative," 502.
39 Don Higginbotham, *Daniel Morgan, Revolutionary Rifleman* (Chapel Hill: University of North Carolina Press, 1961), 107; Henry Lee, *Revolutionary War Memoirs*, 208; Mordecai Gist to Caesar Rodney, Sept. 12, 1780, in Piecuch, *Battle of Camden*, 46.
40 Williams, "Narrative," 505.
41 Piecuch, *Battle of Camden*, 141.
42 Buchanan, *Road to Guilford Courthouse*, 204, 212-13.
43 Buchanan, *Road to Guilford Courthouse*, 218-20, 230-33.

Colonel "Light Horse" Henry Lee successfully abetted General Greene's efforts either by fighting as part of his force or by cooperating with partisan leaders, such as Francis Marion, to harass loyalist or regular British units.
Courtesy of the National Park Service.

General William Smallwood led the Maryland Continentals in many battles in the North and South during the Revolutionary War.
Courtesy of the National Park Service.

Colonel Otho Holland Williams was Howard's friend and also his commander at Guilford Courthouse and Eutaw Springs. He was one of Greene's finest field officers.
Courtesy of the National Park Service.

This portrait of Howard as an older man is from the Maryland Archives. He had served in the Revolution and as Maryland's governor and senator during a long, productive life.
Courtesy of Archives of Maryland Biographical Series.

This is a depiction of the Cowpens Battle. The copy at the Fifth Regiment Armory in Baltimore states that the officer wielding the sword in the picture is Howard. The officer behind the troops is Morgan.
Courtesy of the U.S. Army Center for Military History, painting by H. Charles McBarron.

This is a depiction of the Battle of Guilford Court House.
Courtesy of the U.S. Army Center for Military History, Painting by H. Charles McBarron.

Nathanael Greene was Washington's choice to succeed Gates. His clever application of Washington's instructions led to the ultimate defeat of General Cornwallis at Yorktown.
Courtesy of the National Park Service.

General Daniel Morgan won credit as one of the most innovative tacticians in the Continental Army. He devised a successful disposition of militia and regular army units with which he defeated the British at the Cowpens in South Carolina.
Courtesy of the National Park Service.

William Washington was a tireless cavalry leader who fought throughout the Southern Campaign. He made a pivotal attack on Tarleton's left flank at Cowpens. In the end he was wounded and captured at Eutaw Springs in September, 1781. He was George Washington's cousin.
Courtesy of the National Park Service.

This is a painting of British Lieutenant Colonel Banastre Tarleton, one of Cornwallis' most aggressive and able officers, who earned the nickname "Bloody Tarleton" and was accused of the massacre of Colonel Buford's Continental troops after they surrendered at the Waxhaws after the Battle of Camden.
Courtesy of the National Park Service.

A portrait of John Eager Howard when he was a young regimental commander.
Courtesy of the National Park Service.

George Washington's remarkable leadership was again evident when devising a winning strategy for the Southern campaign. His insightful choice of officers for the mission and his unwavering support for their efforts led to an improbable victory in a little more than a year.
Courtesy of Independence National Historical Park.

Major General Baron de Kalb was a brave and experienced French officer who volunteered to fight with the Marquis de Lafayette in America in 1777. He led the first troops of the Maryland and Delaware Continental Line south to confront the British at Camden in South Carolina. He was killed in the battle.
Courtesy of the National Park Service.

General Horatio Gates, victor at Saratoga and appointed by Congress, lost the Battle of Camden and rode all the way to Charlotte, leaving his troops behind.
Courtesy of National Park Service.

CHAPTER FOUR

TRIUMPH AT THE COWPENS

Horatio Gates has been harshly criticized by his contemporaries as well as historians for the disastrous outcome of the Battle of Camden. However, during his tenure as commander of the southern army, Gates was responsible for three major accomplishments that would change American fortunes in the South. First, he lured Daniel Morgan out of self-imposed retirement. Second, he created a corps of light troops that proved highly effective throughout the remainder of the southern campaign. Finally, he revived the hopes of southern Whigs, bringing many back into the fight against the British occupiers and their Loyalist allies.

Daniel Morgan had played a crucial role in Gates' victory over the British at Saratoga. He later rejoined George Washington's army in New Jersey, where he assumed temporary command of Brigadier General William Woodford's Virginia brigade. Woodford, who had been on leave, resumed command of his brigade in June 1779. Morgan was not disappointed, since Washington decided to create a corps of light troops. Given his proven success and experience as a battlefield leader, Morgan believed that he should receive command of the new unit, along with promotion to brigadier general. Washington, however, assigned Brigadier General Anthony Wayne to the position. Angered at what he considered an unacceptable slight, Morgan resigned from the army on June 30.[1]

During the spring of 1780, Morgan made several visits to Traveller's Rest, the Virginia home of his old Saratoga comrade, Gates, who was on leave. The visits came to an end when Morgan suffered an attack of sciatica, an ailment that he had contracted during the 1775 Quebec campaign. While Morgan was incapacitated, Congress appointed Gates to command the Southern Department and Gates told Congress that he needed Morgan, urging that his fellow Virginian be promoted. Congress complied, but the new brigadier general was unfortunately too ill to join Gates immediately. Morgan did not report to Gates at Hillsborough, North Carolina, until late September, 1780. Morgan's promotion to brigadier general went into effect a few weeks later, on October 13th.[2]

Gates had the perfect assignment in mind for Morgan: command of the army's light troops. Gates knew that an infantry unit unencumbered by baggage, wagons, and any other unnecessary accouterments would be invaluable in the South, where rapid movement could mean the difference between victory and defeat. Gates also realized that such a unit required especially able officers, and from his experience at Saratoga he recognized that Morgan would be the ideal man to command the light troops. As he told Samuel Huntington, President of the Continental Congress, it was his intention to place Morgan "at the Head of a Select Corps from whose services I expect the most brilliant success." In canvassing his army for the officer best-suited to lead the light infantry under Morgan, Gates selected Lieutenant Colonel John Eager Howard.[3]

The twenty-eight-year-old Howard and forty-five-year-old Morgan were very different individuals and much depended on their ability to work together. While Howard was the educated son of a prosperous Baltimore-area planter, placid and reserved, Morgan was the child of poor immigrants, who grew up on the frontier, and who had a volatile personality. In 1755, as a wagon driver on General Edward Braddock's ill-fated expedition against the French at Fort Duquesne, Morgan had struck a British officer and received several hundred lashes as punishment. His experiences during Braddock's campaign earned him the nickname "The Old Waggoner" and instilled in him an enduring hatred of the British. Yet despite all of their differences, Morgan and Howard shared a deep commitment to the cause of American liberty, an ability to lead men in battle, and a natural grasp of military tactics. These attributes would make them a highly effective team on the battlefield.[4]

At the end of September another able officer arrived: Lieutenant Colonel William Washington. He commanded the combined 1st and 3rd Continental Light Dragoons, whose hundred men had been trickling into Gates' camp throughout the month. The two regiments had been badly cut up by the British in battles during the siege of Charleston the previous spring, and since then had been refitting in North Carolina. Washington was a Virginian and cousin of General George Washington. He was the same age as Howard, although more flamboyant. Gates assigned Washington and his cavalry to Morgan's light corps, along with a company of sixty riflemen. Howard's light infantry consisted of three companies of one hundred men each, two from Maryland and one from Delaware.[5]

When Morgan's detachment took the field, they would be able to count on substantial assistance from the southern militia. Gates' hasty march into South Carolina may have overtaxed his army and led to a costly defeat, but it inspired southerners who believed that the Continental Congress would abandon them. Gates had written to American militia officers on July 29th and asked them to assure the Whigs in their districts that he was coming to their aid. He also offered pardon to all who had taken an oath of allegiance to the British government "from the Necessity of protecting their persons and property." Shortly afterward Gates issued a proclamation announcing his offer of amnesty. The plan succeeded. Colonel Robert Gray of the South Carolina Loyalist militia noted that Gates's advance appeared "to be a signal for a general revolt" of backcountry Whigs. Earl Cornwallis informed Sir Henry Clinton that Gates's arrival in South Carolina "very much intimidated our friends, encouraged our enemies, and determined the wavering against us." The backcountry was inflamed as the Whigs took up arms and attacked both the Loyalist militia and British detachments.[6]

Cornwallis expected that his smashing victory at Camden would put an end to harassment from the Whig militia, but was sorely disappointed. Neither the defeat of

Gates nor the destruction of Thomas Sumter's partisan corps two days later quelled the opposition. More than two months after the Battle of Camden, Lieutenant Colonel Francis, Lord Rawdon, observed that "the approach of General Gates's Army unveiled to Us a Fund of disaffection" in South Carolina, "of which we could have formed no Idea; And even the dispersion of that force, did not extinguish the Ferment which the hope of its support had raised."[7]

Lacking the patience to conduct lengthy antipartisan operations, Cornwallis marched to Charlotte and was expected to advance deeper into North Carolina. Gates responded by dispatching Morgan's force, which came to be known as "The Flying Army," to move closer to the British army, gain intelligence, and delay them when they resumed their march. The little corps, minus Washington's cavalry, left Hillsborough on October 7. Eight days later they arrived at Salisbury, where Morgan allowed them three days of rest. Hearing nothing from the British, Morgan decided to continue toward Charlotte. His troops arrived at New Providence on October 22nd, only fourteen miles from Charlotte. There they were joined by Washington's dragoons and two battalions of North Carolina militia under Brigadier General William Davidson.[8]

Sometime after October 25, Morgan learned that Cornwallis had left Charlotte. On October 7, Whig militia had annihilated Major Patrick Ferguson's corps of Loyalist militia at King's Mountain, only twenty-five miles from Charlotte. Ferguson had been covering Cornwallis's western flank, and the British commander, now finding himself exposed to attack from that direction, had retreated into South Carolina. The Old Waggoner put his men in motion, passed through Charlotte, and continued south toward Camden, expecting the British to have returned to their base in the latter town. The corps arrived at Rugeley's Mill, thirteen miles from Camden, on November 6. Morgan remained there for three days, apparently taking time to ascertain that while Cornwallis had left a small garrison at Camden, he had taken the main British army elsewhere. Unable to accomplish anything further, Morgan withdrew to the vicinity of Charlotte, where Gates joined him with the rest of the army on November 11. Gates ordered his men to build huts and prepare to go into winter camp, although he expected the Flying Army to remain active. Still plagued by shortages of provisions and other supplies, Gates worried about his army's ability to survive the harsh season ahead. He asked the secretary of the Congressional Board of War:

> "How can men continue in the field in Winter, without Tents or Blanketts? For want of Cartridge Boxes, Belts, and Froggs [bayonet holders] the Ammunition and Bayonets are lost, or Spoiled, & the Arms rendered useless; For want of Tents, & Blankets the men desert or die."[9]

The Flying Army had tents, but they did not stay in them for long. On the morning of November 28th, the men received orders "to hold our selves in readiness in a moments warning to March." Further instructions arrived shortly afterward, and as Captain Robert Kirkwood, commander of the Delaware light infantry company, noted the troops "left our tents standing with all our sick behind" and headed south. Those soldiers who lacked shoes but were otherwise healthy remained behind to guard the camp. Morgan, Howard, and Washington led the Flying Army to Rugeley's Mill once again. This time the enemy was waiting for them. Colonel Henry Rugeley had fortified his barn, and ignoring orders to withdraw his Loyalist militia to the safety of Camden, prepared to resist. Morgan sent Washington to scout the post with his cavalry on the evening of December 1st, but the ambitious young lieutenant colonel decided to capture it on his own. Mounting a pine log on a wheeled carriage so that in the darkness it appeared to be a cannon, Washington demanded Rugeley's surrender. The ruse worked, and Rugeley and more than one hundred militiamen were made prisoners. Satisfied with this success, Morgan set out for Charlotte the next day, arriving on December 4.[10]

When the troops arrived in Charlotte, they found a new commander waiting for them. On October 5th, in response to criticism of Gates' performance during the Camden campaign, Congress voted to make a formal inquiry into his actions. When the representatives also asked George Washington to name a replacement for Gates, the commander-in-chief selected Major General Nathanael Greene of Rhode Island, perhaps his most trusted subordinate. Since 1778, Greene had served as quartermaster general of the northern army, an administrative post he disliked but had taken at Washington's urging. Congress criticized Greene's work and hinted that the general had profited excessively from his department's operations, sparking a controversy that caused Greene to tender his resignation. Unwilling to lose such a valuable officer, Washington allowed Greene to give up the quartermaster's position and appointed him to command the important post at West Point, New York. Greene had barely taken up his duties there when he received word of his new assignment as commander of the Southern Army.[11]

When Greene reached Charlotte on December 2nd to relieve Gates, some of the army's officers expected an ugly scene. Greene was intensely loyal to Washington, while Gates was widely believed to have schemed to obtain the commander-in-chief's position for himself. Greene could have scorned Gates for his defeat at Camden and subsequent flight to Hillsborough. Gates, who could still claim the victor's laurels from Saratoga, might have countered by reminding Greene of his bungled performance at Fort Washington in 1776. (The Rhode Islander had convinced Washington that the isolated New York fort could be held, only to see it fall to the British with a heavy loss of men and supplies.) Both men, however, were professionals, and handled the change of command with tact and dignity. Otho Williams, describing their meeting, noted:

"a manly resignation marked the conduct of General Gates on the arrival of

his successor, whom he received at headquarters with that liberal and gentlemanly air which was habitual to him. General Greene observed a plain, candid, respectful manner, neither betraying compassion nor the want of it .... In short, the officers who were present had an elegant lesson of propriety on a most delicate and interesting occasion."[12]

Some of the army's officers were glad to see Gates go. Characteristically, the taciturn John Eager Howard left no record of his personal feelings at the time. Because of their difference in rank and the fact that Howard and Gates were often at different locations, the two probably interacted very little; it is certain that there was no close friendship between them. However, the quiet Marylander later indicated that he respected his former commander and in fact had warm personal feelings for him. On a trip to Virginia near the end of the war, Howard stopped at Gates' home to comfort the grieving general, whose wife had died on June 1st, 1783. In a short letter that he wrote to Daniel Morgan on September 12th, Howard informed Morgan that he would not be able to visit the Old Waggoner, because "the General's [Gates] Situation has detained us here some days and we find it difficult to leave him, as he will be entirely alone after we go." These remarks demonstrate the respect and affection that Howard felt for Gates and the Marylander was sufficiently concerned about him to forego visits to other valued friends.[13]

Whatever his feelings toward Gates may have been, as a soldier Howard's first duty was to carry out the orders of his new commander. They would not be long in coming, for Greene had been giving careful thought to his army's future operations while he was traveling southward. His experience with the operations around the Delaware River in 1776 and 1777 helped him realize the importance of the southern rivers. Even before he arrived in Charlotte, Greene had assigned various officers "to explore carefully ... the Depth of the Water, the Current, & the Rocks, & every other Obstruction that will impede the Business of Transportation" on rivers such as the Dan, Yadkin, and Catawba. He also ordered shallow-draft boats to be constructed so that they would be available to the army if crossing a river became necessary. Upon taking command of the army in Charlotte, Greene spent the entire night of December 2nd conferring with Gates' commissary general, Colonel Thomas Polk, questioning Polk about every detail including the state of his troops and of supplies, the surrounding territory, and the strength and condition of the British army.[14]

Greene was doing all he could to prepare for the upcoming campaign, but he would not have the assistance of his highest-ranking general. William Smallwood, having secured his promotion to major general, believed that he should have been named to command the Southern Department. Greene's appointment rankled him, and word of his dissatisfaction soon made its way to his new commander. "The General and I met at least upon very civil terms," Greene told his old friend Alexander Hamilton; however, it quickly became apparent "that Smallwood was not a little mortified at my being appointed to this department." Greene defused the situation by ordering Smallwood back to Maryland to raise recruits and secure supplies for the army, thus helping to assure that both the army command and the Maryland officer corps would be spared the controversies that Smallwood had repeatedly provoked.[15]

Having familiarized himself with his army's situation and dealt with Smallwood, Greene turned to the most pressing problem he faced: supply shortages. He noted that his army seemed to consist of only

> "a few ragged, half-starving troops in the wilderness, destitute of everything necessary for either the comfort or convenience of soldiers ... the country is almost laid waste and the inhabitants plunder one another with little less than savage fury. We live from hand to mouth."

Greene acted quickly and decisively to correct this desperate situation. His experience as quartermaster general of the northern army gave him a unique understanding of supply problems, and he knew that the best remedy was to assign reliable men to manage the supply and feeding of the southern army. He appointed Lieutenant Colonel Edward Carrington to be quartermaster general. Although Carrington had been an artillery officer, Greene was impressed with his intelligence and energy. During his all night discussion with Polk, Greene concluded that despite the colonel's commitment to the American cause, his age and health would make it difficult for him to continue to serve effectively. To replace him, Greene selected Major William Richardson Davie, a North Carolinian who had already established a reputation as a daring partisan leader. Davie was not pleased with his new assignment, and tried to change Greene's mind, but the general insisted.[16]

Carrington and Davie would prove to be wise choices. However, it would take time for their efforts to bring results, and meanwhile Greene needed to feed his men. Added to his core of 950 Continentals, the arrival of additional militia had increased his numbers to about 2,300 men, but less than 1,500 were fit for duty. They could not remain at Charlotte, Greene concluded, because there was simply not enough food in the area. He therefore dispatched his engineer officer, Polish volunteer Tadeusz Kosciuszko, to find a more suitable site for a camp. Kosciuszko selected a location at Cheraw, South Carolina. Greene decided to move part of his army there, while sending the Flying Army to disrupt the British farther west.[17]

In formulating his plan, Greene defied the military maxim that a general should never divide his army in the face of a superior enemy. Yet Greene was confident in his own ability to handle his own force, and trusted Morgan, Howard, and William Washington to manage the Flying Army with sagacity. The rapidity of their movements, he declared, would be their best defense. Furthermore, Greene hoped that his maneuver would induce Earl Cornwallis to divide the British forces, giving the Americans an opportunity to defeat them in detail. During his earlier invasion of

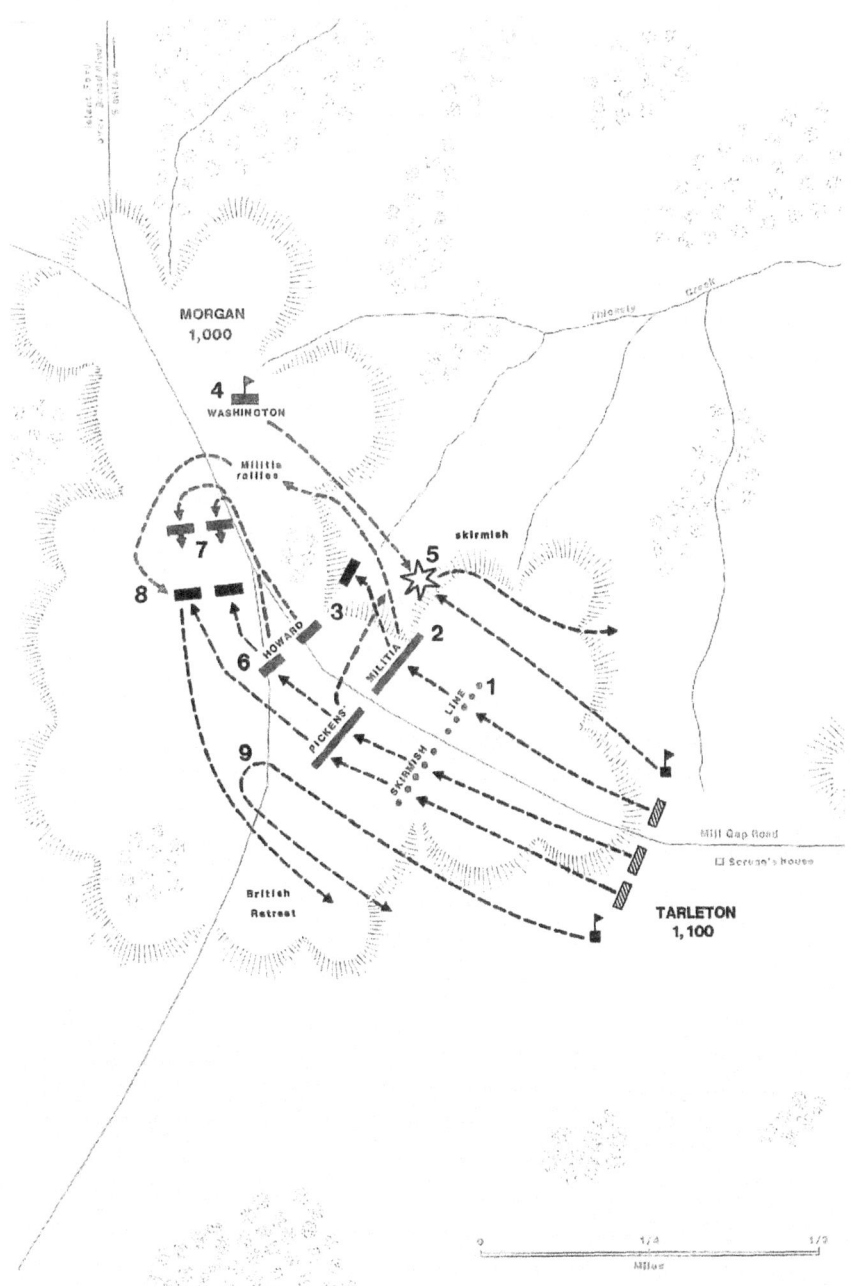

North Carolina, Cornwallis seemed to have lost sight of Ferguson, enabling the Whig militia to win at King's Mountain. Perhaps, Greene reasoned, the Earl would repeat his mistake. Even if this did not occur, a more aggressive stance would encourage South Carolina's Whigs, which would increase the numbers of partisans operating against the British and Loyalist posts.[18]

Before leaving Charlotte, Greene issued his orders to Morgan on December 16. Morgan was to have the command of his own Flying Army (320 Maryland and Delaware Continentals and Washington's 100 dragoons), plus 200 Virginia riflemen, most of whom had previously served in Continental regiments. After leaving Charlotte, Morgan was to march to the west side of the Catawba River and rendezvous with Brigadier General William Davidson's 120 North Carolina militia and a party of South Carolina militiamen under Colonel Andrew Pickens. Green instructed Morgan:

> "This force and such others as may join you from Georgia you will employ against the enemy on the West side of the river, either offensively or defensively as your own prudence and discretion may direct, acting with caution and avoiding surprizes by every possible precaution. The object of this detachment is to give protection to that part of the country and spirit up the people, to annoy the enemy in that quarter; collect the provisions and forage out of the way of the enemy."

If the British moved "in force" toward Greene's position he explained, "you will move in such direction as to enable you to join me if necessary, or to fall upon the flank or into the rear of the enemy as occasion may require." It was a complex, risky mission, one fraught with dire consequences if Morgan failed.[19]

Upon receiving his orders from Morgan, Howard prepared his light infantry for the march. It took several days to get the men ready, and the Flying Army did not leave Charlotte until December 21st, one day after Greene marched with the rest of the army for Cheraw. Morgan's corps covered thirty-six miles in three days without encountering any opposition. At two o'clock in the morning on December 24th, Howard's pickets discerned several mounted men approaching the light troops' encampment in the dark. The sentinels challenged them, received no answer, and opened fire. Howard, concerned about the possibility of a Loyalist raid, ordered his troops to turn out. The light infantry remained alert and under arms all night, but no one else appeared. In the morning the tired soldiers resumed their march. By Christmas Day they had reached the Pacolet River, where Morgan camped.[20]

Morgan contemplated his next move while waiting for the militia to join him. Davidson brought his men as promised and left to get more; Pickens had also come into camp but with only sixty men. With the expected increase in the number of militia, Morgan told Greene on December 31st that he could remain no more than three days in his present location before provisions ran out. He proposed moving westward toward the Appalachians and then marching south into Georgia. In the meantime, he had dispatched William Washington's cavalry and two hundred mounted militia to attack a party of Georgia Loyalists who were harassing the Whigs along Fair Forest Creek. Washington left camp on December 29th, found that the Loyalists had withdrawn upon learning of his approach, and pursued them twenty miles to Hammond's Store. The next day Washington found that the Loyalist commander, Colonel Thomas Waters, had posted his 250 men in a defensive line atop a hill. Washington immediately ordered a charge, and the Loyalists fled without offering any resistance. The American mounted troops cut down 150 of their adversaries and captured 40. The remainder escaped. The Americans did not suffer a single casualty, while the Loyalists' death toll was increased because many of the vengeful militia with Washington executed their prisoners.[21]

Morgan wrote his letter to Greene on December 31st, before he received the one that Greene had written on December 29th. In that letter, Greene warned that he had just received intelligence that Cornwallis was about to be reinforced. Greene advised Morgan to watch British movements "very narrowly," and be prepared to rejoin Greene if it appeared that the British were directing their operations against the main army.[22]

The report Greene received was only partially correct. Additional British troops were indeed on the way to join Cornwallis, but the Earl was not planning to move against Greene—instead, Cornwallis's target was Morgan. Cornwallis had previously asked his superior, Sir Henry Clinton, to send an expedition to Chesapeake Bay to disrupt the flow of American supplies and reinforcements to the Carolinas. Clinton complied, dispatching Major General Alexander Leslie from New York with 2,500 men. However, after Leslie arrived in Virginia on October 29th, had barely begun his operations when Cornwallis ordered him to South Carolina. The Earl wanted to strengthen his forces in the wake of the defeat at King's Mountain. Leslie's men set sail once again reaching Charleston on December 14th.[23]

Leslie, as ordered by Cornwallis, left 1,000 men to reinforce the Charleston garrison and set out with the remainder for Winnsboro. The cold, rainy weather turned the roads to mud, impeding their progress. While Cornwallis awaited Leslie's arrival in late December, he learned of Morgan's and Greene's movements. At first Cornwallis considered advancing north from Winnsboro as soon as Leslie joined him, because such a movement "if executed with tolerable rapidity, might separate the two divisions of the American army, and endanger their being totally dispersed or destroyed." However, Morgan's operations aroused the Earl's concern for the safety of the British post at Ninety Six. On January 1st, 1781, Cornwallis came up with a new plan. He ordered Lieutenant Colonel Banastre Tarleton to cross Broad River with his 550 infantry and cavalry of the British Legion, plus 200 men from the 1st Battalion of the 71st Regiment and drive Morgan out of western South Carolina.[24]

Tarleton set out the next day, advancing twenty miles, and discovered that Morgan posed no threat to Ninety Six. He reported that fact to Cornwallis, suggesting that if he continued to pursue Morgan, the earl could advance with the main army east of Broad River and trap Morgan's Flying Army between the two forces. Cornwallis approved of the plan and sent Tarleton a reinforcement of two hundred infantry of the 7th Regiment, most of them recent recruits, and fifty cavalrymen from the 17th Light Dragoons.[25]

Still unaware of Cornwallis's intentions, Morgan wrote to Greene on January 4 to repeat his request for permission to advance into Georgia. "Forage and Provisions are not to be had" at his post on the Pacolet River, Morgan declared. "Here we Cannot subsist, so that we have but one Alternative, Either to Retreat or move into Georgia. A Retreat will be Attended with the Most fatal Consequences," Morgan warned. "The Spirit which now begins to pervade the People and call them into the Field will be destroyed. The Militia who have already Joined will desert us, and it is not improbable, but a Regard to their own safety will induce them to Join the Enemy." The Old Waggoner added that he would "wait with impatience" for Greene's orders, and "till then my Operations must be in a Manner Suspended."[26]

When Greene received Morgan's letter three days later, he must have grimaced in frustration. He had sent the Flying Army to sweep rapidly through northwestern South Carolina, throw the British off balance, and gather provisions, not to sit hungry in camp while awaiting permission to undertake a risky invasion of Georgia. Nevertheless, the Rhode Islander kept his composure. On January 8th he sent a calm yet firm reply, telling Morgan "I have maturely considered your proposition ... and cannot think it warrantable in the critical situation our Army is in .... Should you go into Georgia and the enemy push this way your whole force will be useless." Greene alerted Morgan that intelligence from several sources indicated "that the enemy have a movement in contemplation," although he still believed it would be directed at his own force at Cheraw. Perhaps the best option, Greene suggested, was for Morgan to take position between the Broad and Saluda Rivers and dispatch raiding parties "for annoying the Enemy, intercepting their supplies" and to "harass their rear if they should make a movement this way."[27]

If John Eager Howard was unhappy with Morgan's unexpected passivity, he did not say so. Howard certainly was aware of Greene's intention to have the Flying Army move rapidly, but given his sense of duty it would have been out of character for him to question Morgan or offer him unsolicited advice. Well acquainted with his commander's great abilities and volcanic temper, Howard withheld his opinion.

Greene received additional correspondence from Morgan on January 13th and he wrote an immediate reply. Again he expressed his opposition to a move into Georgia, but tempered the remark by asking Morgan for details "respecting your plan and object in paying a visit" to that state. Greene also passed on some recent intelligence that he had received. "Col. Tarlton is said to be on his way to pay you a visit,"

Greene reported. "I doubt not but that he will have a decent reception and a proper dismission."[28]

Tarleton was driving forward after Morgan, but the heavy rains turned the roads into quagmires and slowed the British march. Cornwallis promised to move in conjunction with Tarleton, but the Earl did not want to march until Leslie joined him, and the rain slowed Leslie's progress to a crawl. Tarleton could not afford to wait because he realized that if he could strike Morgan while the Flying Army remained west of the Broad River, it would make it nearly impossible for the Americans to escape if they were defeated. The British crossed the Ennoree and Tyger Rivers on January 14th. That night Tarleton learned that Morgan had guards posted at all the fords on the Pacolet River, the next obstacle in the British path. At about the same time, Tarleton received a message from Cornwallis reporting that the main British army had left its camp at Winnsboro, and that Leslie had not yet joined them, but he was close behind. Tarleton replied that he would cross the Pacolet "purposely to force General Morgan to retreat towards Broad river." Tarleton asked Cornwallis to "proceed up the eastern bank" of the Broad "without delay, because such a movement might perhaps admit of cooperation, and would undoubtedly stop the retreat of the Americans."[29]

Local Loyalists and Tarleton's own scouts reconnoitered the Pacolet fords on January 15th. Acting on the intelligence they brought, Tarleton marched upstream—a feint intended to draw the Americans' attention—then shifted direction and crossed unopposed at a ferry only six miles from where Morgan was supposed to be encamped. The crossing was completed during the early morning hours of January 16. Tarleton had originally planned to occupy some nearby log buildings as protection in case Morgan planned an attack, but a British cavalry patrol reached the American camp and found it abandoned. Tarleton moved to the site in the afternoon, where his troops feasted on the half-cooked meal the Americans had left behind.[30]

Morgan had first reacted to Tarleton's advance on January 14th, breaking camp and marching to Burr's Mill north of Grindal Shoals on the Pacolet, which he reached the following day. He intended to draw Tarleton farther from Cornwallis' main army, and into territory that had already been picked clean of provisions by the Flying Army and its supporting militia. At the same time, Morgan was moving closer to new sources of provisions and other militia units in the area. Finally, Tarleton's force had been marching for several days longer than the Americans, and every additional mile Morgan forced them to cover made them more exhausted.[31]

When Morgan reached Burr's Mill he was neither happy nor optimistic. For weeks he had been trying without success to secure cooperation from General Thomas Sumter, commander of partisan forces in northwestern South Carolina. With an unquenchable thirst for personal glory and quick to take offense, Sumter had refused to cooperate. The South Carolinian insisted that he was under Greene's command, not Morgan's, and would only take orders from the Rhode Islander. Governor John Rutledge of South Carolina pleaded with Sumter to assist Morgan, to no avail. Nor did

Sumter budge when orders came from Greene himself. Greene thought that assigning Lieutenant Colonel Henry Lee and his newly-arrived legion of Continental infantry and cavalry to assist Sumter might secure more cooperation, but, as Howard noted, "Lee objected to be put under Sumter's command, and Greene well knew that the service would not be promoted by it, for Sumter and Lee were both very tenacious of command and would not have acted cordially together."[32]

Morgan tried to bypass Sumter by sending his commissary, Captain C. K. Chitty, to one of Sumter's subordinates, Colonel William Hill, with orders to gather provisions between the Broad and Catawba Rivers. Chitty returned to camp and reported that he could accomplish nothing. Hill had refused to comply, telling Chitty "that General Sumpter directed him to obey no orders from me [Morgan], unless they came through" Sumter. Since he could not "procure more provisions in this quarter than is absolutely necessary for our own immediate consumption," Morgan announced to Greene that he could accomplish nothing further. "Upon a full and mature deliberation, I am confirmed in the opinion that nothing can be effected by my detachment in this country which will balance the risks I will be subjected to by remaining here." After reviewing the danger he faced from Tarleton and Cornwallis, he requested that the Flying Army "be recalled." He concluded the gloomy dispatch by noting that "Tarleton has crossed the Tyger at Musgrove's Mill .... It is more than probable that we are his object."[33]

In the midst of this despair, Morgan belatedly learned of Tarleton's approach. The South Carolina militia guarding Easterwood Ford, where the British crossed the Pacolet, had been deceived by Tarleton's feint. Morgan remained unaware of Tarleton's proximity until the morning of January 16th. Shaking off the pessimism of the previous day, Morgan ordered an immediate retreat, leaving some North Carolina militiamen behind to slow any pursuit. The militia remained there until noon before withdrawing. Some of Morgan's men were unhappy with their commander's decision. Thomas Young, a soldier in William Washington's cavalry, recalled, "We were very anxious for battle, and many a hearty curse had been vented against General Morgan during that day's march for retreating, as we thought, to avoid a fight."[34]

Morgan had hoped to reach Island Ford on the Broad River by nightfall, some twenty miles from the Burr's Mill camp. When he realized the muddy roads would make it impossible for his men to cover that distance, he decided to seek suitable ground for a battle. If Tarleton caught up with the Flying Army, Morgan knew that the British commander would immediately attack. Selection of the proper terrain could well make the difference between victory and defeat. During his survey of the area, Morgan encountered Captain Dennis Tramell, who showed Morgan an area known as the Cowpens. It was a place, John Eager Howard wrote:

> *"where pens were made, as was the custom at that time, for the purpose of collecting the cattle once a year to give them salt and more especially to mark*

the ears of the young to distinguish the property of different owners, and to alter the males. This was all the attention given to them. Hence the name Cowpens."[35]

Morgan chose his ground well. The Green River Road followed a northwesterly course through the Cowpens. A dirt route some fifteen feet wide, it intersected Coulter's Ferry Road that ran north from the Pacolet River and Island Ford Road and crossed the Broad River northeast of the field. These routes enabled militia to march easily to the Cowpens. The terrain also rose slowly, so Tarleton's men would be fighting uphill if they attacked. A ravine west of Green River Road and a creek to the east constricted the battlefield. The British would be unable to attempt a flanking maneuver; Tarleton would have no tactical options other than a direct frontal assault.[36]

When the Flying Army reached the field, Morgan ordered them to camp. He remained undecided about fighting, not certain whether his force was sufficient to withstand an attack by Tarleton. At sunset, Colonel Andrew Pickens reached the Cowpens with several hundred militia, and their arrival, Howard observed, convinced Morgan that the army should make a stand. The Old Waggoner summoned his officers for a council of war to announce his decision. No one dissented. "All the [militia] officers were anxious to fight," Howard recalled, and "it is certain Morgan did not discourage them. Many of them had suffered much, their houses burnt & families turned out of doors …. Morgan thought from the favorable disposition manifested by all the corps of militia that he might well calculate on victory." Morgan explained his plan carefully calculated to maximize the effectiveness of both the Continentals and militia. He had clearly learned, from the militia's disastrous performance at the Battle of Camden, that it would be foolhardy to deploy the militia in a position where the Continentals could not support them. Therefore, Morgan decided to form his army in three lines. The troops farthest in advance, a screen of militia sharpshooters, would target British officers and noncommissioned officers when Tarleton attacked, then fall back to the second line. The militia in the second line would then stand their ground long enough to fire two or three volleys at Tarleton's soldiers. Then they too would withdraw, finding safety behind the Continentals posted on the highest ground at the northwestern end of the field. The Continentals would then face the weakened British forces, with Washington's cavalry and the reformed militia behind them on the reverse side of the ridge, ready to assist as needed.[37]

The troops butchered some cattle and ate while Morgan roamed through the camp, encouraging the men. He asked for two companies of volunteers from among the mounted militia to strengthen Washington's cavalry, and they readily came forward. This accomplished, Morgan went from campfire to campfire, speaking with the nervous militiamen who well knew the toughness and determination of their adversary. Thomas Young wrote that Morgan:

> "joked with them about their sweethearts, told them to keep in good spirits, and the day would be ours. And long after I laid down, he was going about among the soldiers encouraging them and telling them that the old waggoner would crack his whip over [Tarleton] in the morning, as sure as they lived. 'Just hold up your heads, boys, three fires,' he would say, 'and you are free, and when you return to your homes, how the old folks will bless you, and the girls kiss you for your gallant conduct!'"

Young added that he didn't believe that Morgan "slept a wink that night."[38]

Their rest was constantly interrupted as additional militia came into camp. The officers were disturbed by the arrival of more of Pickens's men; Morgan conversed with them, retired, but "by the time we were asleep again another party came .... This was the case all night and," Howard confessed, "I wished myself further from them that I might sleep in quiet." Like Howard, most of the American soldiers probably got little sleep given the cold, damp night and the constant arrival of militia, although Morgan did his best to assure that his troops got some rest and food before the coming battle.[39]

Banastre Tarleton had Loyalist scouts and cavalry patrols out all night looking for Morgan and he closely questioned them on their return. Their reports and the interrogation of a Whig militia colonel they had captured, gave Tarleton a fairly accurate picture of Morgan's position, along with information that large numbers of American militia were on the march to the Cowpens. This intelligence strengthened Tarleton's conviction that he must attack quickly. He roused his troops at two o'clock in the morning on January 17th and had them underway an hour later, leaving the baggage behind. The British followed Morgan's route, with light infantry in front, followed by the British Legion infantry, the 7th Regiment, the detachment's two three-pounder cannon, the battalion of the 71st Regiment, and the cavalry in rear. The ground "being broken, and much intersected by creeks and ravines, the march of the British troops during the darkness was exceedingly slow," Tarleton noted. Much time was required to scout ahead and on the flanks of the column to avoid an ambush.[40]

Alerted that Tarleton was approaching, Morgan roused his men. James Collins, a South Carolina militiaman whose unit had reached the Cowpens only a few hours earlier, declared that "we were not permitted to remain long idle, for Tarleton came on like a thunder storm .... After the tidings of his approach came into camp,—in the night,—we were all awakened, ordered under arms, and formed in order of battle by daybreak." After overseeing the deployment of the militia, Morgan rode over to consult briefly with Howard and exhort the Continental troops:

> "He reminded them of the confidence he had always reposed in their skill and courage; assured them that victory was certain if they acted well their part; and desired them not to be discouraged by the sudden retreat of the militia,

that being part of his plan and orders."⁴¹

When the British vanguard came within sight of the Americans, Tarleton paused briefly to discuss the topography with Loyalists from the area. Learning that the open woodland occupied by Morgan was the only easily traversed ground, Tarleton made a decision that came naturally, given his aggressive nature and the constraints imposed by the terrain: he would launch a direct frontal assault. Tarleton sent a portion of his cavalry forward to drive in some parties of militia that were screening Morgan's first line, enabling the British commander to observe the American deployment. The odds seemed imposing, as Tarleton accurately estimated Morgan's strength at about two thousand men. Still, most of this force was militia, who had never demonstrated the ability to withstand a charge by British regulars; their panicked flight at Camden five months earlier undoubtedly remained fresh in Tarleton's mind. Furthermore, Cornwallis's last dispatches, written three days earlier, indicated that the main British army was probably close by. Tarleton was unaware that Cornwallis, after promising to march promptly, had not yet moved. Tarleton formed for battle, placing 50 dragoons on his right flank, followed from right to left by the light infantry, Legion infantry, and 7th Regiment, with another 50 cavalry on the far left. The two three-pounders were placed behind the line near the center. The constricted field gave Tarleton no room to deploy the 1st battalion of the 71st Regiment, so he positioned the unit on his left some 150 yards behind the 7th Regiment. An additional 200 cavalry were similarly held in reserve. Altogether, Tarleton's detachment numbered nearly 1,100 men, about half the size of Morgan's force.⁴²

As soon as his troops had formed, Tarleton ordered the charge. Thomas Young and his comrades, thinking themselves secure behind the hill occupied by Howard's infantry, were complaining of the bitter cold and "slapping their hands together to keep warm" when Tarleton's artillery "opened so fiercely upon the center that Colonel Washington moved his cavalry from the center towards the right wing" to avoid the hail of iron balls. Looking towards the enemy position, Young saw the British move forward "at a sort of trot with a loud halloo. It was the most beautiful line I ever saw." James Collins, farther forward with the militia, recalled "the sight, to me at least, seemed somewhat imposing; they halted for a short time, and then advanced rapidly, as if certain of victory."⁴³

The halt seen by Collins was a brief recoil from the American sharpshooters' fire. As the sharpshooters hurried back to the militia line, the British again surged forward, advancing so rapidly that the citizen-soldiers were unable to fire the two or three volleys Morgan had ordered. "We gave the enemy one fire, when they charged us with their bayonets; we gave way and retreated," Collins admitted. Howard noted that as soon as the British had gotten into position, "they shouted and made a great noise to intimidate, and rushed with bayonets upon the militia who had not time, especially the riflemen, to fire a second time. The militia fell into our rear, and part of them fell into the rear of my right flank."[44]

Because Morgan had planned for the militia to withdraw through and around the Continentals, Howard's troops reestablished their formation as soon as the militia had passed. The British also took the opportunity to pause and redress their ranks, since the militia's fire had inflicted significant casualties. Meanwhile, Tarleton ordered the company of the 17th Light Dragoons on his right to pursue the fleeing militia. The British troopers waded into the running men, slashing with their sabers, but William Washington responded with a counterattack that forced the British horsemen to withdraw.[45]

Now, as the British line surged forward once again, the fate of the day depended on Howard and his Continentals. Young, behind them, saw that "the regulars, under the command of Col. Howard, a very brave man, were formed in two ranks, their right flank resting upon the head of the ravine on the right." Captain Andrew Wallace's Virginia Continentals were posted on Howard's right, their flank guarded by a small force of North Carolina state troops. The veteran Maryland and Delaware Continentals occupied the center, with experienced Virginia militia to their left along with some South Carolina militiamen under Samuel Hammond. Howard rode back and forth along the rear of the line, encouraging his troops to stand fast. Altogether, Howard had just 350 men to face the bulk of Tarleton's force.[46]

Howard gave the order to fire as the British line neared, and the volley checked Tarleton's onslaught. "The british advanced until my regiment commenced firing," Howard reported. For perhaps ten minutes the two lines blazed away at each other, men dropping out of line as they fell dead or wounded. The Continentals stood firm. Tarleton saw an opportunity to commit the 1st battalion of the 71st Regiment and gain the upper hand. He believed that "the advance of the 71st into line, and a movement of the cavalry ... to threaten the enemy's right flank, would put a victorious period to the action." He ordered Major Archibald McArthur to move beyond the left of the 7th Regiment, fire a volley, and then advance. The forward movement of the 71st would be the signal for the other infantry units to renew the attack. "No time was lost in performing this manoeuvre," Tarleton wrote.[47]

The advance of the cavalry and 71st Regiment, accompanied by the wail of the Highlanders' bagpipes, sent the North Carolina state troops on Howard's right fleeing. Howard estimated that his force now faced some 800 British troops, although he showed no sign of dismay at the disparity in numbers. Coolly appraising the situation, he realized that the Legion cavalry and 71st Regiment made his right vulnerable to a flank attack. If the Highlanders of the 71st got into position, they would be able to rake the length of his line with musketry while the cavalry rampaged behind the Americans. Defeat would be certain. Howard therefore ordered Captain Wallace to withdraw his company and reform it at a right angle to the original line, protecting the flank. Instead, Wallace began retreating. "Whether my orders were not well understood or whether it proceeded from any other cause, in attempting this movement some disorder ensued in this company which rather fell back than faced as I wished them," Howard explained. "The rest of the line expecting that a retreat was ordered, faced about and retreated but in perfect order."[48]

To Banastre Tarleton, to Daniel Morgan, and perhaps to every observer on the battlefield except John Eager Howard, it appeared that a crushing British victory was at hand. "The continentals and back woodsmen gave ground: The British rushed forward: An order was dispatched to the cavalry to charge," Tarleton later recorded, his memory rekindling that moment of exhilaration he felt as victory seemed to unfold before him. Morgan, viewing the scene from the opposite perspective, rode to Howard, barely able to control his temper, asked why the Continentals were in retreat. Howard's calm was contagious. He pointed out that his men remained in formation and were not beaten. Morgan told Howard to continue to fall back about a hundred yards and then reform.[49]

Howard had seen an opportunity that neither Morgan nor Tarleton had recognized. The Continentals' withdrawal deceived the British soldiers into thinking that the battle was won. Instead of maintaining their formation, Tarleton's troops broke ranks and rushed forward. Out of formation, their fighting effectiveness was almost nil. As Howard put it,

> *"this retreat was accidental but was very fortunate as we thereby were extricated from the enemy. As soon as the word was given to halt and face about the line was perfectly formed in a moment. The enemy pressed upon us in rather disorder, expecting the fate of the day was decided."*

Howard gave the order to fire when the British were within thirty yards of his line. The results were "unexpected and deadly." Then, Howard ordered a charge executed so promptly that the British never recovered. Howard wrote that at the height of the British charge "an unexpected fire at this instant came from the Americans, who came about as they were retreating, stopped the British, and threw them into confusion .... and an unaccountable panic extended itself along the whole line .... A general flight ensued."[50]

Spurring his horse forward, Howard rode at the head of his troops among the scattered Highlanders. He soon outdistanced the infantry, riding so far ahead that Major Archibald McArthur, commander of the 71st Regiment, initially mistook Howard for a British officer, since the Marylander wore a civilian overcoat that covered his uniform on that cold morning. McArthur later noted that Howard had taken a "great risk" in advancing in such a manner. Howard noted that the British troops "were broken into squads," although some still resisted, killing or wounding several of Howard's soldiers. "I called to them to surrender," Howard reported, "they laid down their arms, and the officers delivered up their swords." According to one account, Howard juggled seven British swords along with the reins of his horse until he handed the trophies off to other soldiers.⁵¹

Captain Duncanson of the 71ˢᵗ's grenadier company, surprised Howard by sticking close to the young Marylander. To Howard's dismay, he found Duncanson "pulling at my saddle, and he nearly unhorsed me. I expressed my displeasure," Howard observed, "and asked him what he was about. The explanation was, that they had orders to give no quarter, and they did not expect any; and as my men were coming up, he was afraid they would use him ill." Howard assigned a sergeant to protect Duncanson, although the officer's comments aroused Howard's concern, since he now heard some of the militiamen shouting "Tarleton's quarters!" The thought that American troops might execute defenseless prisoners horrified Howard, who called out orders to give the British quarter. The soldiers obeyed and no slaughter ensued. Morgan proudly noted that "not a man was killed wounded or even insulted after he surrendered," a result largely attributable to Howard. Duncanson was mistaken about Tarleton's order to give no quarter—the British commander gave no such instructions—but in light of what had occurred three weeks earlier at Hammond's Store, Duncanson's fears were justified. The grateful British officer opened a correspondence with Howard after the war, repeatedly expressing his appreciation of Howard's kindness in the midst of heated battle.⁵²

As the Continentals made their countercharge, Washington's horsemen drove off the British cavalry attempting to outflank the American right. Seeing the British line collapsing, the militia returned to the fight, sweeping around both sides of the hill where Howard's troops had been posted and nearly encircling the British. Tarleton, having failed to rally the infantry, rode back to his cavalry reserve and ordered them to charge and extricate the British infantry. Tarleton rode forward only to find that a mere handful of troopers had followed him; the rest had fled. After a hand-to-hand encounter with William Washington, Tarleton had no choice but to leave the field, too.⁵³

Only the British artillerists fought their cannon to the last. After turning over the prisoners of the 71ˢᵗ to the militia with orders that they be treated well, Howard led his Continentals against the guns. He shouted to some officers to seize the nearest cannon, and Captain Richard Anderson of Maryland outraced a comrade by using his spontoon, a short pike carried by some officers, to pole-vault forward onto the gun and stab the cannoneer an instant before he could fire. Then Howard saw some of his troops surrounding the second gun, about to bayonet an artillerist who refused to give up the match he used to light the cannon fuses. Intervening, Howard spared the man's life. The gunner joined more than 700 of his comrades in captivity, 200 of them wounded. Another 110 had been killed. Morgan's losses, according to one report, were only 10 killed and 55 wounded.⁵⁴

Morgan, Howard, and William Washington had won an overwhelming victory and were nearly bursting with joy. In his excitement, Morgan even kissed a drummer boy. The Old Waggoner then rode over to Howard and cheerfully remarked:

"My dear Howard, you have given me victory and I love and honor you; but had you failed in your charge which you risked without orders, I would have shot you." Laconic as ever, Howard simply replied "Had I failed, there would have been no need of shooting me." Shortly afterward, some American officers brought Howard a distinguished prisoner, Major McArthur. Curious about Tarleton's actions, Howard asked McArthur why the British attacked in such haste, a move that the Marylander had not expected. The crusty old Scot grumbled, Howard wrote, that even though McArthur "was an officer before Tarleton was born" his advice had been ignored, and "that the best troops in the service were put under 'that boy' to be sacrificed." McArthur did not realize, or chose not to admit, that the "boy" he held in such contempt would have won a major victory if not for the brilliant leadership of Howard and his colleagues.[55]

When Morgan's report reached Greene on January 23rd, the Rhode Islander relayed the information to George Washington. "The event is glorious," Greene asserted. The general dashed off similar messages to Samuel Huntington, president of the Continental Congress, Virginia governor Thomas Jefferson, and the Baron von Steuben. The camp at Cheraw erupted into celebration, and Greene ordered a special ration of rum. "We have had a *feu de joie* [celebratory musket fire], drunk all your healths, swore you were the finest fellows on earth, and love you, if possible, more than ever," one of Greene's men told a comrade in Morgan's force. Unfortunately, the happiness would be short-lived. Lord Cornwallis was furious at the news of Tarleton's defeat, and resolved to destroy the American army and recover the British prisoners.[56]

---

1 Higginbotham, *Daniel Morgan*, 94-96.
2 Higginbotham, *Daniel Morgan*, 101-05.
3 John Austin Stevens, "The Southern Campaign, 1780, Gates at Camden," *Magazine of American History*, Vol. 5, No. 4 (October 1880), 282 (quotation); Williams, "Narrative," 508.
4 Higginbotham, *Daniel Morgan*, 2, 4-5.
5 Stephen E. Haller, *William Washington, Cavalryman of the Revolution* (Bowie, MD: Heritage Books, 2001), 65-66.
6 Piecuch, *Three Peoples, One King*, 191.
7 Lord Rawdon to General Alexander Leslie, October 24, 1780, Lord George Germain Papers, Vol. 13, William L. Clements Library, Ann Arbor, Michigan.
8 Robert Kirkwood, "The Journal and Order Book of Captain Robert Kirkwood of the Delaware Regiment of the Continental Line," ed. Rev. Joseph Brown Turner, in *Papers of the Historical Society of Delaware*, Vol. 56 (Wilmington: Historical Society of Delaware, 1910), 11-12; William Seymour, "A Journal of the Southern Expedition, 1780-1783," in *Papers of the Historical Society of Delaware*, Vol. 15 (Wilmington: Historical Society of Delaware, 1896), 8-9.
9 Kirkwood, "Journal," 12; Seymour, "Journal," 9-10; Williams, "Narrative," 509; Paul David Nelson, *Horatio Gates: A Biography* (Baton Rouge: Louisiana State University Press, 1976), 250 (quotation).
10 Kirkwood, "Journal," 12-13 (quotation); Seymour, "Journal," 10; Piecuch, *Three Peoples, One King*, 234.
11 Theodore Thayer, "Nathanael Greene: Revolutionary War Strategist," in George Athan Billias, ed., *George Washington's Generals and Opponents: Their Exploits and Leadership* (New York: Da Capo Press, 1994), 118-20.
12 Williams, "Narrative," 510.

13 John Eager Howard to Daniel Morgan, Sept. 12, 1783, in Theodorus Bailey Myers, *One Hundred Years Ago. The Story of the Battle of Cowpens* (Charleston, SC: News & Courier, 1881), 51-52.
14 Burke Davis, *The Cowpens-Guilford Courthouse Campaign* (Philadelphia: Lippincott, 1962), 57; George Washington Greene, *Historical View of the American Revolution* (New York: Hurd & Houghton, 1876), 270; Nathanael Greene to Edward Stevens, Dec. 1, 1780, in Showman, ed., *Papers of Greene*, 6:512-13 (quotation).
15 Davis, *Cowpens-Guilford Courthouse Campaign*, 62; Showman, ed., *Papers of Greene*, 6:539n; Greene to Alexander Hamilton, Jan. 10, 1781, in Showman and Dennis Conrad, eds., *Papers of Greene*, 7:89 (quotation).
16 Davis, *Cowpens-Guilford Courthouse Campaign*, 59 (quotation); Greene to Edward Carrington, Dec. 4, 1780, in Showman, ed., *Papers of Greene*, 6:516-17; Pancake, *This Destructive War*, 129.
17 Pancake, *This Destructive War*, 130-31.
18 Showman, ed., *Papers of Greene*, 6:588; Buchanan, *Road to Guilford Courthouse*, 294-95.
19 Pancake, *This Destructive War*, 131; Greene to Morgan, Dec. 16, 1780, in Showman, ed., *Papers of Greene*, 6:589-90.
20 Seymour, "Journal," 12; Kirkwood, "Journal," 13.
21 Morgan to Greene, Dec. 31, 1780, in Showman and Dennis Conrad, eds., *Papers of Greene*, 7:30-31; Haller, *William Washington*, 80-81.
22 Greene to Morgan, Dec. 29, 1780, in Showman and Conrad, eds., *Papers of Greene*, 7:22.
23 Henry Clinton, *The American Rebellion. Sir Henry Clinton's Narrative of His Campaigns, 1775-1782, With an Appendix of Original Documents*, William B. Willcox, ed. (New Haven: Yale University Press, 1954), 220-21, 231.
24 Banastre Tarleton, *A History of the Campaigns of 1780 and 1781, in the Southern Provinces of North America* (London: T. Cadell, 1787), 207-08, 210-11.
25 Tarleton, *History of the Campaigns*, 211-12.
26 Morgan to Greene, Jan. 4, 1781, in Showman and Conrad, eds., *Papers of Greene*, 7:50-51.
27 Greene to Morgan, Jan. 8, 1781, in Showman and Conrad, eds., *Papers of Greene*, 7:72-73.
28 Greene to Morgan, Jan. 13, 1781, in Showman and Conrad, eds., *Papers of Greene*, 7:106.
29 Lawrence E. Babits, *"A Devil of a Whipping": The Battle of Cowpens* (Chapel Hill: University of North Carolina Press, 1988), 9; Tarleton, *History of the Campaigns*, 212-13 (quotation), 248-49.
30 Tarleton, *History of the Campaigns*, 213-14.
31 Babits, *Devil of a Whipping*, 52.
32 Buchanan, *Road to Guilford Courthouse*, 304; Pancake, *This Destructive War*, 132; Howard to William Johnson, n.d. (c. 1822), Lee Family Papers, Robert E. Lee Memorial Association, Stratford Hall, Virginia (quotation).
33 Morgan to Greene, January 15, 1781, in Showman and Conrad, eds., *Papers of Greene*, 7: 127-28.
34 Babits, *Devil of a Whipping*, 52-53; Thomas Young, "Memoirs of Major Thomas Young," *The Orion*, Vol. III (October 1843), 88.
35 Babits, *Devil of a Whipping*, 53; Buchanan, *Road to Guilford Courthouse*, 313-14; Howard to William Johnson, n.d. (c. 1822), Lee Family Papers (quotation).
36 Babits, *Devil of a Whipping*, 61-65.
37 Babits, *Devil of a Whipping*, 54-55; Buchanan, *Road to Guilford Courthouse*, 316-17; Howard to William Johnson, n. d. (c. 1822) Lee Family Papers.
38 Young, "Memoirs," 88; Morrill, *Southern Campaigns*, 128.
39 Howard to Johnson, (c. 1822), Lee Family Papers.
40 Tarleton, *History of the Campaigns*, 214-15.
41 James P. Collins, *Autobiography of a Revolutionary Soldier*, John M. Roberts, ed. (Clinton, LA: Feliciana Democrat Print, 1859), 56; Henry Lee, *Revolutionary War Memoirs*, 227-228.
42 Tarleton, *History of the Campaigns*, 215-16; Babits, *Devil of a Whipping*, 30-42, 150-51. In his official report, Morgan claimed that his force consisted of less than 1,000 men. Lawrence E. Babits, after a careful study of the records, has shown this figure to be a vast understatement; Morgan only counted a small portion of the militia who were on the field. Morgan's decision not to include all of the militia in his count was rooted in a dispute that had raged in the Continental Congress and among governors and military officers since 1775. Many Americans distrusted professional soldiers, fearing that a European-style standing army would become a threat to liberty. Thomas Jefferson and Horatio Gates were among those who shared this concern, while George Washington, Nathanael Greene, and Morgan were staunch advocates of a professional military. The defeats of Continental forces at Charleston and Camden in 1780, followed by the American militia's important victory at King's Mountain, seemed to demonstrate the greater effectiveness of militia in the fight for independence. Morgan, unwilling to give the critics of a professional army

further proof of militia's value, and reluctant to diminish the crucial role of the Continentals in the victory at Cowpens, omitted most of the militia when he reported his strength.

43 Young, "Memoirs," 100; Collins, *Autobiography*, 56-57.
44 Collins, *Autobiography*, 57; Howard to [John Marshall], n. d. (c. 1804), Bayard Papers.
45 Babits, *Devil of a Whipping*, 97-98, 100
46 Babits, *Devil of a Whipping*, 101-03; Young, "Memoirs," 100 (quotation); Seymour, "Journal," 295.
47 Howard to [Marshall], n. d. (c. 1804), Bayard Papers; Tarleton, *History of the Campaigns*, 217; Morrill, *Southern Campaigns*, 131.
48 Howard to [Marshall], n. d. (c. 1804), Bayard Papers.
49 Tarleton, *History of the Campaigns*, 217; Howard to [Marshall], n. d. (c. 1804), Bayard Papers.
50 Howard to [Marshall], n. d., (c. 1804), Bayard Papers; Tarleton, *History of the Campaigns*, 217.
51 Howard to Johnson, n. d., (c. 1822), Lee Family Papers; Howard to [Marshall], n.d., (c. 1804), Bayard Papers; Babits, *Devil of a Whipping*, 119; "Papers used in preparing the Biography of J. E. Howard," Oct. 1833, Bayard Papers.
52 Howard to Johnson, n. d., (c. 1822), Lee Family Papers; Babits, *Devil of a Whipping*, 122-23; Morgan to Greene, Jan. 19, 1781, in Showman and Conrad, eds., *Papers of Greene*, 7:153.
53 Buchanan, *Road to Guilford Courthouse*, 326; Tarleton, *History of the Campaigns*, 217-18.
54 Howard to [Marshall], n. d. (c. 1804), Bayard Papers; Babits, *Devil of a Whipping*, 120; Showman and Conrad, eds., *Papers of Greene*, 7:161n. Morgan probably did not report the losses for the militia units he omitted when calculating his force's strength. Babits's study indicates that the actual American losses were at least twice as high as the figures commonly given. Babits, *Devil of a Whipping*, 151-52.
55 Buchanan, *Road to Guilford Courthouse*, 329; Howard to Johnson, n. d., (c. 1822), Lee Family Papers.
56 Greene to George Washington, Samuel Huntington, Thomas Jefferson, and Baron von Steuben, all dated January 24, 1781, in Showman and Conrad, eds., *Papers of Greene*, 7:181-87; Buchanan, *Road to Guilford Courthouse*, 329.

CHAPTER FIVE

THE RACE TO THE DAN

There were two paradoxical developments during the weeks following Cowpens. As news of the victory spread across the United States, American morale soared. Morgan and his subordinate officers were lauded. John Eager Howard at last received the well-deserved recognition for his service. However, at the same time, events in the Carolinas seemed to have taken a decisive turn in favor of the British. Nathanael Greene's army was in full retreat and Lord Cornwallis' redcoats were in hot pursuit. Many Americans shifted their opinion and concluded that Cowpens had been a hollow triumph. Only a few months later they would realize that Greene's apparently ignominious flight had led to the unraveling of the entire British campaign in the South.

At first the American horizon appeared unclouded. Otho Holland Williams, the southern army's adjutant general, expressed his delight to Morgan, with whom he had served in the rifle units at Boston in 1775:

> *"Next to the happiness a man feels at his own good fortune is that which attends his friend. I am much better pleased that you have plucked the laurels from the brow of the hitherto fortunate Tarleton, than if he had fallen by the hands of Lucifer. Vengeance is not sweet if it is not taken as we would have it."*

In a letter to Henry Lee written a week after the battle, Greene praised his officers for their victory. "General Morgans success was glorious and the action was conducted with great good conduct. Lt Colonel [John Eager] Howard and [William] Washington were the heroes of the day."[1]

Morgan sent his aide-de-camp, Major Edward Giles, to carry news of the Cowpens victory to Congress in Philadelphia, a trek that would take the major a full month to complete. When Giles arrived in Baltimore in early February, the *Maryland Gazette* published an account of Cowpens which praised the actions of Howard, the hometown hero. The *Gazette* reported:

> *"When the enemy charged our infantry, they received a severe and well directed fire, but the superiority of their numbers enabled them to gain our flanks, which obliged the infantry to retreat, which they did in good order, and took a new position about 60 paces and then advanced, and gave the enemy a heavy fire, which threw them into confusion. Col. Howard observing this, gave orders to charge bayonets, which was done with such address that they fled with the utmost precipitation, and abandoned their artillery."*

The article made no mention that the Continentals' retreat had been unplanned.[2]

Howard received additional praise from George Washington in the commander-in-chief's General Orders of February 14, issued at New Windsor, New York. The highest honor came from Congress; the representatives resolved on March 9 "that a medal of gold be presented to Brigadier General Morgan, and a medal of silver to Lieutenant Colonel W. Washington, of the cavalry, and one of silver to Lieutenant Colonel Howard, of the infantry of the United States; severally with emblems and mottos descriptive of the conduct of those officers respectively on that memorable day." Congress also approved the presentation of a sword to Colonel Andrew Pickens of the South Carolina militia for his contribution at Cowpens. One side of Howard's medal was to read in part: *"the enemy's Army just thrown into disorder by the fire from the line under his Command, and the latter instantly charging, victory hovering over both Armies and dropping a branch of Laurel to be instantly snatched by Lt. Colonel Howard."* The other side was to carry the inscription: *"In honor of the prompt and decisive conduct and gallantry of Lt. Col. Howard in the action of the victory obtained at the Cowpens 17th of January 1781."*[3]

Unfortunately, nearly a decade passed before Howard, Morgan, and Washington received their medals. Such intricate items could not be produced in the United States, so Congress contracted the work to the Academie des Inscriptions et Belles-Lettres in Paris. Thomas Jefferson eventually procured the medals during one of his sojourns in France and personally carried them back to the United States. In March 1790, President George Washington finally forwarded Howard's medal to the Marylander, along with a letter of congratulations. The President wrote:

> *"You will receive this with a medal struck by order of the late Congress in commemoration of your much approved conduct in the Battle of Cowpens—and presented to you as a mark of the high sense which your country entertains of your service on that occasion. This medal was put into my hands by Mr. Jefferson; and it is with singular pleasure that I now transmit it to you."*[4]

Congress may have had the luxury to move slowly, but the armies in the South did not. The fighting at Cowpens ended by eight o'clock on the morning of January 17th. Morgan, concerned that Cornwallis might be approaching, knew that his Flying Army would be badly overmatched if forced to fight a much larger force of British regulars. Accordingly, Morgan made the astute decision to retreat from the battlefield as quickly as possible in order to move his prisoners out of the reach of Cornwallis and to get his own troops on the road to rejoin Greene, who was in camp more than 120 miles away at Cheraw on the Pee Dee River. Morgan dispatched William Washington and the cavalry to pursue the British dragoons, while he and Howard remained on the battlefield to handle the numerous details involved in readying the troops for rapid movement. They paroled British officers, organized the captured enlisted men for the march (they were to be sent to Virginia), and assigned Pickens and the militia to care for the wounded and bury the dead. By noon, Morgan, Howard, and the Flying Army were marching toward the Broad River, which they crossed that afternoon.[5]

Meanwhile, Cornwallis remained in his camp, having moved not an inch since January 14th, when he had informed Tarleton of his plan to march up the east side of the Broad in concert with Tarleton's detachment. The Earl had no idea of what transpired at the Cowpens, or even that a battle had been fought, until the evening of January 17th, when a few British dragoons straggled into camp with news of the defeat. Cornwallis remained skeptical until Tarleton arrived the next morning to report what had happened. According to an American prisoner in Cornwallis's camp, the Earl was leaning on his sword while listening to Tarleton's account. As his anger grew so did the pressure he exerted on the sword, until the blade snapped. Cornwallis vowed to recover the prisoners. That same morning, Alexander Leslie's reinforcements finally reached the British camp.[6]

The British army marched on January 19, two days after the Battle of Cowpens, heading in a northwesterly direction in the logical expectation that Morgan's force had remained close to the battlefield. The next day, Cornwallis ordered Tarleton to take his cavalry and the Hessian jaegers, the highly skilled light infantrymen who had arrived with Leslie's detachment, to cross Broad River and locate Morgan's force. Tarleton learned that Morgan had long gone, and rejoined the main army that night to inform Cornwallis. Cornwallis redirected his march on January 21st and reached Ramseur's Mill, North Carolina, four days later, only to find that Morgan was still twenty miles ahead of him and on the opposite side of the Catawba River, at Sherrald's Ford.[7]

Cornwallis realized that the loss of most of his light troops had reduced his ability to move rapidly and to gather intelligence. In addition, during the British march to Ramseur's Mills "the train of waggons ... met with great obstacles ... which considerably impeded the progress of the army." The Earl decided that if he was to catch Morgan, he would have to rid his army of all excess baggage, in effect converting the whole force to light infantry. Therefore, he resolved to destroy all of the nonessential wagons and supplies so that his army could pursue the retreating Americans as swiftly as possible. He ordered this done upon arriving at Ramsour's Mills, and set the example for his men by personally throwing his own belongings into the fire. Except for the wagons carrying medical supplies, salt, and ammunition, along with four wagons reserved for use as ambulances, everything was consigned to the flames. The lengthy task of destruction, combined with heavy rains that made the roads nearly impassable, kept Cornwallis in place until January 28th, when he resumed his pursuit of Morgan.[8]

Shorn of its unnecessary baggage, the British army moved much more quickly. During the first two weeks of February, Cornwallis's troops marched about 230 miles, an astonishing distance given the poor roads and foul weather.[9] The army had only covered one-third that distance in the two preceding weeks. Cornwallis had lost several precious days while he destroyed wagons and supplies. In committing his troops to a campaign of rapid movement, he was attempting to beat the Americans at their own game, one in which they had most of the advantages. Furthermore, he had placed his army in a tenuous situation, forcing the soldiers to undertake a difficult campaign without a guaranteed supply of provisions or an opportunity to replenish ammunition or receive reinforcements. The Earl had staked everything on the chance to destroy Morgan and free the British prisoners, a gamble he could not afford to lose.

Morgan, keenly aware of the importance of the prisoners, was determined to prevent their rescue. On his march toward the Catawba River, Morgan put Major Francis Triplett and his Virginia militia in charge of the captives. He sent them in a more northerly direction, so that they crossed the Catawba at Island Ford, seventeen miles upstream from Morgan's crossing point at Sherrald's Ford. This enabled Morgan to keep his detachment between the prisoners and the British army. Shortly after reaching Sherrald's, Morgan ordered another Virginia militia officer, General Edward Stevens, to assume control of the prisoners. Stevens' men had completed their tours of duty and were returning home, so their use as guards would not reduce the strength of Morgan's force. Uncertain of Cornwallis's intentions, Morgan decided to remain at Sherrald's until he received further instructions from Greene.[10]

Morgan had little choice but to remain in camp, since the heavy rain impeded his movement just as it did the British. Furthermore, he had suffered a relapse of sciatica; he informed Greene on January 24th that despite his "sanguine expectations to do something clever," he felt "oblig'd to give over the persuite, by reason of an old pain returning upon me." The next day, Morgan reported to his commander that Cornwallis had reached Ramseur's Mill. He believed the Earl intended to march to Virginia to unite with a detachment under General William Phillips operating along Chesapeake Bay, and that if such was Cornwallis's goal, Greene's army at Cheraw was in a poor position. The Old Waggoner added that his own force was too weak to make any effective opposition.[11]

When he received Morgan's letters, Greene responded with a mixture of optimism and alarm. According to one account, the news that Cornwallis had destroyed most of his wagons and baggage prompted Greene to exclaim: "Then he is ours." Even if this story is exaggerated, Greene certainly recognized that the Earl planned a long and rapid march. Doing so would present the Americans an excellent opportunity to exhaust or assail the British army. Greene told his second-in-command, General Isaac Huger, "I am not without hopes of ruining Lord Cornwallis if he persists in his mad scheme of pushing through the Country." However, Greene also worried about Morgan's condition and realized that Cornwallis could dash his hopes if the British caught Morgan's detachment before it could unite with the main American army.

He therefore ordered Huger to march the troops from Cheraw to Salisbury, North Carolina, recalled Henry Lee's Legion from detached duty with instructions to join Huger, and told Colonel Edward Carrington to assemble boats on the Dan River in case the army was forced to make a rapid retreat. Greene boldly set out on January 28th for Morgan's camp, determined to assist the Old Waggoner as he struggled to evade Cornwallis. Greene was accompanied by an escort of three cavalrymen, an aide, and a guide. The little group succeeded in making the 120-mile journey through Loyalist-infested territory in just three days, without incident.[12]

John Eager Howard was not present to greet the Rhode Islander; he had already left Morgan's camp at the head of the Continental light infantry, heading for Salisbury and a junction with Greene's main army under Huger. "We marched all night in the rain & mud," Howard recounted, "and a most fatiguing march it was." Howard and his troops stopped "4 miles short of Salisbury" at dawn on February 2nd, where he ordered a halt "to get dry and for the men who had fallen out of the ranks from fatigue, to catch up."[13]

On January 31st, Greene convened a council of war consisting of himself, Morgan, William Washington, and General William Lee Davidson of the North Carolina militia. The rain had abated, the water level in the Catawba was falling, and Greene knew that with his army so widely dispersed he could not risk battle. After listening to his officers' views, he decided that Morgan and Washington would march to Salisbury, leaving Davidson and his three hundred militia to guard the fords on the Catawba and to delay Cornwallis's crossing. In an effort to strengthen Davidson's force, Greene wrote a letter to be distributed to the militia officers in Salisbury district, exhorting them to turn out with their men. "If ... you neglect to take the field and suffer the enemy to over run the Country you will deserve the miseries ever inseparable from slavery," Greene warned them.[14]

The Americans left none too soon because Cornwallis had decided to cross the Catawba that night. British cavalry patrols and Loyalist informants brought word of Greene's arrival at Sherrald's, as well as news that the main American army had left Cheraw. Suspecting that Greene planned to unite his force and contest the Catawba crossings, Cornwallis sent units to create diversions "at the most frequented and shallowest" fords while marching the bulk of his army to a little-used ford called Cowan's (or McCowan's). The Earl planned to begin the crossing at one o'clock on the morning of February 1st, but poor roads, darkness, and the overturning of an artillery piece prevented his vanguard from reaching the ford until just before dawn. Wading through cold, waist-deep water, Brigadier General Charles O'Hara's brigade of Guards slogged across the river. Forced to hold their muskets and cartridge boxes over there heads to keep them dry, they were unable to fire at the 250 militiamen who "commenced a galling and constant fire" that killed several British soldiers and wounded thirty-six. Once upon the opposite shore, however, the Guards dispersed the militia. Davidson, who correctly predicted where the British would cross and was directing the defense, was killed. Cornwallis hastened his troops across the river and Tarleton, in advance with the cavalry, learned that the militia was assembling at Torrence's (also called Tarrence's or Tarrant's) Tavern, ten miles from the Catawba. Tarleton raced ahead with his horsemen. Late that afternoon he caught about five hundred unsuspecting militiamen at the tavern. With shouts of "Remember the Cowpens" the dragoons struck, killing over fifty Americans, wounding many more, and dispersing the remainder.[15]

Greene and Morgan, who had taken separate routes, reunited at Island Ford on the Yadkin River, several miles north of Salisbury, on February 3. They found Howard and his troops awaiting them. Greene, although pleased to have Howard's Continentals at hand again, was nonetheless disappointed at the small numbers of North Carolina militia who had turned out thus far. As usual, when the Continental Army was retreating or otherwise appeared to be in a difficult position, the militia was reluctant to take the field, and the proximity of Cornwallis's army made them even more hesitant. Greene estimated that the British troops had been twenty-five miles behind him on the previous night. He ordered his troops to cross the Yadkin the next day. The movement was made none too soon, Greene noted, "before we got over all the baggage and stores the enemy were at our heels. A pretty smart skirmish" ensued. The Americans held off O'Hara's Guards long enough to complete the crossing in safety. Greene reported, "We had secured all the boats, and the river was so high that the enemy could not follow us."[16]

The rapid British pursuit made a junction of American forces at Salisbury impossible, since that town was now in the rear of Cornwallis's army. Greene ordered Huger to redirect his march to the town of Guilford Courthouse to meet Morgan's men. The latter had little time to recover from their exhausting marches; on the night of February 4th, Greene found "that the river … was falling so fast, that it might be forded" the next morning. On February 6th, Morgan and Howard immediately led the troops on another night march, reaching Guilford Courthouse, forty-seven miles from where they crossed the Yadkin. Greene remained optimistic, despite his concern that if Cornwallis defeated his army "he compleats the reduction of the State" of North Carolina. Greene told Huger, "It is not improbable from Lord Cornwallises pushing disposition, and the contempt he has for our Army, we may precipitate him into some capital misfortune."[17]

Greene had overestimated the rate at which the water level in the Yadkin was dropping. When Cornwallis arrived at the river's bank, he found to his chagrin that the Americans had escaped and that the river was unfordable. Perhaps in frustration, he brought up his artillery and fired ineffectually at the American rear guard on the opposite shore. Greene, who had stayed behind to supervise the defense if the British tried to cross, calmly attended to his correspondence, while ignoring the six-pound iron balls that thudded into the mud nearby.[18]

The Earl waited until February 6th for the river to fall only to find the water was still too deep to attempt a crossing, so he dispatched Tarleton to reconnoiter upstream with the cavalry and 23rd Regiment. Tarleton discovered that the several tributaries that joined to form the Yadkin several miles northwest of Island Ford could be crossed easily and without significant opposition. Upon receiving Tarleton's report, Cornwallis ordered his army to march on that route. The British reached the town of Salem, twenty-five miles west of Guilford Courthouse, on February 9.[19]

High water and lack of boats had forced Cornwallis to make a lengthy detour, but it gave his tired soldiers something of a respite. Tarleton observed, "The mild and hospitable disposition of the inhabitants, being assisted by the well-cultivated plantations in their possession, afforded abundant and seasonable supplies to the King's troops during their passage through this district." Cornwallis welcomed the opportunity to feed his troops, but but did not allow them to pause and rest. Determined "to intercept the Americans, and force them to action to the southward of the Roanoke [the Dan River becomes the Roanoke a short distance below Irwin's and Boyd's Ferries]," he pushed ahead toward the upper reaches of the Haw River. On the way, he learned that on February 9 Greene had succeeded in reuniting the scattered American forces at Guilford Courthouse.[20]

The American commander's task had not been easy. He explained to George Washington that he had hoped to assemble his forces sooner. "Heavy rains, deep creeks, bad roads, poor horses and broken harness as well as delays for want of provisions prevented our forming a junction as early as I expected," Greene reported. Knowing that his situation remained precarious, on February 8th Greene had ordered Captain Joseph Marbury to move the hospital and some supplies to Virginia but to send arms and ammunition to Guilford to arm the North Carolina militia. However, Greene continued to be disappointed by the small numbers of militiamen who turned out to join his army. He decided that the army would have to continue its retreat. Greene organized a new "light army" to act as a rear guard, "harrass the enemy in their advance, check their progress and if possible give us an opportunity to retire without a general action." This command consisted of the Continental cavalry, the infantry of Henry Lee's Legion, sixty riflemen from Virginia, and John Eager Howard and his 280 Continental light infantry. The force had a total strength of seven hundred men; Greene gave overall command to Howard's friend and fellow Marylander, Colonel Otho Williams, because Morgan was incapacitated. On February 10th, Greene granted a leave of absence to the Old Waggoner, who was in agony from sciatica and now suffering from other ailments as well.[21]

Morgan had fought his last battle, but he had also helped to change the course of the war. Greene lamented his departure, remarking that "great generals are scarce—there are few Morgans to be found." Howard was also sorry to see his commander and comrade go. In the few months that they were comrades-in-arms, he and Morgan shared danger, privation, grueling marches, and cooperated to achieve victory at Cowpens. They also forged a bond of friendship and mutual respect that lasted until

Morgan's death in 1802.²²

With Morgan gone, Greene carefully selected his best officers: Williams, Howard, William Washington, and Lee, to command the light army. The task that the commander had in mind for this unit demanded proven fighting men of the highest quality. The reunited American army numbered over two thousand men, and Greene intended that Williams, Howard, and their third of the force would keep the British at a distance while Greene led the remaining two-thirds across the Dan River to safety in Virginia. Once the light army had accomplished its assignment, it would also withdraw; in the meantime, it would be engaged in the risky task of fending off Cornwallis's 2,400 veterans, buying as much time as possible while avoiding a pitched battle that would certainly result in its destruction. As the light army left camp at Guilford Courthouse on February 10th, its officers knew that they had very little margin for error in the conduct of their operations.²³

Cornwallis marched from Salem the same day, heading for the upper part of the Dan River. He was aware that Greene had not received reinforcements from Virginia and that the North Carolina militia had not turned out in significant numbers to support him; he wrote:

> *"I concluded he would do every thing in his power to avoid an action on the south side of the Dan; and it being my interest to force him to fight, I made great expedition, and got between him and the upper fords; and being assured that the lower fords are seldom practicable in winter, and that he could not collect many flats [flatboats] at any of the ferries, I was in great hopes he would not escape me without receiving a blow."*

Unfortunately for the Earl, his information was inaccurate, and he in fact was doing exactly what Greene hoped he would do. While Greene and the bulk of the army marched for Boyd's and Irwin's ferries on the Dan, Williams and the light army marched to the northwest to lure Cornwallis in that direction.²⁴

If the light army was to deceive Cornwallis, Williams had to make sure that the Earl knew his location. During his march on February 11, Williams learned that the British advance units were "within six or Eight miles" and sent Lee's cavalry to find them. Howard and the light infantry followed to support Lee. Before the infantry could arrive, Lee's dragoons attacked the British van and captured a few prisoners, who reported that "the whole British Army preceeded by Coll Tarltons Legion is close in our rear." Williams had done his job and it was time to hurry away to rejoin Greene and the main army.²⁵

Greene, hastening toward Boyd's and Irwin's ferries on the Dan, "sent off the baggage and stores" that remained with the army on the evening of February 11th, "with orders to cross as fast as they got to the river." The few North Carolina militia who had joined his army "have all deserted us, except about 80 men," he told Williams.

"It is very evident the enemy intend to push us in crossing the river." Greene now feared that in carrying out his assigned task, Williams might endanger his detachment, whose loss the Americans could not afford. "You have the flower of the army, don't expose the men too much, lest our situation should grow more critical," Greene warned the Marylander.[26]

Williams had his own worries in addition to the hard marching, frequent skirmishing, and renewed deluge of rain—his priority was insuring that the main army made it safely across the Dan, regardless of the risk to the light army. On February 13th, the same day that Greene cautioned him not to expose his force, Williams learned that the main army was still "25 miles from the ferry." Cornwallis was only twenty-two miles behind Greene and ten miles behind Williams, maneuvering so adeptly that he had forced Williams to abandon the "Strong position" at Chambers' Mill, where the light army had hoped to delay the British. Williams decided that Cornwallis was too close to risk moving farther north. Williams told Greene, "Rely on it, my Dr Sir it is possible [for you] to be overtaken before you can cross the Dan even if you had 20 Boats, and your present situation obliges me to lay within reach ... of the Enemy." If the light army moved fast enough to evade the British, Williams predicted, they would be driven to the main army's position before it could cross the Dan. The only alternative, he declared, was that he must risque the Troops he had the Honor to command. Williams, Howard, Lee, and Washington were prepared to sacrifice their troops and their own lives in a last stand if necessary to enable the rest of the army to escape.[27]

Greene's main army started crossing the Dan in the early morning hours of February 14th, and he ordered Williams to start moving his light army toward Irwin's Ferry. That afternoon, Greene dashed off a quick note to Williams to report that the main army was safely across the river, and that "I am ready to receive you and give you a hearty welcome." Williams and Howard were still fourteen miles from the ferry when they received Greene's letter. Assigning Lee to command the rear guard, they led their infantrymen forward. The exhausted soldiers, invigorated by the news that the rest of the army had eluded Cornwallis, covered the distance in a few hours. By evening they had crossed the Dan, and Lee arrived at the ferry with his cavalry before nine o'clock. Waiting boats conveyed the men across the river, their horses swimming alongside. Lee and Greene's quartermaster general, Edward Carrington, were in the last boat. The British army reached the scene six hours later and took possession of some abandoned earthworks.[28]

Greene and his army had won what would become known as "the Race to the Dan," and in doing so they had frustrated Cornwallis's desperate gamble and survived to fight another day. The Earl, although praising "the patience and alacrity of the officers and soldiers under every species of hardship and fatigue," made excuses for his failure to catch and destroy the American army. "Our intelligence was faulty," he told the Secretary of State for the American Department, Lord George Germain, "which, with heavy rains, bad roads, and the passage of many deep creeks, and bridges destroyed by the enemy's light troops, rendered all our exertions vain." Tarleton gave a more objective assessment in his memoirs, crediting Greene for his successful withdrawal. He wrote,

> "Owing to an excellent disposition, which was attended with some fortunate contingencies, General Greene passed the whole army over the river Dan … without their receiving any material detriment from the King's troops. Every measure of the Americans, during their march from the Catawba to Virginia, was judiciously designed and vigorously executed."[29]

Much of the credit for Greene's escape belonged to the soldiers who had demonstrated such fortitude throughout the grueling campaign. "It must be expected that the army, especially the light troops, were very much fatigued both with travelling and want of sleep," Sergeant William Seymour of Delaware wrote after his arrival in Virginia. "We marched for the most part both day and night, the main army of the British being so close in our rear, so that we had not scarce time to cook our victuals." In addition, when the light army did camp, "the duty, severe in the day, became more so at night; for numerous patrols and strong pickets were necessarily furnished by the light troops, not only for their own safety, but to prevent the enemy from placing himself … between Williams and Greene," Henry Lee noted. "Half of the troops were alternately appropriated every night to duty; so that each man, during the retreat, was entitled to but six hours' repose in forty-eight." Lee added that the troops marched in "worn out" shoes, "much tattered" uniforms, and four men had to share a blanket. The officers fared little better, with three sharing a single blanket, and all ranks ate only one meal per day. On February 15th, even Greene confided to Virginia governor Thomas Jefferson that he was "almost fatigued to death."[30]

John Eager Howard had borne more of the burden of the campaign than any officer of equal or greater rank in the army. In less than two months he led his troops from Charlotte to within twelve miles of Camden, back to North Carolina, and into northwestern South Carolina with Daniel Morgan. There he was pursued by Tarleton, fought at Cowpens, participated in the long retreat to Guilford Courthouse and then commanded the Maryland and Delaware light infantry in Williams's detachment. He was among the last American soldiers to reach Virginia. Throughout the hard winter marches after Cowpens he exercised the same steady leadership that he had shown on the battlefield, holding his troops together under the relentless pressure of Cornwallis's pursuit.

Although Greene's retreat was later recognized as a masterful achievement, at the time most Americans considered it a disaster. Looking at the positions of the two armies on a map, it appeared that Cornwallis had driven Greene out of North Carolina. Henry Lee observed that "no operation during the war attracted the public attention than this ... the safety of the South, hanging on its issue, excited universal concern. The danger of this contingency alarmed the hearts of all .... The stoutest heart trembles lest the Potomac should become the boundary of British dominion." Greene understood the public's concern. He also understood that if he remained too long in Virginia, Cornwallis might use the time to mobilize North Carolina's Loyalists and that the beleaguered patriots in South Carolina and Georgia might lose heart and submit to British rule. But Greene was too good a general to wait idly for such events to occur. He had barely crossed the Dan River when he began formulating plans to carry the war back to North Carolina. For John Eager Howard and the rest of the American army, their respite in Virginia would be brief.[31]

---

1 Buchanan, *Road to Guilford Courthouse*, 329; Greene to Henry Lee, Jan. 26, 1781, in Showman and Conrad, eds., *Papers of Greene*, 7:203.
2 *Journals of the Continental Congress*, Feb. 17, 1781, Library of Congress. The delegates granted Giles $5,100 in inflated Continental currency to defray the expenses incurred on his journey; *Maryland Gazette*, Feb. 8, 1781.
3 George Washington, "General Orders," Feb. 14, 1781, Washington Papers; *Journals of the Continental Congress*, March 9, 1781, Library of Congress.
4 John Boles, ed., *Maryland Heritage: Five Baltimore Institutions Celebrate the American Bicentennial* (Baltimore: Maryland Historical Society, 1976), 162; George Washington to Howard, March 25, 1790, Bayard Papers (quotation). An identical version of this letter, addressed to Anthony Wayne and minus the postscript, includes a note that copies were sent to Howard, Morgan, and William Washington along with their medals, see George Washington to Anthony Wayne, March 25, 1790, George Washington Papers, Library of Congress.
5 Morgan to Greene, Jan. 19, 1781, in Showman and Conrad, eds., *Papers of Greene*, 7:154 (quotation); Buchanan, *Road to Guilford Courthouse*, 332.
6 Tarleton, *History of the Campaigns*, 219, 222; Davis, *Cowpens-Guilford Courthouse Campaign*, 71.
7 Buchanan, *Road to Guilford Courthouse*, 337-40; Tarleton, *History of the Campaigns*, 222-23.
8 Davis, *Cowpens-Guilford Courthouse Campaign*, 72; Higginbotham, *Daniel Morgan*, 147; Pancake, *This Destructive War*, 161; Tarleton, *History of the Campaigns*, 223 (quotation).
9 Davis, *Cowpens-Guilford Courthouse Campaign*, 100.
10 Morgan to Greene, Jan. 23, 1781, in Showman and Conrad, eds., *Papers of Greene*, 7:178; Buchanan, *Road to Guilford Courthouse*, 337.
11 Morgan to Greene, Jan. 24, 1781; Morgan to Greene, Jan. 25, 1781, in Showman and Conrad, eds., *Papers of Greene*, 7:190 (quotation), 199-200.
12 Charles Bracelen Flood, *Rise and Fight Again: Perilous Times Along the Road to Independence* (New York: Dodd, Mead & Co., 1976), 383; Greene to Isaac Huger, Jan. 30, 1781, in Showman and Conrad, eds., *Papers of Greene*, 7:220 (quotation); Buchanan, *Road to Guilford Courthouse*, 342.
13 Howard to William Johnson, [c. 1822], Lee Family Papers
14 Buchanan, *Road to Guilford Courthouse*, 342-43; Greene to Samuel Huntington, Jan. 31, 1781; Greene to the Officers Commanding the Militia in the Salisbury District of North Carolina, Jan. 31, 1781, in Showman and Conrad, eds., *Papers of Greene*, 7:225-26, 227 (quotation).
15 Tarleton, *History of the Campaigns*, 223-26 (quotations); Buchanan, *Road to Guilford Courthouse*, 346-48; Davis, *Cowpens-Guilford Courthouse Campaign*, 78-79.
16 Greene to Baron von Steuben, Feb. 3, 1781; Greene to George Washington, Feb. 9, 1781, in Showman and Conrad, eds., *Papers of Greene*, 7: 242-43, 267-68 (quotations).
17 Greene to Huger, Feb. 5, 1781, in Showman and Conrad, eds., *Papers of Greene*, 7:251-52 (quotation); Kirkwood, "Journal," 13.
18 Buchanan, *Road to Guilford Courthouse*, 350.
19 Tarleton, *History of the Campaigns*, 227-28; Davis, *Cowpens-Guilford Courthouse Campaign*, 100; Buchanan, *Road to Guilford Courthouse*, 354.
20 Tarleton, *History of the Campaigns*, 228.

21 Greene to Joseph Marbury, Feb. 8, 1781; Greene to George Washington, Feb. 9, 1781 (quotations); Greene to Morgan, Feb. 10, 1781, in Showman and Conrad, eds., *Papers of Greene*, 7:257, 268, 270n, 271.
22 Buchanan, *Road to Guilford Courthouse*, 351 (quotation); Higginbotham, *Daniel Morgan*, 180.
23 Buchanan, *Road to Guilford Courthouse*, 352; Pancake, *This Destructive War*, 168.
24 Cornwallis to Lord George Germain, March 17, 1781, in Tarleton, *History of the Campaigns*, 264 (quotation); Williams to Greene, Feb. 11, 1781, in Showman and Conrad, eds., *Papers of Greene*, 7: 282; Pancake, *This Destructive War*, 168.
25 Williams to Greene, [Feb. 11, 1781], in Showman and Conrad, eds., *Papers of Greene*, 7:283 (quotations); Tarleton, *History of the Campaigns*, 228.
26 Greene to Williams, Feb. 13, 1781, in Showman and Conrad, eds., *Papers of Greene*, 7:285.
27 Williams to Greene, Feb. 13, 1781, in Showman and Conrad, eds., *Papers of Greene*, 7:285-86.
28 Greene to Williams, [Feb. 14, 1781], three letters of this date, in Showman and Conrad, eds., *Papers of Greene*, 7: 287 (quotation from letter written at 5:30 p.m.); Lee, *Memoirs*, 246-47; Tarleton, *History of the Campaigns*, 229.
29 *Cornwallis to Germain, March 17, 1781, in Tarleton, History of the Campaigns, 264; Tarleton, History of the Campaigns, 229*.
30 Seymour, *Journal*, 17; Lee, *Memoirs*, 238, 248n.; Greene to Thomas Jefferson, Feb. 15, 1781, in Showman and Conrad, eds., *Papers of Greene*, 7: 289.
31 Lee, *Memoirs*, 247; Pancake, *This Destructive War*, 172.

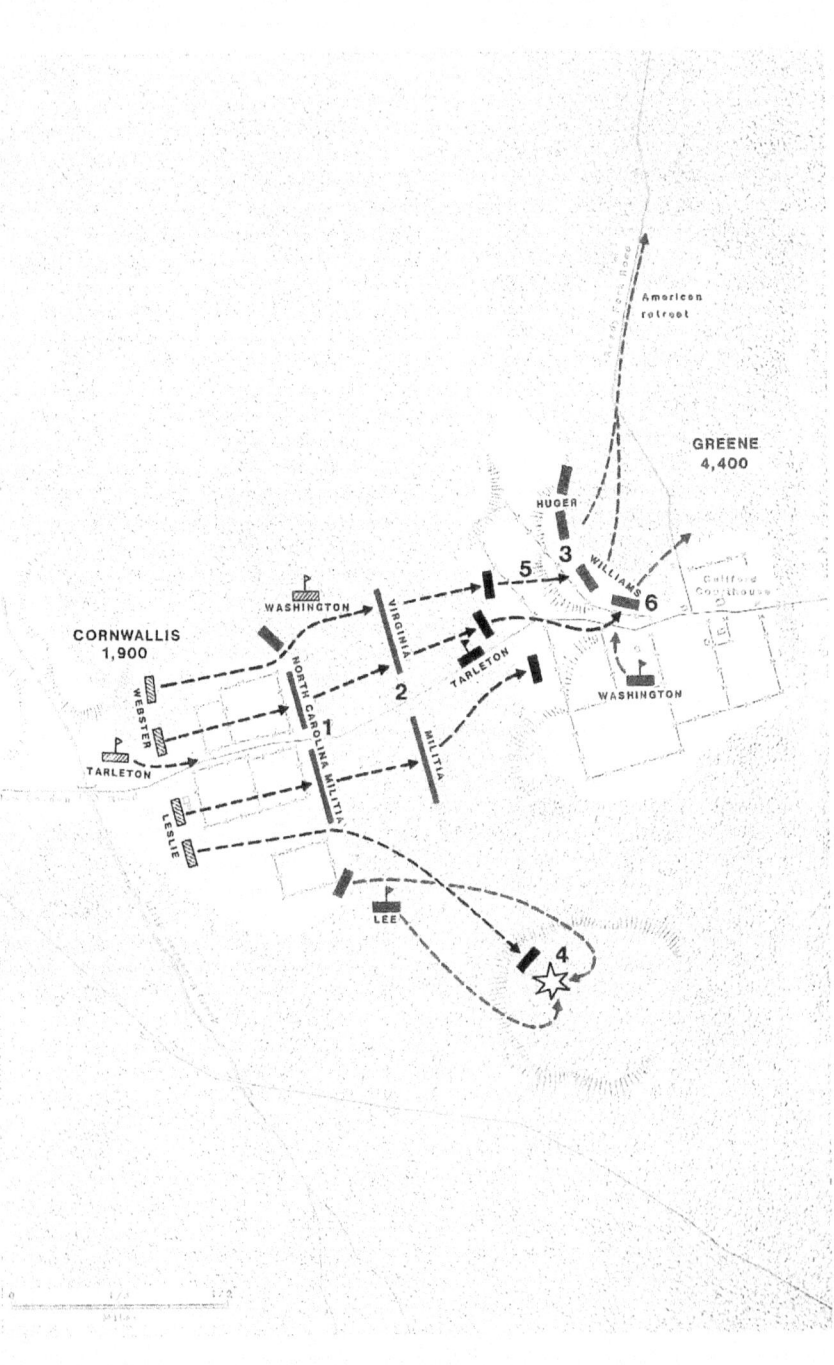

CHAPTER SIX

GUILFORD COURTHOUSE

In the American army's camp at Halifax, Virginia, Nathanael Greene weighed his strategic options while a frustrated Earl Cornwallis fell back with his worn out British troops to Hillsborough, North Carolina. Greene had thwarted the Earl's plans and earned a breathing space, but he had won only one round of the contest. The struggle to control the southern states still hung in the balance. Both generals knew that the outcome would be determined on the battlefield, and not by skillful retreats or clever maneuvers. Greene soon resolved to return to North Carolina and challenge Cornwallis, and the always aggressive Earl welcomed the prospect of a head-on confrontation.

Meanwhile, the American troops enjoyed the opportunity to recuperate from the arduous campaign. They were in friendly country, protected by the formidable barrier of the Dan River, and could now spend several days resting, healing, and enjoying the rare luxury of ample food supplies. Rumors that large numbers of fresh troops were on the way to reinforce them also elevated their spirits. Henry Lee wrote:

> *"In the camp of Greene, joy beamed in every face; and as if every man was conscious of having done his duty, the subsequent days to the reunion of the army on the north of the Dan were spent in mutual gratulations; with the rehearsal of the hopes and fears which agitated every breast during the retreat; interspersed with the many simple but interesting anecdotes with which every tongue was sprung."*

Lieutenant Colonel John Eager Howard was undoubtedly just as relieved as his comrades to be safe from British pursuit, and to relish the few days of rest and abundant food. He and his men had certainly earned such luxuries. Given Howard's taciturn nature, however, it is unlikely that he was among those sharing "simple but interesting anecdotes." He would have stayed quietly in the background attending to his duties, insuring that his troops recovered from their exertions while he prepared for the next phase of the campaign. Howard was content to let others spin stories around the campfires.

Earl Cornwallis and his British army faced a more difficult situation. They found themselves in territory that had been picked clean of all provisions. They were more than 150 miles from the nearest British supply base at Wilmington, North Carolina, and 240 miles from their original base at Camden, South Carolina. Cornwallis decided that his army was "ill suited to enter … so powerful a province as Virginia," consequently after allowing his troops a day of rest on the south bank of the Dan, he "proceeded by easy marches to Hillsborough," the former capital of North Carolina, sixty-two miles from the Dan River ferries. The slow pace was necessary given the exhausted condition of the British soldiers and the fact that many of them had worn out their shoes during the pursuit of Greene. The army reached its destination on February 20.[1]

At Hillsborough Cornwallis found some provisions, but not enough to sustain his troops for long. Charles Stedman, a Pennsylvania Loyalist who served as the army's commissary general, reported that "such was the condition of the British army, that [I] with a file of men, was obliged to go from house to house, throughout the town, to take provisions from the inhabitants, many of whom were greatly distressed by this measure." One such foray discovered a trove of salt pork, beef, and live hogs, resources that were quickly consumed. Cornwallis reluctantly ordered his troops to seize oxen found on area farms, and at last slaughtered many of his own draft horses to feed his men. Other troops were assigned the tasks of making shoes from animal hides and repairing uniforms and equipment.[2]

Assessing his situation, Cornwallis grew pessimistic. "The immense extent of this country, cut with numberless rivers and creeks, and the total want of internal navigation, will make it very difficult to reduce this province to obedience by a direct attack upon it," he informed Lord George Germain.[3]

Cornwallis knew that he would have a better chance to pacify North Carolina if he could obtain Loyalist assistance, so he called upon Loyalists in the region to take up arms in the royal cause. Shortly after reaching Hillsborough, he "invited, by proclamation, all loyal subjects ... to stand forth and take an active part in assisting me to restore order and constitutional government." The poor response discouraged the Earl. Even though the British had alienated many potential supporters by impressing supplies in and around Hillsborough, hundreds of Loyalists did come to Cornwallis's camp. However, the sight of the bedraggled, hungry British soldiers did not inspire them with confidence; instead it had the opposite effect. They realized that the British "could neither feed nor equip them." Many Loyalists expressed concern that the Continental Army would soon return. Aware of what happened to Loyalists in Hammond's Store, Kings Mountain, and elsewhere in South Carolina, they admitted that their "dread of violence and persecution prevented their taking a decided part in a cause which yet appeared dangerous." A few stalwart Loyalists who came to Hillsborough did promise that they would raise men to serve with the British, and Cornwallis and Josiah Martin, the colony's former royal governor, issued them military commissions.[4]

As he had done in South Carolina, Cornwallis soon complained that the Loyalists of North Carolina were not as numerous as he had been led to believe, and they were timid if not outright cowards. Tarleton, whose Legion was composed almost entirely of Loyalists, understood them better and later explained their reluctance to serve. He wrote:

> "The King's troops had never made any serious effort to assist the well affected in North Carolina since the commencement of the war," he wrote. Since then, "the variety of calamities which had attended the exertions of the loyalists, had not only reduced their numbers and weakened their attachment, but had confirmed the power and superiority of the adverse party, and had occasioned a general depression in the King's friends."

This attitude "would not easily have been shaken off in the most prosperous times, and therefore was not likely to be warmed into action with the present appearance of public affairs."[5]

Events soon proved that the Loyalists' fears were well founded. Greene had hoped that Cornwallis might be lured into crossing the Dan, where Greene believed he would be able to fight a battle on advantageous terms. If the British did not follow, he told North Carolina Governor Abner Nash, "the moment the enemy move towards Hillsborough I shall fall into their rear." Greene took the first step on February 18th, only four days after his army had crossed the Dan, by ordering Henry Lee with his Legion, along with Andrew Pickens's South Carolina militia and two companies of Maryland Continentals under Captain Edward Oldham, back across the river. Their orders were to harass the British army and check any Loyalist efforts to organize in support of Cornwallis. Greene personally crossed the Dan to meet secretly with Lee and Pickens, thus assuring that his plans were understood. He promised that the main army would follow them into North Carolina in a few days.[6]

On February 25th, Lee and Pickens got their opportunity to strike at the Loyalists when their detachment encountered a force of between three and four hundred men riding to join Cornwallis. Doctor John Pyle, a North Carolinian who lived between the Haw and Deep rivers, had raised the loyalist force. Pyle notified Cornwallis that he was en route to Hillsborough, and on February 23rd the Earl dispatched Tarleton with 200 cavalry, 150 British infantry, and 100 Hessian light infantrymen known as jaegers, to meet the Loyalists and escort them safely to the army's camp. Tarleton met a party of American militia the next day, dispersed them, and learned from the prisoners that a Continental force might be in the area. He sent orders to Pyle to speed his march, and he repeated them later in the day upon confirming that Lee's troops were nearby. The Loyalists, however, did not hurry, stopping frequently to visit friends along their line of march. Pyle's advance scouts met a mounted unit on February 25th, and he assumed that the green-jacketed cavalrymen were Tarleton's soldiers. Instead, they had met Lee's Legion. Lee seized the opportunity to carry out a ruse, pretended to be Tarleton, and sent the scouts back to Pyle with orders to form his troops along the road to allow the regulars to pass. Pyle obeyed and Lee proceeded having ordered Pickens to follow but keep his militia concealed. Lee's men rode past the mounted Loyalists, whose muskets were laid across their saddles or slung or over their shoulders. Upon reaching Pyle at the far end of the Loyalist column, Lee was about to seize him when some Loyalists at the opposite end of the line spied Pickens's men and realized the deception. Before the Loyalists could react, Lee's and Pickens's troops attacked them. Lee claimed that ninety were killed; Tarleton put the number at two hundred. The Americans suffered no casualties. "We lost not a man, and only one horse," Lee reported.[7]

Lee himself admitted that some Loyalists were killed despite their attempts to surrender and their appeals for mercy, defending such actions with the assertion that in war the "first injunction is to take care of your own safety." Some accounts indicate that a few Loyalists were taken prisoner, and that six were later hacked to death with broadswords in retaliation for alleged British atrocities. Cornwallis stated that "a number" of Pyle's men "were most inhumanly butchered, when begging for quarter, without making the least resistance." Greene, who normally decried excessive violence, conceded that his troops "made a most dreadful carnage" of the Loyalists: "upwards of 100 were killed, and most of the rest cut to pieces." He accepted the bloodshed as necessary, noting that "Pyle's Massacre," as the event came to be known, "had a very happy effect on those disaffected Persons, of which there are too many in this Country." Greene told Pickens that "the defeat of the Tories was so happily timed, & in all probability will be productive of such happy consequences, that I cannot help congratulating you on your success." The Rhode Islander's assessment was correct. Pyle's Massacre crushed any enthusiasm that remained among North Carolina's Loyalists, and put an end to Cornwallis's slender hopes of securing substantial support from that colony's loyal inhabitants.[8]

Greene had already returned to North Carolina, having recrossed the Dan on February 22, three days before Pyle's defeat. Greene once again put Otho Williams in command of a screening force composed of Howard's infantry, Lee's Legion, and William Washington's cavalry. Their task, as Lee described it, was to play "that arduous game of marches, countermarches, and manoeuvres, which greatly contributed to baffle ... Lord Cornwallis." The American army's advance sent most of the Loyalists still with the British scurrying back to their homes, and forced Cornwallis to recall his detachments. The British army left Hillsborough on February 26 and headed for the Haw River, which it crossed the next day. Cornwallis took position near Alamance Creek and waited for Greene's next move.[9]

Williams anticipated Cornwallis's departure from Hillsborough, but his and Howard's desire to press the British nearly resulted in a near brush with disaster for Howard and his troops. On February 25 Williams was at Mitchell's Mill, only sixteen miles from Hillsborough and Howard's infantry had been detached and was even closer to the enemy. Reports indicated that the British had left Hillsborough and taken position south of the town. Williams planned to unite his force with Howard's and probe the enemy the next day. Howard, having gotten the same information, decided to push toward the town without waiting for Williams. Williams wrote, "Lt Coll Howard got within four Miles of Hillsborough Yesterday before he recd information of the Enemy's not being gone." One of Howard's soldiers, Thomas Anderson, believed that the force was within two miles of the town before Howard learned that the British were still there. Howard ordered a hasty withdrawal. The troops "faced about and marched back quick time," Anderson noted. They joined Williams on February 26 and set off on another rapid march, trying to link up with Lee and Pickens while simultaneously tracking the route of the British army.[10]

Over the next week, Williams and Howard stayed close to Cornwallis, sparring occasionally with British detachments as the Earl probed for an opportunity to isolate some of the dispersed American units and overwhelm them. Williams, reinforced by several hundred militia under Colonel William Campbell, spread his force over a relatively broad area. When Cornwallis learned of the American dispositions on March 5, he saw an opportunity to separate Williams's screening force from Greene's main army. The Earl rushed his troops toward Weitzel's Mill on Reedy Fork Creek to take a position between the two American forces. Learning of Cornwallis's movement, Williams marched his men toward the Mill while Campbell's militia and William Washington's cavalry tried to delay the British advance. Williams was able to place his main force in a good defensive position on the north side of the creek before Lieutenant Colonel James Webster and the leading British units drove back Campbell and Washington and reached the creek. Webster ordered his three regiments to ford the stream and assault the Americans. Howard's infantry stood their ground, delivering a steady fire that checked the initial British attack. Supported by the fire of four artillery pieces, Webster's soldiers regrouped and drove back the Continentals. Howard's staunch resistance had given Williams time to gather his forces and withdraw safely. The British pursued Williams for several miles but Cornwallis, having received a report that Greene was marching in his direction, recalled his cavalry. Tarleton considered the move a mistake, believing that the army had a chance to get between the scattered American units and defeat some of them before they could unite, or prevent their junction. Cornwallis dismissed his subordinate's advice, and ordered his army to march to the southwest.[11]

The Earl had been eager for weeks to bring Greene to action, and Greene had deftly avoided every attempt. Now the American commander was ready to stand and fight because he was finally able to assemble a force that was large enough to take on Cornwallis's professional army. The arrival of large numbers of militia from Virginia and North Carolina, plus an additional 550 Virginia Continentals, raised the strength of the American army to over 4,600 men, including about 2,000 combat veterans. Greene's army was now considerably larger than Cornwallis' army. The British force had been reduced to about 2,000 men by their loss of some 500 soldiers through desertion, illness, and combat casualties during the previous weeks' grueling campaign. Nevertheless, Cornwallis's force of experienced regulars had triumphed before against superior numbers, and he was confident that they could do so again.[12]

After several days of maneuvering, on March 14th Greene took a strong position near Guilford Courthouse, an area that he had examined closely when he passed through on the retreat to Virginia. He originally considered attacking the British, but decided that the ground afforded him more advantage on the defensive. Greene had studied the tactics that Daniel Morgan had used so effectively at the Battle of Cowpens. Morgan, with whom Greene continued to correspond after the Old Waggoner had returned home, urged Greene to employ the three-line defense in future combat. The ground at Guilford Courthouse was well suited to the plan, as it was very similar to the terrain at Cowpens. The New Garden (or Salisbury) Road on which the British were expected to advance bisected fields that sloped upward, giving Greene the advantage of high ground. "Timber and thick under brush" bordered the fields, making any British effort to mount a flank attack difficult. Greene posted the North Carolina militia under Generals John Butler and Thomas Eaton in the front line, supported by two pieces of artillery. To guard against possible flanking attacks, Greene assigned William Washington's cavalry, Captain Robert Kirkwood's Delaware Continentals acting as light infantry, and Colonel Charles Lynch's militia riflemen to protect his right. Lee's Legion, some additional light infantry, and Colonel William Campbell's riflemen secured his left. These experienced and capable troops would support the first line at the start of the battle, but Greene intended that they fall back to each successive line and assist with the defense as the British advanced.[13]

Greene's second line was three hundred yards behind the first line, in a strip of forest that divided the fields. He deployed the Virginia militia, commanded by Robert Lawson and Edward Stevens, in these woods. Stevens had been humiliated at the Battle of Camden the previous August when his militia had panicked and fled at first contact with the British. He was determined that his troops would stand and fight this time. Stevens placed a group of tough veterans behind his brigade with orders to shoot any men who attempted to flee. The third line, three hundred yards behind the second, consisted of the Virginia Continentals under Brigadier General Isaac Huger and the Maryland Continentals under Colonel Otho Williams. Lieutenant Colonel John Eager Howard was with the 1st Maryland Regiment, where he served as second-in-command to Colonel John Gunby, who had recently joined Greene's army.[14]

Many officers, after having commanded a unit for any considerable period of time, would have resented being superseded, especially if they had performed as well as Howard when he commanded the 1st Maryland. Yet Howard, attentive as always to military protocol, made no protest about being relegated to a subordinate role under Gunby, under whom Howard had previously served. Howard merely noted that the officers and men of the light infantry that had comprised the part of the screening force he had commanded "were ordered to join our respective regiments, and I then acted as Lt. Colo. under Gunby." However, Howard quickly realized that the arrival of reinforcements from Maryland had created problems in his home state's units. He wrote:

> *"There was a new regiment sent out from Maryland ... and it was thought that the officers had been more favored than the officers of the old regiments. It joined us a few days before the action and there were such jealousies among the officers that Genl. Greene sent all the new officers home, and made a new arrangement of the two regiments. The most of the new men were thrown into the second regiment which was very deficient in officers."*

Amidst this controversy, Greene must have appreciated Howard's tactful, uncomplaining acceptance of a post subordinate to Gunby.[15]

Cornwallis learned of Greene's arrival at Guilford Courthouse on March 14, the same day the Americans reached that location. Since the British army was camped only twelve miles away, the Earl immediately resolved to attack the next day. After sending off his baggage to Bell's Mill on Deep River with a strong escort, Cornwallis "marched with the rest of the corps at daybreak on the morning of the 15th, to meet the enemy, or attack them in their encampment." Greene ordered Lee to advance down the New Garden Road with his Legion and some of Campbell's riflemen to provide advance warning of Cornwallis's approach and delay the British advance. Tarleton's cavalry, riding ahead of the main army, encountered them about four miles from Greene's position. A "very severe skirmish" ensued, Lee was forced back, and his troops resumed their assigned position on the left of the American first line for the impending battle. Tarleton took several prisoners, but to Cornwallis's dismay, they were not familiar with the ground around Guilford Courthouse, nor did they have any useful information about the American deployment. An effort to procure intelligence from local residents proved equally futile. Cornwallis had to plan his attack with almost no information on the terrain or on the disposition of Greene's army.[16]

The Earl examined the ground as best he could. "I resolved to attack the left wing of the enemy," he reported. Cornwallis placed Major General Alexander Leslie in command of his right, with the 71st Regiment of Scottish Highlanders and the Hessian regiment Von Bose in the front line and the 1st Battalion of Guards in reserve. Lieutenant Colonel James Webster commanded the 23rd and 33rd Regiments on the left, supported by the grenadiers and 2nd Battalion of Guards under Brigadier General Charles O'Hara. Cornwallis had already deployed his artillery farther to the left, and the guns opened fire to cover the British troops while they moved into position. The American six-pounders quickly answered the British cannonade, and the frontline troops on both sides came under artillery fire in the opening minutes of the battle. Cornwallis sent the light infantry of the Guards and the Hessian Jaegers beyond the guns to secure his left flank, leaving Tarleton's cavalry "in the road, ready to act as circumstances might require." By 1:30 in the afternoon the British preparations were complete. The Earl halted his cannonade, which had lasted twenty minutes, and ordered Leslie to open the attack.[17]

Recent rain had soaked the ground, and the British troops plodded forward, stepping to the beat of drums and the skirling of the 71st Regiment's bagpipes. Observing that the American line extended far beyond his right, Leslie ordered up the 1st Guards Battalion to extend his line in that direction. At about the same time, Cornwallis directed Webster to move forward and support Leslie's left. The North Carolina militia watched from behind a rail fence as the veteran British troops moved into place with precision. The long, straight lines, the bright uniforms and shining bayonets, the drums and bagpipes, and the steely determination on the faces of their adversaries had the desired effect on the North Carolinians, who fired their first, ragged volley when the advancing British lines were some 140 yards away. John Eager Howard observed the action from his position in the third line, and noted that some of the militia in the front line did not even fire one shot, but turned and ran as the British approached. Cornwallis's troops moved forward relentlessly, and even though the fire of the remaining militiamen became more effective as the range closed, the threat of facing a bayonet charge proved more than most of them could stand. "To our infinite distress and mortification, the North Carolina militia took to flight," Henry Lee lamented. "Every effort was made by the officers ... to stop this unaccountable panic," but without success. "So thoroughly confounded were these unhappy men that, throwing away arms, knapsacks, and even canteens, they rushed like a torrent headlong through the woods."[18]

Some of the militia showed more determination, ignoring the flight of their comrades and holding their ground as long as possible. Opposite the British 23rd Regiment, the North Carolinians held their fire until the king's troops were within forty yards and then staggered them with a well directed volley. Webster rode to the front of his men and urged them forward in an assault that routed the defenders. On Greene's left, some of Thomas Eaton's militia posted near Campbell's riflemen and Lee's Legion stood fast. Leslie ordered the Hessian regiment and 1st Guards Battalion to drive back these troops and secure his right flank. Lee and Campbell fought doggedly but were slowly pushed back. Instead of retreating toward the American second line, they drifted in an easterly direction. By the time the battle ended, they were about a mile away from the rest of the army.[19]

On Greene's right, Kirkwood's Delaware veterans and Lynch's riflemen delivered "a heavy fire" into the exposed flank of the 33rd Regiment, checking the British advance. With the North Carolina militia gone and Captain Anthony Singleton having withdrawn his two pieces of cannon, Webster was able to order a change of front to his left. Calling up the jaegers and Guards light infantry in support, he drove off Lynch and Kirkwood, who retreated to the American second line. Webster then shifted front to face the main American force once again, having brought up the grenadiers and 2nd Battalion of the Guards to fill the gap between his force and Leslie's force.[20]

Their flanks cleared, Leslie and Webster reformed their line of battle and resumed the advance. Cornwallis ordered the artillery to move forward along the road at the same pace as the infantry. None of the British commanders knew what lay ahead, but their battle-hardened soldiers confidently pressed forward. Beyond the field, the ground was forested, and the Virginia militia of Lawson and Stevens were deployed in these woods, awaiting the British advance. Greene worked to insure that these Virginia troops were more carefully selected and better led than the group that fled so ignominiously at Camden seven months earlier. Howard reported that during the retreat across North Carolina, Greene wrote to Stevens, Lawson, and the other Virginia militia officers to demand that they bring reliable men to the field. Greene "pressed them to come out with their neighbours, for that the militia sent out under your laws were useless," Howard wrote, knowing the accuracy of Greene's statement from his own experience at Camden, and perhaps having influenced his commander's action by recounting it. "High bounties were given to worthless substitutes who deserted from county to county to get new bounties, and when they were got into the field they had no intention of fighting." Howard noted the effect of Greene's prodding: "officers of character joined Genl. Greene with their neighbours the yeomanry of the country," and he witnessed "the brave conduct of these men" at Guilford Courthouse.[21]

The Virginians took full advantage of the woods and the numerous ravines on this part of the field, taking cover behind trees and in the depressions to fire at the advancing line of British troops. Unable to see their adversaries, the British soldiers could only press forward doggedly until they reached the trees. The bitter fighting in these woods lasted almost a half hour. Cornwallis reported, "The excessive thickness of the woods rendered our bayonets of little use, and enabled the broken enemy to make frequent stands, with an irregular fire, which occasioned some loss, and to several of the corps great delay." The British experienced the greatest difficulty on their left, where Kirkwood and Lynch were able to fire into their flank, and some of Lynch's riflemen even circled behind the British to fire into their rear before the 33rd Regiment finally drove them off. Cornwallis grew so concerned that despite having his own horse shot from under him just minutes before, he took a horse from a cavalryman and rode alone across the open field to where the 23rd Regiment had temporarily halted. His exhortations sent the troops surging forward.[22]

As the fighting in the woods intensified, some of the militia who had not yet been engaged became alarmed when they saw British troops on their flank and rear, and they fled. "Holcombe's regiment and ours instantly broke off without firing a single gun and dispersed like a flock of sheep frightened by dogs," St. George Tucker admitted. This left the rest of Lawson's brigade in a bad position, and the men soon fell back. Stevens's brigade fought longer. However, they lost cohesion when they were outflanked on their right. Stevens was wounded in the thigh. The loss of their commander increased the Virginians' confusion in an already chaotic situation. Continuing their determined (if by now disorganized) advance, the British forced the last of the militia from the woods. Greene anticipated that his second line would delay but not stop the British advance and he was pleased with the men's performance, noting that "the Virginia Militia gave the Enemy a warm reception and kept up a heavy fire for a long time" before "being beat back."[23]

Some British units moved through the woods more rapidly than others. Their pace was determined by the difficulty of the terrain, density of the forest, and the resistance from the militia opposite them. Instead of approaching the final American line in a unified, orderly body, the British emerged from the woods piecemeal to find that a solid line of 1,400 fresh Continental soldiers waited for them some three hundred yards ahead. As Tarleton described it, "some corps meeting with less opposition and embarrassment than others, arrived sooner in presence of the continentals, who received them with resolution and firmness."[24]

First out of the woods were the light infantry of the Guards, the 33rd Regiment, and the Hessian jaegers, with Webster at their head. The field sloped downward before rising again to the crest where the 1st Maryland waited, with Kirkwood's Delaware Continentals to their right. Webster did not even pause to ascertain the location of the rest of the British army. He ordered his men forward, and they charged into the hollow and up the opposite side—straight into the waiting Continentals. The Americans held their fire until the British were within one hundred feet, then they delivered a devastating volley. Shaken, the British fell back in disarray but Webster kept control of his men and led them across a ravine to higher ground, despite having received a painful knee wound that would prove mortal. There they took position and reformed their lines while Webster waited for other units to come up.[25]

The next British unit to clear the woods was the 2nd Guards Battalion, now commanded by Lieutenant Colonel James Stuart because Brigadier General Charles O'Hara had suffered two wounds and was out of action. The battalion "found a corps of continental infantry, much superior in number"—the 2nd Maryland—"formed in an open field on the left of the road," Cornwallis wrote. "Glowing with impatience to signalize themselves, they instantly attacked and defeated them, taking two six-pounders." Cornwallis did not exaggerate. Howard stated that the 2nd Maryland "immediately gave way," as the British surged toward them with bayonets leveled, a flight he attributed "to the want of officers & having so many new recruits."[26]

The rout of the 2nd Maryland threatened the American army with destruction. Howard, Gunby, and Huger, who commanded the Virginia Continentals to the right of the 1st Maryland, at first did not even realize their dangerous situation. Howard noted, "The guards pursued" the fleeing men of the 2nd Maryland "into our rear, where they took two pieces of artillery. This transaction was in a great measure concealed from the 1st regiment by the woods and unevenness of the ground." Howard learned what was happening when a staff officer rode over to him and shouted that the British "were pushing through the cleared ground and into our rear, and that if we would face about & charge them, we might take them." Howard, posted on the left of his regiment, spurred his horse and found Gunby to relay the information.

Although the 1st Maryland was still exchanging fire with Webster's troops, the Continentals were "not hard pressed." Gunby "did not hesitate to order the regiment to face about." The maneuver was carried out just in time to engage the approaching Guards. After trading several volleys with the British troops, the 1st Maryland advanced, the men pausing at intervals to fire.[27]

The counterattack had barely begun when Gunby's horse was shot, pinning the colonel beneath it. Howard immediately assumed command of the regiment, and instantly assessed conditions on the field. William Washington had appeared with his cavalry behind the guards. He saw the danger on the left and without waiting for orders, he led his cavalry in a charge aimed at the rear of the Guards. Observing Washington's maneuver, Howard realized that the fast-moving mounted troopers would be upon the Guards before his own infantry could reach the British position. Therefore he ordered a bayonet charge that was perfectly timed to follow the cavalry's assault. The 1st Maryland moved "very quickly," Howard wrote, "and we passed through the guards, many of whom had been knocked down by the horse without being much hurt. We took some prisoners and the whole were in our power." The Marylanders also retook the artillery. Tarleton reported that Howard and Washington "repulsed the guards with great slaughter." Lieutenant Colonel Stuart was killed, and the cavalry drove the Guards all the way back into the woods.[28]

The arrival of the 23rd and 71st Regiments forced Howard to halt his troops. He caught sight of the Highlanders of the latter unit "near the Court House and other columns of the enemy appearing in different directions." Howard noticed that Washington had "gone off" with his cavalry, leaving the 1st Maryland alone in an open field. Consequently Howard "found it necessary to retire, which I did leisurely," although not without loss. "Many of the guards who were laying on the ground & who we supposed were wounded, got up and fired at us as we retired," he remarked.[29]

Howard's account contradicts one of the more colorful tales of the Battle of Guilford Courthouse. According to many historians, the 1st Maryland became entangled in bloody, hand-to-hand fighting with the Guards. Cornwallis, over the protests of his officers, ordered his artillery to open fire with grapeshot on the crowd of struggling men in order to check Howard's attack and prevent the annihilation of the Guards, even though many British soldiers were killed and wounded by the blasts of grapeshot. It is a dramatic tale, and in most versions, the British cannon are powerful six-pounders. However, neither Howard, Greene, Cornwallis, O'Hara, nor Tarleton reported any such incident. Cornwallis did state that he had ordered his artillery and cavalry to advance up the New Garden Road, keeping pace with the infantry. Seeing the 2nd Guards Battalion "driven back into the field by Colonel Washington's dragoons," the Earl ordered Lieutenant John McLeod to deploy his cannon against the charging horsemen. "The enemy's cavalry was soon repulsed by a well-directed fire from two three-pounders just brought up by Lieutenant Macleod, and by the appearance of the grenadiers of the guards, and of the 71st Regiment," Cornwallis reported.

His account is consistent with that of Howard, who had lost sight of Washington's cavalry and would not have seen their pursuit of the Guards and subsequent repulse by the British artillery.[30]

Greene watched the raging battle so closely that at one point he was nearly been taken captive by the British. Now he thought carefully about his next move. His only remaining fresh troops were Colonel John Green's Virginia Continentals. All of the other American units had either left the field or were still engaged with the enemy. Webster extended his line and was pushing troops past Huger's position on the American right. Lee and Campbell were far away on the left, their situation unknown to the commanding general. Efforts to reform the 2nd Maryland and return the regiment to the battlefield had failed. Howard's battered 1st Maryland stood alone on the left to face the British 23rd and 71st Regiments, the remnants of the 2nd Guards Battalion, Tarleton's Legion, and the royal artillery. Howard and his tough Marylanders had saved the American army twice on this bloody day, and might be able to do so again, but Greene refused to gamble. Like George Washington, he understood that it was more important to keep an effective army in the field than it was to risk the destruction of his force in a desperate effort to chalk up a victory. Greene ordered his troops to retreat along the Reedy Fork Road, with John Green's Virginia Continentals acting as rear guard. It was about 3:30 in the afternoon. The bitter fighting had lasted two hours.[31]

Cornwallis sent the 23rd and 71st Regiments and part of the Legion cavalry to pursue Greene. He ordered Tarleton and the rest of his mounted troops to the right where the Earl could still hear "a heavy fire." Tarleton arrived to find the British forces in a desperate situation. "Owing to the nature of the light troops opposed to them," Tarleton realized, the regulars "could never make any decisive impression: As they advanced, the Americans gave ground in front, and inclined to their flanks." The British cavalry first encountered wounded men of the 1st Guards Battalion and Hessian regiment, guarded by American militia. They drove off the militia, freed the captives, and rode forward, where Tarleton found General Leslie. A brief conference ensued, the officers agreeing on a plan. "The guards and the Hessians were directed to fire a volley upon the largest party of the militia, and, under the cover of the smoke, Lieutenant-colonel Tarleton doubled round the right flank of the guards, and charged the Americans with considerable effect. The enemy gave way on all sides." Tarleton's charge had saved Leslie's troops from disaster. After the war, John Eager Howard met the Hessians' commander, Major De Buy, in Philadelphia. De Buy told Howard that "he lost a number of men ... and that his regiment would have been cut up if Tarleton had not so seasonably come to his relief."[32]

This encounter brought the fighting to a close. Huger, commanding Greene's rear guard, held off the exhausted British troops who tried to pursue the retreating Americans. Greene fell back only three miles, halting after his army forded Reedy Fork Creek. Calculating the bloody balance sheet, he reported 57 Continentals killed, 111 wounded, and 161 missing. The militia figures were 22 killed, 73 wounded, and 885 missing, many of the militiamen headed directly for home rather than returning to the main army. As at Cowpens, the official figures for the militia killed and wounded were probably estimates, with the actual losses being higher. Greene also lost all four of his six-pounder cannon and two ammunition wagons. He had harsh criticism for the North Carolina militia, but praised the Virginia militia, Lee's and Washington's troops, and "the first Regiment of Marylanders commanded by Colo Gunby, and seconded by Lieutt Colo Howard." Greene also reported that his army's morale remained high, noting that "Our Men are in good spirits and in perfect readiness for another field Day."[33]

Cornwallis had won an impressive tactical victory against heavy odds, but he actually had little cause for celebration. His troops had earned the praise he lavished on them for "their persevering intrepidity in action." However, it had come at the price of substantial losses. Lieutenant Colonel James Stuart had been killed, the reliable and courageous Lieutenant Colonel James Webster lay mortally wounded, and Brigadier General Charles O'Hara was out of action with two wounds. Total British casualties amounted to 93 dead, 413 wounded, and 26 missing, an aggregate loss of 532 men, which was more than one-fourth of the army's strength. Cornwallis made no effort to claim that the Battle of Guilford Courthouse had been a decisive victory. He knew that he had not put Greene's army out of action, and that he had not yet secured North Carolina for the crown. Instead of making such claims, he noted in his official report that the area around the battlefield was "destitute of subsistence," and he would leave behind "about seventy of the worst of the wounded" at the Quaker meetinghouse at New Garden and withdraw the rest of his army toward Wilmington.[34]

Brigadier General Charles O'Hara offered an even more somber assessment of the battle's results. He wrote, "I wish it had produced one substantial benefit to Great Britain. On the contrary, we feel at the moment the sad and fatal effects of our loss on that Day." He added that the troops were "completely worn out by the excessive Fatigues of the campaign," the rigors of which had "totally destroyed this Army." Morale was low; "no zeal or courage is equal to the constant exertions we are making." The demoralizing effects of the battle extended to the British Parliament in London. Reviewing the casualty returns that accompanied Cornwallis's letter reporting the British victory, Charles James Fox, a leading opponent of the war in the House of Commons, declared that "another such victory would ruin the British army."[35]

It began raining heavily soon after the battle, and the downpour forced Cornwallis to linger at the mournful scene of combat for the remainder of March 15th and the next day and night as well. Lacking both food and tents, the British troops sought shelter among the trees from "a violent and constant Rain that lasted above Forty hours." The men huddled among the scattered bodies of the dead of both armies, listening to the screams of the wounded begging for assistance, yet unable to "administer the smallest comfort to many."[36]

Greene and his soldiers also had to contend with the rain, although their elevated spirits made their situation more tolerable. On March 18, Greene informed his wife Catharine of the battle, conceding that Cornwallis had forced the American army from the field but "the enemy suffered so severely in the action that they dare not move towards us since." To Joseph Reed of Pennsylvania, Greene wrote that he had "never felt an easy moment since the enemy crossed the Catawba until the defeat of the 15th; but now I am perfectly easy, being perswaded it is out of the enemies power to do us any great injury."[37]

Once again Greene correctly gauged the enemy's situation. Cornwallis marched to Cross Creek, a settlement of Scots Loyalists, where he hoped to open a supply line via the Cape Fear River to the British base at Wilmington. When he arrived, he received a letter from the commander at Wilmington, Major James Craig, stating that it was impractical to establish water communication to Cross Creek. Craig explained that the high banks along the narrow river gave the rebels numerous opportunities to harass the boats, making the shipment of supplies dangerous and unreliable. A quick examination of the terrain verified Craig's assessment. Under the circumstances, Tarleton believed that the army should fall back to Camden in South Carolina, where it could help defend that province from an American effort to retake it. Cornwallis, however, decided to go to Wilmington, arriving there on April 7. The British found some needed food and equipment in the port town, but not enough to meet their needs. Tarleton noted, "Unluckily for many of the troops, and for the cavalry in particular, the supplies transported from Charlestown to Wilmington were inadequate to the deficiencies." Cornwallis "meditated the future operations of his army" and would soon come up with a new plan. With the benefit of hindsight, Tarleton later concluded that "it may be deemed unfortunate that so eligible a plan" as the march from Cross Creek to Camden for the purpose of defending South Carolina "was not carried into execution."[38]

Greene followed Cornwallis toward Wilmington at a safe distance, reaching the Deep River on March 26. The next day, Greene learned that many of his North Carolina and Virginia militiamen had decided to return home, since they calculated the time it would take to get there as part of their term of service. Nevertheless, Greene responded to a report that Cornwallis was still on the same side of the Deep River as the American army by marching aggressively toward Ramsey's Mill on March 28. Cornwallis was gone and Greene called off his pursuit. He sent Henry Lee and some North Carolina militia to follow Cornwallis, but instructed them to keep a wide interval between themselves and the Redcoats. Greene did not press the pursuit further because he had been mulling a new plan for some time. On March 29th he revealed his intentions to George Washington. Greene wrote:

> "If the Enemy falls down towards Wilmington they will be in a position

where it will be impossible for us to injure them. In this critical and distressing situation I am determined to carry the War immediately into South Carolina. The Enemy will be obliged to follow us or give up their posts in that State. If the former takes place it will draw the War out of this State .... If they leave their posts to fall they must lose more there than they can gain here. If we continue in this State the Enemy will hold their possessions in both. All things considered I think the movement is warranted by the soundest reasons both political and military."

Greene's logic was indeed sound, but to turn his back on Cornwallis and march for South Carolina was a move fraught with risk. He admitted. "The Manoeuvre will be critical and dangerous; and the troops exposed to every hardship," he told Washington, but this would be at least partially offset because "the movement will be unexpected to the Enemy." Greene would march in five days, and he had already sent orders to partisan leader Thomas Sumter to gather his militia to assist the Continentals.[39]

Eight months earlier, John Eager Howard and seven Maryland Continental regiments had marched into South Carolina. Since that time, Howard had fought three major battles, winning only one despite displaying outstanding leadership and conspicuous gallantry in all of them. The seven Maryland regiments were now reduced to two, and of the leaders Howard had fought under, Baron Johann De Kalb was dead, Horatio Gates had been shelved in disgrace, and Daniel Morgan incapacitated by illness. With the army heading once again toward Camden, as it had in 1780, Howard could only hope that a better fate lay ahead as they approached the town where they had been so soundly defeated the previous August.

---

1 Cornwallis to Germain, March 17, 1781, in Tarleton, *History of the Campaigns*, 265 (quotation); Pancake, *This Destructive War*, 172; Buchanan, *Road to Guilford Courthouse*, 359; Treacy, *Prelude to Yorktown*, 156.
2 Buchanan, *Road to Guilford Courthouse*, 360 (quotation); Davis, *Cowpens-Guilford Courthouse Campaign*, 118.
3 Buchanan, *Road to Guilford Courthouse*, 359.
4 Cornwallis to Germain, March 17, 1781, in Tarleton, *History of the Campaigns*, 265 (quotation); Treacy, *Prelude to Yorktown*, 156-57 (quotation); Davis, *Cowpens-Guilford Courthouse Campaign*, 119; Tarleton, *History of the Campaigns*, 230-31 (quotation).
5 Davis, *Cowpens-Guilford Courthouse Campaign*, 119; Tarleton, *History of the Campaigns*, 231 (quotation).
6 Greene to Joseph Clay, Feb. 17, 1781; Greene to Abner Nsh, Feb. 17, 1781, in Showman and Conrad, eds., *Papers of Greene*, 7:300-01, 303 (quotation); Henry Lee, *Memoirs*, 253.
7 Pancake, *This Destructive War*, 173; Lee, *Memoirs*, 256-58 (quotation); Tarleton, *History of the Campaigns*, 231-33.
8 Lee, *Memoirs*, 258 (quotation); Buchanan, *Road to Guilford Courthouse*, 364; Cornwallis to Germain, March 17, 1781, in Tarleton, *History of the Campaigns*, 265 (quotation); Greene to Thomas Jefferson, Feb. 29 [28], 1781 and Greene to Andrew Pickens, Feb. 26, 1781, in Showman and Conrad, eds., *Papers of Greene*, 7:367 (quotation), 353 (quotation); Pancake, *This Destructive War*, 173.

9 Lee, *Memoirs*, 588 (quotation); Tarleton, *History of the Campaigns*, 233-34; Pancake, *This Destructive War*, 175.
10 Williams to Greene, Feb. 25, 1781, Feb. 26, 1781, and Feb. 27, 1781, in Showman and Conrad, eds., *Papers of Greene*, 7:350, 360 (quotations), 366.
11 Williams to Greene, March 7, 1781, in Showman and Conrad, eds., *Papers of Greene*, 7:407-08; Angus Konstam, *Guilford Court House 1781: Lord Cornwallis's Ruinous Victory* (Westport, CT: Praeger Publishers, 2004), 49-53; Pancake, *This Destructive War*, 176-77; Tarleton, *History of the Campaigns*, 237-39.
12 Pancake, *This Destructive War*, 177; Buchanan, *Road to Guilford Courthouse*, 369.
13 Buchanan, *Road to Guilford Courthouse*, 369; Pancake, *This Destructive War*, 178; Lee, *Memoirs*, 277; Greene to Samuel Huntington, March 16, 1781, in Showman and Conrad, eds., *Papers of Greene*, 7:433-34.
14 Buchanan, *Road to Guilford Courthouse*, 369; Pancake, *This Destructive War*, 178; Lee, *Memoirs*, 277; Greene to Samuel Huntington, March 16, 1781, in Showman and Conrad, eds., *Papers of Greene*, 7:433-34.
15 Howard to William Johnson, n.d. (c. 1822), Bayard Papers.
16 Cornwallis to Lord George Germain, March 17, 1781, in Tarleton, *History of the Campaigns*, 272, 304 (quotation); Greene to Huntington, March 16, 1781, in Showman and Conrad, eds., *Papers of Greene*, 7:434 (quotation).
17 Cornwallis to Germain, March 17, 1781, in Tarleton, *History of the Campaigns*, 304-05 (quotations); Greene to Huntington, March 16, 1781, in Showman and Conrad, eds., *Papers of Greene*, 7:434; Morrill, *Southern Campaigns*, 153.
18 Buchanan, *Road to Guilford Courthouse*, 375; Cornwallis to Germain, March 17, 1781, in Tarleton, *History of the Campaigns*, 305: Howard to William Johnson, n.d. (c. 1822), Bayard Papers; Greene to Samuel Huntington, March 16, 1781, in Showman and Conrad, eds., *Papers of Greene*, 434; Lee, *Memoirs*, 277-78 (quotation).
19 Buchanan, *Road to Guilford Courthouse*, 375-76; Lee, *Memoirs*, 277-78.
20 Cornwallis to Germain, March 17, 1781, in Tarleton, *History of the Campaigns*, 305 (quotation); Tarleton, 273; Buchanan, *Road to Guilford Courthouse*, 376.
21 Treacy, *Prelude to Yorktown*, 182; Howard to William Johnson, n.d. (c. 1822), Bayard Papers (quotation).
22 Treacy, *Prelude to Yorktown*, 183; Davis, *Cowpens-Guilford Courthouse Campaign*, 157, 158-59; Morrill, *Southern Campaigns*, 155; Cornwallis to Germain, March 17, 1781, in Tarleton, *History of the Campaigns*, 305-06 (quotation).
23 Davis, *Cowpens-Guilford Courthouse Campaign*, 157 (quotation); Treacy, *Prelude to Yorktown*, 183; Greene to Huntington, March 16, 1781, in Showman and Conrad, eds., *Papers of Greene*, 7:435 (quotation).
24 Tarleton, *History of the Campaigns*, 274.
25 Tarleton, *History of the Campaigns*, 274; Buchanan, *Road to Guilford Courthouse*, 378; Treacy, *Prelude to Yorktown*, 184.
26 Cornwallis to Germain, March 17, 1781, in Tarleton, *History of the Campaigns*, 306 (quotation); Buchanan, *Road to Guilford Courthouse*, 378; Morrill, *Southern Campaigns*, 156; Howard to William Johnson, n.d. (c. 1822), Bayard Papers (quotation).
27 Howard to William Johnson, n.d. (c. 1822), Bayard Papers.
28 Howard to William Johnson, n.d. (c. 1822), Bayard Papers (quotation); Tarleton, *History of the Campaigns*, 274 (quotation).
29 Howard to Willliam Johnson, n.d. (c. 1822), Bayard Papers (quotation); Tarleton, *History of the Campaigns*, 274.
30 For accounts of the British artillery firing into the crowd of Marylanders and Guards, see Pancake, *This Destructive War*, 183; Davis, *Cowpens-Guilford Courthouse Campaign*, 161; Treacy, *Prelude to Yorktown*, 185; Buchanan, *Road to Guilford Courthouse*, 379. Eyewitness accounts make no mention of this incident: Greene to Huntington, March 16, 1781, in Showman and Conrad, eds., *Papers of Greene*, 7:433-35; Howard to William Johnson, n.d. (c. 1822), Bayard Papers; Cornwallis to Germain, March 17, 1781, in Tarleton, *History of the Campaigns*, 305, 306 (quotation); Charles O'Hara to Duke of Grafton, April 20, 1781, in "Letters of Charles O'Hara to the Duke of Grafton," ed. George C. Rogers, Jr., *South Carolina Historical Magazine*, Vol. 65, No. 3 (July 1964), 173-79; Tarleton, *History of the Campaigns*, 275.
31 Greene to Huntington, March 16, 1781, in Showman and Conrad, eds., *Papers of Greene*, 7:435; Davis, *Cowpens-Guilford Courthouse Campaign*, 162; Buchanan, *Road to Guilford Courthouse*, 379.

32 Cornwallis to Germain, March 17, 1781, in Tarleton, *History of the Campaigns*, 307; Tarleton, *History of the Campaigns*, 275-76 (quotations); Howard to William Johnson, n.d. (c. 1822), Bayard Papers (quotation).
33 Greene to Huntington, March 16, 1781, in Showman and Conrad, eds., *Papers of Greene*, 7:434-35 (quotation), 441n.
34 Cornwallis to Germain, March 17, 1781, "Return of the killed, wounded, and missing ... in the action at Guildford," in Tarleton, *History of the Campaigns* 308-09 (quotation), 310-11.
35 Buchanan, *Road to Guilford Courthouse*, 381-82 (quotation); Craig L. Symonds, *A Battlefield Atlas of the American Revolution* ([Annapolis, MD]: Nautical & Aviation Publishing Co., 1986), 93.
36 Lee, *Memoirs*, 286; Pancake, *This Destructive War*, 381 (quotation).
37 Greene to Catharine Greene, March 18, 1781; Greene to Joseph Reed, March 18, 1781, in Showman and Conrad, eds., *Papers of Greene*, 7:446 (quotation), 450 (quotation).
38 Tarleton, *History of the Campaigns*, 280-82.
39 Treacy, *Prelude to Yorktown*, 191-92; Pancake, *This Destructive War*, 190; Greene to George Washington, March 29, 1781, in Showman and Conrad, eds., *Papers of Greene*, 7:481 (quotations).

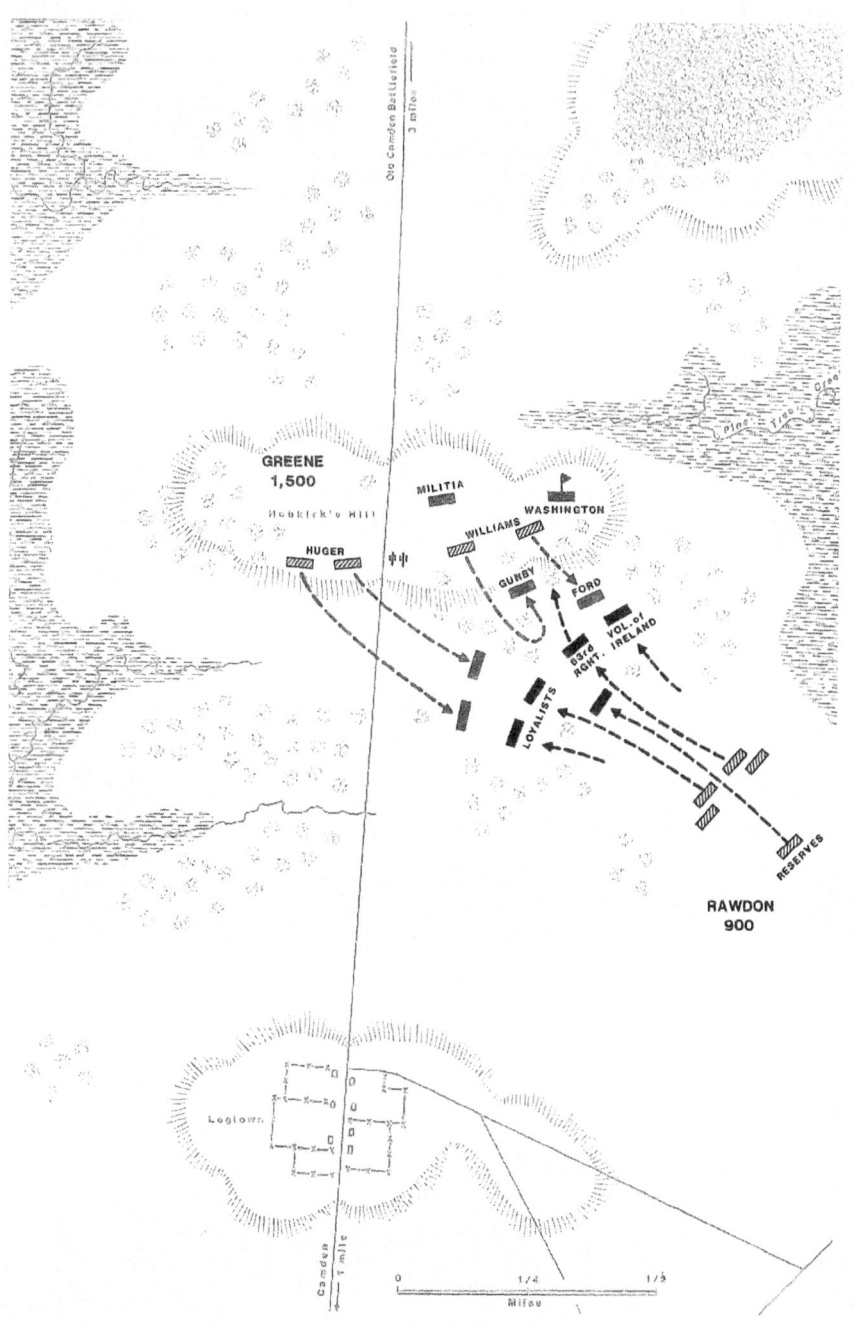

CHAPTER SEVEN

THE SECOND FIGHT FOR CAMDEN—HOBKIRK'S HILL

As Nathanael Greene led his army on the difficult march into South Carolina, he thought long and hard about the challenges ahead. The 5,200 British, German, and provincial troops in the state outnumbered his army by more than two-to-one, and they were ably commanded by Lieutenant Colonel Francis, Lord Rawdon, a twenty-six-year-old Irish nobleman who had served with distinction since the Battle of Bunker Hill in 1775. Should Lord Cornwallis follow Greene back to South Carolina, as seemed probable, the American army might be trapped between the British forces. Yet Greene had two significant, offsetting advantages. First, the most important British posts in the interior of South Carolina, at Camden and Ninety Six, depended on Charleston for supplies and reinforcements and thus dangled at the end of a long, precarious line of communications with the coast. Most of Rawdon's troops were tied down in fixed garrisons to protect the supply line and the strategic inland towns. Second, Greene could count on the assistance of several thousand partisans to augment his army or strike at the scattered British posts. To take advantage of these irregular forces, Greene detached Henry Lee and his Legion on April 6 to unite with Francis Marion's command and attack Fort Watson on the Santee River, an essential link in the British line of communications. Greene took the rest of the army toward Camden, where Rawdon had his headquarters.[1]

The Americans received an unexpected but welcome bit of assistance from Cornwallis. While his army recuperated in Wilmington, the Earl pondered his options and convinced himself that his best move was to march northward, into Virginia. He concluded that he could not accomplish much with his own army, reduced now to 1,600 men. To undertake a march from Wilmington back to Camden meant exposing his troops to further hardship, as they would be passing through a region that would provide only scant provisions and require crossing numerous creeks and rivers. One alternative was to march a shorter distance south to British-occupied Georgetown, South Carolina, and put his troops aboard ships there to return to Charleston, but in the Earl's opinion this might appear to be a "disgraceful" retreat and an admission of defeat. On the other hand, if he moved north to Virginia, where Major General William Phillips was operating in Chesapeake Bay with a 5,500-man British expedition, Cornwallis could assume command of Phillips's force and, at the head of 7,000 regulars, perhaps force the Old Dominion to submit to British rule.[2]

Cornwallis explained his thinking in an April 10 letter to his superior, General Henry Clinton. "Until Virginia is in a manner subdued, our hold of the Carolinas must be difficult, if not precarious," the Earl asserted. "The Rivers in Virginia are advantageous to an invading army; but North Carolina is of all the provinces in America the most difficult to attack." Cornwallis' insistence that operations in Virginia would secure British control of South Carolina was necessary to demonstrate that the Earl's impending move complied with Clinton's earlier orders to hold South Carolina at all costs. Privately, Cornwallis realized that his plan jeopardized British control of that province. In a letter to his protégé Lieutenant Colonel Nisbet Balfour, commander of the Charleston garrison and the highest-ranking British officer in South Carolina and Georgia, Cornwallis conceded that the British might be "so unfortunate as to lose some of the Outposts and the Country of S. Carolina," but that at least "Charleston is not in danger." The Earl added that even if he pursued Greene, he would arrive too late to aid Rawdon. On April 25, Cornwallis led his troops out of Wilmington and headed north toward Virginia. On the very same day, Greene, John Eager Howard, and their soldiers were engaged in a bloody fight with Rawdon's redcoats just outside Camden, a battle that might determine the fate of South Carolina.[3]

Like Cornwallis, Greene had his own problems with supply and a sometimes hostile populace, although he did not allow these to impede his operations. "Most of our Men are naked for want of Overalls," he informed his wife Catharine shortly before setting out for South Carolina. On April 7th, Thomas Sumter replied to Greene's request for assistance from the partisans with more bad news. Sumter pledged to cooperate, but could do little to provide food for Greene's soldiers, as nearly all of the grain in upper South Carolina was in areas controlled by the British. Loyalists added to Greene's difficulties. He wrote, "Most of the Inhabitants between Peedee and Haw River are disaffected," and thus the army "found the greatest difficulty in procuring supplies and obtaining intelligence. Our reconnoitring Parties were frequently shot down by the Tories."[4]

Sergeant William Seymour of the Delaware Continentals also alluded to the hardships attending the march, noting that the Americans traveled "over the same ground which our army went the last summer along with General Gates. This is a poor barren part of the country. The inhabitants are chiefly of a Scotch extraction, living in mean cottages, and are much disaffected, being great enemies to their country."[5]

Nevertheless, Greene, Howard, and their troops persevered. They had pushed to within two miles of Camden by late in the afternoon of April 19, having covered 130 miles since leaving Guilford Courthouse. To his consternation, Greene found "the Garrison of Camden ... much greater than I expected." He decided to probe toward Log Town, a cluster of log houses half a mile north of Camden. Greene ordered Captain Robert Kirkwood and his Delaware veterans to seize the village that night. After a two-hour firefight in the darkness, Kirkwood's Continentals drove the British pickets from the cabins. A small British force tried to dislodge Kirkwood at sunrise the next morning, provoking a sharp skirmish but failing to drive out the Americans. Rawdon made only a limited attempt to retake the position because, he noted, "I cannot afford to risque the Men necessary to maintain" the post at Log Town. Greene arrived with the rest of the army two hours later, decided that the position Kirkwood had won was unfavorable, and instead occupied better defensive ground on Hobkirk's Hill a half-mile farther north.[6]

After sending his light troops to reconnoiter the British position, Greene assessed his situation. It was not encouraging. In addition to finding that the town's garrison was larger than he had anticipated, Greene also learned that "their Works ... were found to be much stronger than had been represented." Furthermore, expected reinforcements from Virginia and South Carolina had not arrived. In mid-March, Greene asked Virginia officials to provide fifteen hundred militia, and they had agreed, but not a militiaman had appeared yet, nor was there any indication that they were even on the way to join Greene's army. Sumter had promised to send Greene one thousand South Carolina militia by April 18, yet these too had failed to appear. Thus the American army "was too small either to invest the Town or storm the Works." On April 22nd, Greene warned Samuel Huntington, the President of Congress, that "if more effectual support cannot be given than has been, or as I can see any prospect of, I am very apprehensive that the Enemy will hold their ground."[7]

One cause of Greene's frustration was that he had hoped to surprise Rawdon by appearing unexpectedly before Camden, but instead the British commander was well aware of the Americans' approach and ready to meet them. Rawdon had received a report on April 10 that Greene had crossed the Pee Dee River, yet he remained skeptical of the information until the morning of April 12th, when an escaped prisoner from the Royal North Carolina Regiment arrived at Camden with a detailed description of Greene's recent movements. The young Irishman had no doubt of the Americans' objective. "I am sure from all accounts Camden is Greens object," he informed Balfour. "This post is infamous but if we are tried we shall do what becomes us."[8]

Realizing that Rawdon intended to hold Camden, Greene tried a variety of methods to lure the British out of their fortifications. First, he sent Washington's cavalry and Kirkwood's infantry to attack a redoubt on the west side of the town on April 20. While the Continentals exchanged fire with the British defenders, they managed to set fire to a house inside the redoubt; however, the Continental detachment was too weak to mount a serious attack and the British did not sally from their defenses. Next, Greene began a march around Camden on April 22nd, completing the circuit the next day and reoccupying Hobkirk's Hill in the evening. Again Rawdon did not stir from the fortified lines.[9]

Rawdon did wish to attack the Americans if opportunity offered, but he had to be cautious. At about the same time he learned that Greene was approaching Camden, he received a letter from Lieutenant Colonel Balfour, relaying instructions from Cornwallis to abandon the South Carolina backcountry and withdraw to a defensive position behind the Santee River. With the American army so close, the move was impossible to execute without exposing the British troops to attack while on their march. Rawdon wrote that under the circumstances, he "conceived some immediate effort necessary," adding that "I did not think that the disparity of numbers was such as should justify bare defense."[10]

Having resolved to strike Greene, Rawdon waited for reinforcements. On April 22nd, the South Carolina Royalists arrived at Camden from Ninety Six, augmenting Rawdon's strength by 130 officers and men. Rawdon waited a few days longer, hoping that Lieutenant Colonel John Watson and his five hundred troops would return from their foray to the east against American partisans. When Watson did not arrive and intelligence reports indicated that Greene was likely to be reinforced by Sumter and Marion, Rawdon decided that he could not delay much longer. An American deserter brought a report on the night of April 24th, which convinced Rawdon that the time to attack had come. The young man, a drummer in one of the Maryland regiments, accurately described Greene's strength and position to Rawdon, and he added an important detail: Greene had sent his artillery to the rear, escorted by the American militia. Rawdon immediately recognized his opportunity and began preparing to attack the next morning.[11]

During the night Rawdon scoured Camden for men to strengthen his army. He wrote, "By arming our musicians, our drummers, and in short everything that could carry a firelock, I mustered above nine hundred men for the field" including sixty cavalry. Officers even combed the hospital and organized fifty of the fittest men into a company designated "Convalescents." Those soldiers too ill or badly injured to march were left, along with the local militia and some armed slaves, to hold the fortifications. Only the 63rd Regiment and the Convalescents were British regulars; the remainder of Rawdon's force, nearly three-fourths of his total strength, consisted of American Loyalists, most of whom were well trained veterans.[12]

The British infantry, supported by Major John Coffin's cavalry and two six-pounder cannons, marched at about ten o'clock in the morning of April 25th. To deceive any Americans who might be watching their movements, they headed south from Camden, and then turned east into the woods when they reached Pine Tree Creek. They followed the stream and one of its tributaries in a northeasterly direction and reached the far left flank of the American picket line unobserved.[13]

Rawdon needed every advantage because Greene's army was larger than his and the Americans occupied a strong defensive position. Furthermore, Greene had ordered his regiments to camp in the positions they would occupy in his line of battle so that they would be ready for the attack he hoped would come. The Great Wagon Road that ran north from Camden bisected Greene's line. East of the road, Colonel John Gunby's 1st Maryland Regiment was posted, with Howard as second-in-command. The 2nd Maryland, under Lieutenant Colonel Benjamin Ford, was deployed to their left on the army's eastern flank. Colonel Otho Williams had overall command of the two Maryland Continental regiments. The 2nd Virginia Continentals, led by Lieutenant Colonel Samuel Hawes, stood west of the road. Lieutenant Colonel Richard Campbell's 1st Virginia Regiment was on the right, holding the flank. Brigadier General Isaac Huger commanded these Virginia troops. The Continental light infantry companies, including Kirkwood's Delaware troops, were dispersed in a picket line that Howard estimated was "about three hundred yards in front" of the main American line. Greene held Washington's cavalry, a company of Maryland Continentals, and Colonel James Read's regiment of North Carolina militia in reserve. Altogether, Greene's force numbered about 1,500 men.[14]

At about 11 a.m. Rawdon's vanguard, the light infantry and grenadiers of the Volunteers of Ireland approached Greene's pickets on the far left of the American line. As he had desired, Rawdon achieved tactical surprise. The Americans had not received provisions. Some were cooking the meager amounts of food that remained, while others had gone to a spring east of Greene's main position to wash their clothing. They had no warning of the British advance until "the Flank Companies of the Volunteers of Ireland which led our Column fell in with the Enemy's Picquets," Rawdon noted. The firing alerted the American troops, and, Howard reported, without waiting for orders "the officers made every exertion" to form their men for battle. Rawdon, riding near the head of his column, watched as Greene's pickets "were instantly driven in, & followed to their Camp."[15]

Howard estimated that the British infantry reached the main American line about six or eight minutes after their initial contact with the pickets. Given the short amount of time they had to prepare for the attack, Howard found that "the line was not well formed, and many of the men who were washing never joined us." Rawdon sad that "the Enemy were in much confusion, but notwithstanding, formed; and received us bravely. I believe they imagined us to be much weaker than we were."[16]

Despite taking his foe by surprise, Rawdon had to surmount several difficulties. His direction of march forced him to attack the American line at an angle while most of his troops were still in column in the rear. At first he could get only two regiments in line, the 63rd on his right and the King's American Regiment on his left. The British charged "with great spirit;" however, Rawdon found that Greene's line overlapped both of his flanks. He ordered the Volunteers of Ireland forward to take position to the right of the 63rd Regiment. Then, as the King's American Regiment moved westward to cross the Great Wagon Road, "heavy showers of Grape Shot" blasted the Loyalists. Greene's artillery returned just minutes before the battle, giving the British an unwelcome shock. Sergeant William Seymour declared that the cannon fire "put the enemy in great confusion, having killed and dangerously wounded great numbers of them as they crossed the main road."[17]

Finding that "the Enemy were ...advancing only with a small front," Greene tried to strike Rawdon simultaneously in the front, both flanks, and the rear. He ordered the 1st Maryland and 2nd Virginia Regiments in his center to make a frontal counterattack with fixed bayonets. He directed the 2nd Maryland and 1st Virginia on his wings to shift direction and assail the British flanks. At the same time, he instructed William Washington "to turn the Enemies right flank and charge them in the rear."[18]

The storm of artillery fire and the unexpected counterattack checked the British advance. "The whole line was soon engaged in close firing," Greene wrote. Undaunted, Rawdon deftly ordered forward his remaining units as they reached the field. The light infantry hastened forward to extend the British right. The New York Volunteers rushed ahead through the hail of musket fire to fill the gap that had opened between the 63rd and the King's American Regiment. Apparently not slowed by their ailments, the Convalescent Company rapidly marched west, braved the grapeshot sweeping the road, and took position on the British left. Rawdon held the South Carolina Royalists and Coffin's cavalry in reserve.[19]

The thickness of the pine woods prevented both sides from seeing one another "until they were close in." The British and American soldiers traded musket volleys at short range for several minutes. Soon the Americans' superior numbers and strong position began to tell. "The Enemy were staggered in all quarters, and upon the left were retiring," Greene reported. For the moment, everything seemed to be going Greene's way. Then, in a few short minutes, the advantage that the Americans had gained began to crumble.[20]

William Washington's threat to the British army never materialized. A cavalry charge into the rear of the already shaken British troops might have finished Rawdon's force, but after circling past the British right and getting behind their lines, Washington became distracted from his mission by the alluring opportunity to take a large number of prisoners. "On the ground from which [the British] had first driven the Enemy" lay dozens of wounded soldiers, along with army surgeons attending to them. Catching sight of this defenseless lot, Washington appeared to forget his assignment. Instead he and his troops busied themselves paroling some of the wounded soldiers and hoisting others onto horses behind the cavalrymen. By the time he finished dealing with men who were already out of action, the battle had been decided. Having missed his chance to make a decisive assault on the British rear, Washington led his men back to rejoin Greene's army.[21]

Atop Hobkirk's Hill, the American situation had suddenly and drastically deteriorated. As Gunby and Howard led the 1st Maryland forward, a Loyalist sharpshooter killed Captain William Beatty, the capable and respected commander of the company on the regiment's right. A simultaneous volley inflicted several more casualties among the troops. The loss of their commander and a number of men threw the company into disorder, which quickly spread to the adjacent company. Rather than try to rally the units where they stood, Gunby, who was overseeing the right of his regiment while Howard supervised the left, ordered both companies to fall back about fifty yards to reform.[22]

Howard was still leading the 1st Maryland's four other companies forward "when [he] observed that the right had given way." Moments later, a messenger brought Howard Gunby's order to withdraw the rest of the regiment and realign it with the broken companies. Howard obeyed, and upon reaching Gunby's position found the colonel "exerting" himself "in forming the regiment."[23]

Gunby's decision helped to change the course of the battle. At the start of the action, his and Ford's regiments had been separated by a gap of 150 yards. When Gunby withdrew the 1st Maryland while Ford continued to push the 2nd Maryland forward, the distance increased and left Ford's troops isolated. The British promptly took advantage of the situation, pouring fire into the front and exposed right flank of the 2nd Maryland. Ford had no choice but to retreat, and Rawdon's troops surged to the crest of the hill. Rawdon considered this to be the decisive moment of the battle. He asserted, "The rout of the Enemy was immediately decided."[24]

Other British troops advanced towards the 1st Maryland which had retreated again. Although the Virginians continued to fight on the west side of the road, they found it impossible to hold their ground. The 1st Virginia on the far right had faced the least resistance of any American regiment, but they somehow managed to get "into some disorder," perhaps due more to the difficult terrain than to the handful of British troops who had reached that part of the field. Only Samuel Hawes and his 2nd Virginia Continentals remained organized and in action. They had "advanced some distance down the Hill," driving back the British left, but, as Greene explained, "the Maryland line being gone the Enemy immediately turned their flank, while they were engaged in front. ... This obliged me to order Lieutenant Colo Haws to retire." The American army retreated from the field.[25]

Rawdon pursued Greene's force for "about three Miles," but not aggressively. "The Enemy's Cavalry greatly surpassing ours as to number, horses, & appointments, our Dragoons could not risque much, nor could I suffer the Infantry to break their order in hopes of overtaking the fugitives," explained Rawdon. One bright spot emerged for the Americans during the confusion of their retreat: they succeeded in saving their artillery. "The Enemy's Cannon escaped by mere accident," Rawdon noted. "It was run down a steep hill among some thick brush wood, where we passed without observing it, & it was carried off whilst we pursued the Infantry in a contrary direction." Unable to accomplish anything further, Rawdon returned to Camden, leaving Coffin's cavalry on the summit of Hobkirk's Hill. Late in the afternoon, Greene sent Washington and Kirkwood back to the field to round up any American wounded and stragglers who might have avoided capture. The detachment used a ruse to lure Coffin from the hill and into an ambush. The ploy succeeded; however, as soon as he realized his situation, Coffin turned his troopers in the opposite direction and rode into Camden.[26]

Both sides tallied their losses. Colonel Otho Williams reported American officer casualties as one killed, three badly wounded including Lieutenant Colonel Ford of the 2nd Maryland, three slightly wounded, and one captured. Williams also recorded 18 enlisted men killed, 108 wounded, and 136 missing. Of the latter, he had learned that 47 were wounded and in the British hospital in Camden, some had been killed, and a few were roving about the country. It was hoped that these stragglers would soon find their way back to the army and return to duty. Apparently many did not; Rawdon remarked that "a Number" of American soldiers, "finding their retreat cut off, went into Camden & claimed protection as Deserters." British losses numbered 38 killed, 177 wounded, and 43 missing. Although the total number of casualties was low, the losses were high in proportion to the small number of troops engaged. Rawdon had lost more than a quarter of his force, while Greene lost over twenty percent. The fighting had been brief, but it had been intense. Given the outcome of the battle, a bitterly disappointed Greene was less effusive in praising his soldiers' performance. He commented only that "the troops were not to blame in the ... affair."[27]

In addition to losing the battle, the American army lost three important officers at Hobkirk's Hill. Greene lamented the death of Captain Beatty, whom he described as "a most excellent Officer and an ornament to his profession." On April 27th, Benjamin Ford died from the wound he received in his elbow. The third officer whose services were lost to the army as a result of this battle was Colonel John Gunby, who was unhurt in the fighting but whose career was damaged by Greene's insistence that he had been the sole cause of the defeat.[28]

Greene was enraged at Gunby. An opening victory in his campaign to drive the British from South Carolina had been in the American general's grasp, only to be snatched away by what Greene considered the inexplicable performance of the normally reliable 1st Maryland Regiment. This same unit performed brilliantly at Guilford Courthouse barely a month before, and under the same leaders, Gunby and Howard. However, at Guilford Courthouse Gunby had been incapacitated early in the action, leaving Howard to exercise command.[29]

Greene's criticism of Gunby was public and widespread. The Maryland colonel requested a court martial to try to clear his name. Greene approved the request on April 28 and the court convened on May 2nd. It was comprised of three officers: General Isaac Huger, Colonel Charles Harrison, and Lieutenant Colonel William Washington. As Gunby's second-in-command, Howard was a key witness. After hearing testimony, the court released its findings the same day. "It appears to the court that Colonel Gunby received orders to advance with his regiment, and charge bayonets without firing," the officers stated in their review of events. Gunby, they found, complied with the order and the 1st Maryland "advanced cheerfully for some distance," engaged the British, and "soon after two companies on the right of the regiment gave way." The court recounted Gunby's order to Howard to withdraw the other four companies and that when Howard joined Gunby "at the foot of the hill" (not the actual base of the hill but a depression in the uneven ground along the ridge), Howard "found Colonel Gunby actively exerting himself in rallying the two companies that broke from the right, which he effected, and the regiment was again formed and gave a fire or two at the enemy." The court cited other witnesses in addition to Howard, who confirmed that Gunby "was active in rallying and forming his troops." Thus far Gunby had been vindicated, but the court's conclusion dealt him a severe blow. The officers wrote, "It appears, from the above report, that Colonel Gunby's spirit and activity were unexceptionable. But his order for the regiment to retire, which broke the line, was extremely improper and unmilitary, and, in all probability, the only cause why we did not obtain a complete victory." Greene announced the court's verdict to the entire army in the day's general orders.[30]

Gunby felt that he had been unjustly humiliated and could no longer serve under Greene. He volunteered to return to Maryland on recruiting detail, but Greene eventually assigned him to Charlotte, where he collected and forwarded supplies to the army.[31]

Gunby labored long afterward to clear his name, and he tried to enlist Howard's support. Howard answered one of Gunby's inquiries in March 1782, less than a year after the battle, with what was essentially a repetition of his testimony at the court martial. The tone of Howard's reply reflected his discomfort discussing the matter, as he was apparently torn between his sense of fairness in defending the actions of his direct superior and his hesitation to challenge openly the army's angry commanding general. Howard was still uncomfortable revisiting the affair some forty years later when he provided a very circumspect answer to Greene biographer William Johnson's inquiry about Hobkirk's Hill. Howard struggled to provide a definitive explanation for the 1st Maryland's poor performance in that battle. "No doubt Beatty's being killed was one cause" of the 1st Maryland's retreat, Howard asserted. "But there must have been other causes, for the fire of the enemy was not severe, and I have seen the same men on other occasions where such a fire would not have made the least impression." He added that the troops' "having been some days in want of provision and the sudden manner in which they were brought into action had an effect in developing their spirits and producing this bad behavior." Then, with his characteristic honesty, he declared: "The truth is they behaved bad." He concluded with a positive description of Gunby's actions that day, adding that Greene considered Gunby's order for the regiment to fall back "very unfortunate."³²

Howard provided no support for Greene's accusations against Gunby. Greene's vindictive persecution of Gunby must have disturbed Howard, as it was wholly out of character for the Rhode Islander. Most of Greene's subordinates generally agreed with Henry Lee's assessment that "no man was more familiarized to dispassionate and minute research than General Greene. He was patient in hearing every thing offered, never interrupting or slighting what was said." These attributes temporarily vanished after the Battle of Hobkirk's Hill. William Washington's failure to carry out his assigned mission proved costly, yet Greene praised him lavishly in his official report. Thomas Sumter had utterly failed to make good his promise to join Greene with substantial militia reinforcements, which Howard identified as a key factor in the defeat. The 1st Virginia Regiment, facing more opposition from pine trees than from British soldiers, fell into disorder and withdrew from the battle without orders. Greene entirely ignored those aspects of the battle. As one historian noted, "this was Greene at his worst: petulant, filled with self-pity, and desperately trying to protect his reputation from those confounded critics who were ever so willing to find fault with him. He chose Gunby as a scapegoat when, in fact, his own decisions ... may have tipped the battle in Rawdon's favor."³³

Perhaps Greene's focus on Gunby had more to do with the commanding general's anger at himself for the use he had made of Gunby, rather than with any actual failings on the part of the Marylander. When Gunby joined the army before the Battle of Guilford Courthouse, Greene could have bent military protocol and assigned him to command the 2nd Maryland, leaving Howard in charge of the 1st Maryland. The combination of Howard's outstanding performance at Cowpens and the lack of experienced officers in the 2nd Maryland, a problem Greene and Otho Williams had acknowledged before the Battle of Guilford Courthouse, would have been sufficient justification for such action. Howard's subsequent stellar performance at Guilford Courthouse after Gunby was pinned under his horse must have made Greene wonder, after the Battle of Hobkirk's Hill, if Howard might have handled the situation in the 1st Maryland better had he been in command, and thus changed the outcome of the contest. The fact that Howard was not in a position to do so was neither his fault nor Gunby's, but Greene's. Since Greene could not openly criticize himself for a decision he now severely regretted, his best option was to shift the blame to Gunby.

Greene continued his persecution of Gunby for months. On August 6, 1781, nearly four months after the battle, the Rhode Islander told Joseph Reed that "Gunby was the sole cause of the defeat" at Hobkirk's Hill "and I found him much more blameable afterwards than I represented him in my public letter." After admitting that his army's casualties in the battle had been higher than initially reported—twenty-five percent of the American force—Greene went on to declare that "we should have had Lord Rawden and his whole command prisoners in three Minutes, if Col Gunby had not orderd his Regiment to retire. ... I was almost frantick with vexation at the disappointment." Two months later, on October 4, Greene was still complaining about Gunby to his predecessor, Horatio Gates. "At Camden, not far from the ground where you fought Lord Cornwallis, we met with a repulse by Lord Rawdon," Greene wrote. "I was almost sure of capturing the whole garrison, and nothing prevented, but Colonel Gunby's Ordering a Regiment to retreat, instead of advancing and charging bayonet, agreeable to the Order he received. How cruel fortune! How uncertain military Fame! The repulse mingled our misfortunes together, and as ours was last, it drew a veil over yours." Six months had passed since the battle, yet the injury Greene believed had been inflicted on his reputation still stung.[34]

Greene's furor was, in the end, much ado over very little. As he had noted two days after the battle in his report to the President of Congress, "this little repulse will make no alteration in our general plan of operation." The overall plan was succeeding quite well, thanks to an American victory on April 23 that proved far more consequential in the long term than the engagement at Hobkirk's Hill. Henry Lee and Francis Marion had surrounded Fort Watson on the Santee River on April 15, and forced the 114 British and Loyalist defenders to surrender eight days later. The fort was a key link in the supply line between Charleston and Camden. Rawdon depended on Charleston for arms and other military supplies; he could normally secure food for his troops from the area around Camden, but the proximity of the American army now made that impossible. On May 2nd he reported that he had only a two-week supply of provisions on hand. If he could not destroy Greene's army, he would have to evacuate Camden.[35]

Greene had retreated to Rugeley's Mill, putting thirteen miles between his army and Rawdon's while making another British surprise attack impossible. Rawdon chose to wait for the long overdue arrival of Watson's detachment before moving against the Americans. Hoping to disrupt any plans Rawdon may have formed as well as obtain provisions from a region that supplied Camden, Greene crossed the Wateree River on May 4 and took a strong position behind Twenty-five Mile Creek the next day. Rawdon soon learned of the move; however, he was unwilling to risk battle unless reinforced. Watson finally reached Camden on May 7. To Rawdon's disappointment, he found the detachment "much reduced in number, thro' Casualties, Sickness," and Watson's decision to leave some of his detachment as a reinforcement for the garrison at Georgetown. In addition to Watson's having failed to achieve anything to compensate for his losses, that officer brought the news that Lee and Marion had surrounded Fort Motte, located on the Congaree River close to where it joined the Wateree to form the Santee. The post was another key link in the British supply chain.[36]

Rawdon knew that he could delay no longer. Despite the poor condition of Watson's troops, he "thought it first requisite to attempt reaping some advantage from the additional strength which I had received." That same night his army crossed to the west side of the Wateree River. The British commander hoped to "turn the flank & attack the rear of Greene's army, where the ground was not strong, tho' it was very much so in front." Greene, however, anticipated the move. While Rawdon was ferrying his troops across the river they moved the camp from " twenty-five Miles creek to Sandy creek, five miles higher up the river," the Rhode Islander informed Henry Lee.[37]

Rawdon's Loyalist informants brought him word of Greene's movements just minutes after the British finished crossing the river. Determined to strike regardless of the changed situation, Rawdon pushed forward, only to find that Greene did not like the new position and had withdrawn another four miles to better ground behind Sawney's Creek. Rawdon reported:

> After "having driven in [Greene's] Picquets, I examined every point of his situation. I found it every where so strong, that I could not hope to force it without suffering such loss as must have crippled my force ... & the retreat lay so open for him that I could not hope Victory would give us any advantage sufficiently decisive to counterbalance the loss."

Further inspection revealed that the Americans could easily evade any attempt to flank them. The disappointed Irish nobleman led his soldiers back to Camden.[38]

That same evening, on May 8th, Rawdon concluded that he had to evacuate Camden. Only a week's provisions remained, and they would be needed to sustain the troops during their retreat. Rawdon announced his intentions the next day. That evening he sent off the baggage, his sick and wounded, except for thirty who were not well enough to be moved, and a large number of Loyalists. "We brought off not only the Militia who had been with us in Camden," Rawdon noted, "but also all the well-affected Neighbors on our Route; together with the Wives, Children, Negroes & Baggage of almost all of them." The last British troops left Camden by mid-morning on May 10.[39]

Later that day, Lieutenant Colonel John Eager Howard and the Maryland Continentals finally entered Camden, nearly nine long months and much hard fighting after their first attempt had failed so disastrously the previous August. The town was ruined. In addition to burning the supplies they could not carry, the British had set fire to the jail, mill, and several houses, leaving Camden, in Greene's words, "little better than a heap of rubbish." The fortifications had been partly destroyed by the British, and Greene ordered the remainder leveled. He did not plan to stay there. The post that one historian described as "the linchpin in the line of British garrisons" in the southern interior had fallen, and Greene knew that a strong push now would drive the British back to the coast. "If proper exertions are made ... the enemy will soon be convinced, that if they divide their forces they will fall by detachments, and if they operate collectively they cannot command the country," Greene told President of Congress Samuel Huntington. The Rhode Islander announced his intention to make "proper exertions" to insure that this was exactly what happened. For Howard and his troops, there would be no time to savor the retaking of Camden. Greene ordered them out in pursuit of Rawdon.[40]

---

1 Piecuch, *Three Peoples, One King*, 244; Henry Lee, *Memoirs*, 325.
2 Tarleton, *History of the Campaigns*, 283-285 (quotation); Pancake, *This Destructive War*, 189.
3 Davis, *Cowpens-Guilford Courthouse Campaign*, 182 (quotation); Pancake, *This Destructive War*, 189-90; Piecuch, *Three Peoples, One King*, 244 (quotation).

4 Nathanael Greene to Catharine Greene, March 30, 1781, in Dennis Conrad, ed., *The Papers of General Nathanael Greene*, Vol. 8 (Chapel Hill: University of North Carolina Press, 1995), 7, 9 (quotations); Thomas Sumter to Greene, April 7, 1781, in Conrad, ed., *Papers of Greene*, 8:67.
5 Seymour, *Journal of the Southern Expedition*, 23 (quotation).
6 Greene to John Butler, April 19, 1781, Greene to Henry Lee, April 19, 1781, in Conrad, ed., *Papers of Greene*, 8:117, 117-18 (quotation); Pancake, *This Destructive War*, 192; Seymour, *Journal of the Southern Expedition*, 24; Kirkwood, *Journal*, 16; Rawdon to Nisbet Balfour, April 21, 1781, Cornwallis Papers, PRO 30/11/6, 24 (quotation).
7 Greene to Samuel Huntington, April 22, 1781, in Conrad, ed., *Papers of Greene*, 8:131.
8 Lord Rawdon to Lt. Col. Small, April 10, 1781; Rawdon to Nisbet Balfour, April 12, 1781; Rawdon to Balfour, April 13, 1781 (quotation), Cornwallis Papers, PRO 30/11/5, 235, 236, 238.
9 Kirkwood, *Journal*, 16; Seymour, *Journal of the Southern Expedition*, 24.
10 Rawdon to Cornwallis, April 26, 1781, Cornwallis Papers, PRO 30/11/5, 262.
11 Rawdon to Cornwallis, April 26, 1781, Cornwallis Papers, PRO 30/11/5, 262; Pancake, *This Destructive War*, 195; Lee, *Memoirs*, 335.
12 Rawdon to Cornwallis, April 26, 1781, Cornwallis Papers, PRO 30/11/5, 262 (quotation); Piecuch, *Three Peoples, One King*, 247.
13 Rawdon to Cornwallis, April 26, 1781, PRO 30/11/5, 262.
14 Greene to Samuel Huntington, April 27, 1781, in Conrad, ed., *Papers of Greene*, 8:155; Pancake, *This Destructive War*, 193, 196; Howard to John Gunby, March 22, 1782, Bayard Papers, MHS (quotation).
15 Rawdon to Cornwallis, April 26, 1781, Cornwallis Papers, PRO 30/11/5, 262 (quotation); Howard to Gunby, March 22, 1782, Bayard Papers (quotation).
16 Howard to Gunby, March 22, 1782, Bayard Papers (quotation); Rawdon to Cornwallis, April 26, 1781, Cornwallis Papers, PRO 30/11/5, 262 (quotation).
17 Rawdon to Cornwallis, April 26, 1781, Cornwallis Papers, PRO 30/11/5, 262 (quotation); Seymour, *Journal*, 25 (quotation).
18 Greene to Huntington, April 27, 1781, in Conrad, ed., *Papers of Greene*, 8:156.
19 Greene to Huntington, April 27, 1781, in Conrad, ed., *Papers of Greene*, 8:156 (quotation); Pancake, *This Destructive War*, 195-96.
20 Howard to William Johnson, n.d., (c. 1822), Lee Family Papers (quotation); Greene to Huntington, April 27, 1781, in Conrad, ed., *Papers of Greene*, 8:156 (quotation).
21 Rawdon to Cornwallis, April 26, 1781, Cornwallis Papers, PRO 30/11/5, 262 (quotation); Pancake, *This Destructive War*, 198.
22 Howard to William Johnson, n.d., (c. 1822), Lee Family Papers; Greene to Huntington, April 27, 1781, in Conrad, ed., *Papers of Greene*, 8:156; Morrill, *Southern Campaigns*, 161.
23 Howard to Gunby, March 22, 1782, Bayard Papers.
24 Howard to Johnson, n.d., (c. 1822), Lee Family Papers; Greene to Huntington, April 27, 1781, in Conrad, ed., *Papers of Greene*, 8:156; Rawdon to Cornwallis, April 26, 1781, Cornwallis Papers, PRO 30/11/5, 262 (quotation).
25 Howard to Gunby, March 22, 1782, Bayard Papers (quotation); Greene to Huntington, April 27, 1781, in Conrad, ed., *Papers of Greene*, 8:156-57, (quotation).
26 Rawdon to Cornwallis, April 26, 1781, Cornwallis Papers, PRO 30/11/5, 262 (quotations); Pancake, *This Destructive War*, 198.
27 "List of the Officers Killed, Wounded, and Taken Prisoners, in the Action Before Camden," April 25, 1781, in Tarleton, *History of the Campaigns*, 470; Rawdon to Cornwallis, April 26, 1781 (quotations) and "Return of the Killed Wounded & Missing" at Hobkirk's Hill, April 25, 1781, Cornwallis Papers, PRO 30/11/5, 262, 267; Greene to Joseph Reed, Aug. 6, 1781, in Conrad, ed., *Papers of Greene*, 9:135 (quotation). The percentage of American losses excludes the estimated 250 North Carolina militia who did not take part in the battle.
28 Greene to Huntington, April 27, 1781, in Conrad, ed., *Papers of Greene*, 8:157 (quotation); Steuart, *History of the Maryland Line*, 81.
29 Pancake, *This Destructive War*, 198.
30 Pancake, *This Destructive War*, 198; "General Greene's Orders," May 2, 1781, in Conrad, ed., *Papers of Greene*, 8:187 (quotations).
31 A. A. Gunby, *Colonel John Gunby of the Maryland Line: Being Some Account of his Contribution to American Liberty* (Cincinnati: R. Clarke Co., 1902), 118-19; Otho Williams to Gunby, July 16, 1781, in Conrad, ed., *Papers of Greene*, 9: 21, 21n.
32 Greene to Gunby, March 22, 1782, Bayard Papers; Howard to Johnson, n.d., (c. 1822), Lee Family Papers (quotations).

33 Henry Lee, *Memoirs*, 325 (quotation); Greene to Huntington, April 27, 1781, in Conrad, ed., *Papers of Greene*, 8:157; Howard to Johnson, n.d., (c. 1822), Lee Family Papers; Pancake, *This Destructive War*, 198-99; Terry Golway, *Washington's General: Nathanael Greene and the Triumph of the American Revolution* (New York: Henry Holt and Co., 2005), 269 (quotation).
34 Greene to Joseph Reed, Aug. 6, 1781 and Greene to Horatio Gates, Oct. 4, 1781, in Conrad, ed., *Papers of Greene*, 9:135 (quotation), 425-26 (quotation).
35 Francis Marion to Greene, April 23, 1781, and "List of Prisoners Taken in Fort Watson," in Tarleton, *History of the Campaigns*, 471, 473; Rawdon to Cornwallis, May 2, 1781, Cornwallis Papers, PRO 30/11/6, 21; Pancake, *This Destructive War*, 195.
36 Greene to Huntington, May 5, 1781, in Conrad, ed., *Papers of Greene*, 8:206; Rawdon to Cornwallis, May 24, 1781, Cornwallis Papers, PRO 30/11/6, 106 (quotation).
37 Rawdon to Cornwallis, May 24, 1781, Cornwallis Papers, PRO 30/11/6, 106 (quotation); Greene to Henry Lee, May 9, 1781, in Conrad, ed., *Papers of Greene*, 8:227 (quotation).
38 Greene to Lee, May 9, 1781, in Conrad, ed., *Papers of Greene*, 8:227-28; Rawdon to Cornwallis, May 24, 1781, Cornwallis Papers, PRO 30/11/6, 106 (quotations).
39 Rawdon to Cornwallis, May 24, 1781, Cornwallis Papers, PRO 30/11/6, 106.
40 Greene to Huntington, May 14, 1781, in Conrad, ed., *Papers of Greene*, 8:250-51 (quotation); Pancake, *This Destructive War*, 195 (quotation).

CHAPTER EIGHT

THE FINAL CAMPAIGN

In the four months after reclaiming Camden, John Eager Howard and the American army would face grueling marches, blistering heat, food shortages, and occasional bloody bouts with the enemy as Nathanael Greene fulfilled his pledge to maintain pressure on the British. The campaign would take them across the breadth of South Carolina, bringing failure and frustration at Ninety Six before culminating in the final open-field battle of the War for Independence at Eutaw Springs near the Santee River.

As Greene pushed his troops past Camden in pursuit of Lord Rawdon's retreating British army, the partisans continued to attack the scattered British posts. Thomas Sumter, getting into action at last, surrounded the British force at Orangeburg on the evening of May 10 and the garrison surrendered the next morning. Sumter told Greene that he believed Rawdon might be cut off if Francis Marion's partisans could reach Nelson's (also called Neilson's) Ferry on the Santee before the British could cross. Unfortunately, Greene did not have any forces to make the attempt because Marion was with Henry Lee at Fort Motte, where they found the earthwork fortifications around the Motte family house "strong" and the defenders "obstinate." The garrison's determination increased, as did Marion and Lee's desperation, when both sides saw the campfires of Rawdon's army burning several miles away on the night of May 11. The American commanders decided they had to burn the house to force the defenders to surrender. Rebecca Motte, the building's owner, not only consented, but according to one source lent the American soldiers bows to shoot flaming arrows at her home. The roof caught fire, the garrison surrendered, and the 140 captured British and Loyalist soldiers then joined Lee's and Marion's troops in extinguishing the flames. Their combined efforts saved the house. "The Stroke was heavy upon me," Rawdon lamented when he heard of the fort's surrender, since he was expecting to find provisions for his troops there.[1]

Greene continued his relentless efforts to force the British out of their chain of forts. Upon learning that Fort Motte had fallen, he ordered Henry Lee to march his legion up the Congaree River and "demand an immediate surrender" of Fort Granby on the road leading from Camden to Ninety Six. Sumter had failed in an attempt to take the fort at the beginning of May, when the garrison of 60 British troops and 300 Loyalists, supported by artillery, had proven too strong for the American partisans. Believing that Rawdon was marching to the defenders' aid, Lee did not want to waste time with a siege. Instead, he visibly began preparations to besiege the fort while opening negotiations with its commander, Major Andrew Maxwell. Doubtful that his troops would be relieved by Rawdon and hoping to avoid capture, Maxwell offered to abandon his post if Lee allowed the British and Loyalist troops to leave unmolested and take along their stock of supplies, which included goods and slaves plundered from the area's rebels. Lee, knowing that it was more important to take the fort than its garrison, agreed. The defenders left on May 15.[2]

Although neither Lee nor Greene knew it, Rawdon was reluctant to risk his army to help with the defense of any of the threatened British posts. When Rawdon arrived at Nelson's Ferry he met Lieutenant Colonel Nisbet Balfour, commandant of Charleston and Rawdon's superior. Balfour brought a grim assessment of the British situation in South Carolina. He told Rawdon that the defenses around Charleston "had been in part levelled to make way for new ones, which were not as yet constructed; that his Garrison was inadequate to oppose any force of consequence," and that Charleston's inhabitants were showing signs of rebelliousness. Rawdon therefore agreed with Balfour "in the conclusion to be drawn from hence; that any misfortune happening to my Corps might entail the loss of the Province."[3]

Nevertheless, having received a reinforcement of 300 infantry and 80 cavalry, Rawdon made an effort "to check the enemy's operations on the Congaree." His troops marched on the night of May 14 and reached McCord's Ferry the next evening, much too late to assist Fort Granby. There Rawdon learned from spies that Greene was marching toward Orangeburg. This information led Rawdon to order a second night march, a withdrawal to Eutaw Springs. Although his spies had brought inaccurate reports, Rawdon's retreat was wise, as Greene's army was on the Congaree dangerously close to the British. A few days later, Rawdon gave up hope of holding the interior of South Carolina and withdrew to Monck's Corner, close to Charleston.[4]

The American campaign was an astonishing success. As Henry Lee observed, "in less than one month since Greene appeared before Camden, he had compelled the British general to evacuate that important post, forced the submission of all the intermediate posts, and was now upon the banks of the Congaree, in the heart of South Carolina, ready to advance upon Ninety-Six (the only remaining fortress in the State, besides Charleston, in the enemy's possession)." Howard and the rest of Greene's troops welcomed the news of these successes, and perhaps wished that they, like Lee, had been participants in some of them.[5]

Lee also noted that the British still held Georgetown, and he accurately predicted that they would not retain it much longer. When Lee took his legion to Fort Granby, Marion led his partisans east, determined to drive the British out of Georgetown by siege if necessary. On June 6, shortly after Marion's force appeared before the British fortifications, the small garrison evacuated the town, going to Charleston by sea. That left Ninety Six as the only British post in the South Carolina interior, and by then Greene already had the town and its defenders surrounded.[6]

Located deep in the backcountry in a region where Loyalists were numerous, Ninety Six was left dangerously isolated when Rawdon withdrew from Camden. On May 14th, after learning that the Americans had captured Orangeburg and Fort

Motte, the British commander "dispatched Emissaries immediately to Ninety Six; desiring Lt. Col. Cruger to retire to Augusta [Georgia]; and I desired Lt. Col. Balfour to forward the same order by different routes." When Rawdon wrote his assessment of the British situation ten days later, he had received no news from Ninety Six and remarked ominously that "should Lt. Col. Cruger not have received this order, I fear his situation will be dangerous." Rawdon added that he "did not think it practicable" to march to the aid of Ninety Six since it could not be done "without running hazards which I judged the General State of the Province would not allow."[7]

None of Rawdon's or Balfour's messengers got through the American lines to Ninety Six—they were either captured or forced to turn back. Thus, when Greene's army appeared before the post on May 22, its commander, Lieutenant Colonel John Harris Cruger, had to deal with the threat as best he could. Fortunately for the British, Cruger was an experienced and highly skilled officer. He had received no instructions from his superiors so the New York Loyalist "thought himself bound to maintain the post." His garrison of 350 veteran New York and New Jersey Loyalists, bolstered by 200 experienced South Carolina Loyalist militiamen, hunkered down behind their recently strengthened fortifications and waited to see what Greene would do.[8]

To his dismay, Greene found Ninety Six "much better fortified and garrison much stronger in regular troops than was expected." His army, reduced by casualties and detachments, numbered only about 1,050 men, too few for a full scale assault on the defenses. A wooden palisade surrounded the town, which was linked on the east side to an earthwork in the shape of a multi-pointed star. West of the stockade, a spring that provided water to the garrison and townspeople ran through a gully, and a covered way led from the main post to the spring and to a smaller wooden fort beyond. Greene decided that formal siege operations would be necessary to take the town.[9]

The American army had little experience with siege warfare. Greene relied on his engineer officer to manage the operations, but Polish-born, European-trained Colonel Tadeusz Kosciuszko opened the siege with a serious blunder. On May 22nds, Kosciuszko decided to focus his efforts on the Star Fort and he sent troops to begin digging a trench only seventy yards from that position. Cruger responded by blasting the work party with artillery and, when they took cover, sending a detachment to attack them. The Loyalists drove off the Americans, and a group of slaves who accompanied the attackers seized the Americans' tools and filled the trench. Greene and Kosciuszko decided to restart their work at a safer distance. Later in the day, the troops started work on an approach trench in the shelter of a ravine and out of effective range of enemy fire.[10]

The tedious work went on day and night as the Americans, assisted by slaves taken from area Loyalists, inched closer to the Star Fort despite occasional sorties by the defenders. Greene found the slow process a strain on his patience, telling Henry Lee on May 29 that "the work goes on slow." Howard and the other officers must have shared Greene's frustration. By June 3, Kosciuszko's laborers finally reached the point where they had originally started digging nearly two weeks before. Greene used that accomplishment to have Colonel Otho Williams send Cruger a summons to surrender. The New Yorker, however, promptly rejected Williams's demand. But for Howard, the bad news that the siege would continue was offset by his assignment to take command of the 2nd Maryland Regiment, although he did not receive a promotion to colonel.[11]

June 3rd proved to be a significant day for the British as well. A messenger dispatched by Cruger on the night of May 31 reached Rawdon to report that Ninety Six was besieged, that Cruger considered his garrison "ample" to defend the town, and that "the fire of the Enemy had no effect" thus far. Cruger's only concern was "that relief might not arrive before his Provisions are expended." That eventuality, however was no longer a concern, because ships carrying three British regiments had arrived off Charleston on the night of June 2nd. The next day the fleet entered the harbor and the troops debarked. Rawdon could now march to relieve Ninety Six without worrying that Charleston might be lost. It took him four days to organize his own troops and the light infantry and grenadier companies of the three newly arrived regiments and to procure sufficient provisions for the march. Rawdon set out from Charleston on June 11th with a powerful force of nearly two thousand men.[12]

Greene, learning from Sumter of the arrival of the British reinforcements, by June 10th began to consider the possibility that the British would try to lift the siege of Ninety Six. Greene's army had also been reinforced, but he realized that he would have to move quickly to insure the capture Ninety Six in the event Rawdon did march to the garrison's relief.[13]

Henry Lee and his legion, along with Andrew Pickens and his South Carolina militia, had joined Greene at Ninety Six on June 8, fresh from their victory at Augusta, Georgia. Greene had sent them to assist Colonel Elijah Clarke's Georgia partisans, who were besieging that key post on the Savannah River. The British garrison surrendered on June 5th after a stubborn defense. Lee and Pickens wasted no time in coming to Greene's assistance, and the Rhode Islander ordered them to focus their efforts on the small, somewhat isolated wooden fort west of the spring. Lee immediately saw that he could position troops to cut off the defenders' access to the spring and by that means perhaps force Ninety Six to surrender. Cruger responded to the new threat by sending naked slaves out at night to fill buckets of water, a method that provided enough water to sustain the garrison and townspeople throughout the rest of the siege.[14]

Greene retained some of Pickens's men to assist in the operations against the Star Fort, assigning them to build a Maham tower. This log structure, devised by South Carolina militia colonel Hezekiah Maham, had been used successfully to force the surrender of Fort Watson. Assembled under cover of darkness, the tower housed sharpshooters who could fire from its top into a fort while sheltered behind protective logs. The exposed defenders would have to abandon their position or surrender.[15]

The tower had worked well at Fort Watson; however, it failed at Ninety Six. Cruger simply ordered his soldiers to raise the parapets an additional three feet with sandbags, negating the effect of the tower. The garrison was buoyed by this small success, and on June 12th they received further encouragement when a Loyalist messenger outwitted the Americans and made his way past the besiegers and into the fort with the good news that Rawdon was bringing his force to relieve the siege. When this daring courier initially approached the fort, he pretended to be a simple country fellow and rode slowly through the American camp, pausing frequently to chat with the troops. Then, when he was opposite the gate to Ninety Six, he spurred his horse and dashed toward the stockade. The surprised Americans shot at him and missed, and he made it safely inside the fortifications. His report insured that Greene would continue to face a tenacious defense.[16]

The American commander was still uncertain of Rawdon's intentions, and with each passing day believed that his operations were coming closer to success. On June 12th, he told North Carolina governor Abner Nash "we are prosecuting our siege at this place with all the dispatch our force will admit. ... We must succeed in time if not interrupted." However, Greene warned that "should the enemy move out in force" from Charleston "they will oblige us to raise the seige." That same day, in a letter to Thomas Sumter, he predicted that the British garrison "will soon get tired of this business." The next day, Greene declared that "a few days more will terminate the seige here." Howard and his fellow officers hoped that Greene's prediction was correct, because their duties were burdensome. In addition to performing their usual tasks such as issuing supplies, performing inspections, and serving as officer of the day, the siege required them to assign some men to dig the approach trenches and others to provide protection against British forays, to make sure that the troops were rotated in these assignments to prevent exhaustion or complaints, and to maintain morale throughout the slow progress of the siege.[17]

Greene's confidence and the hopes of Howard and the rest of the army were shaken soon afterward by news from Thomas Sumter. On June 13th, the South Carolinian warned Greene that the British were "advancing & Giving out that they are Going for Ninty Six." Although he ordered Lieutenant Colonel William Washington to join Sumter and delay the British advance, Greene doubted the accuracy of the report. "I cannot persuade myself yet that the enemy mean to pay a visit to this place," he wrote Sumter on June 15th. It was not until the next night, after receiving another message from Sumter, that Greene decided "it is highly probable" that Rawdon intended "to raise the Seige here."[18]

The Irish nobleman had been marching "as rapidly as the excessive heat would admit," losing over fifty of his men to heat stroke and heat exhaustion along the way, while Greene's instructions to Sumter and other officers to delay the British advance went largely unheeded. Other than token opposition, the only serious encounter between Rawdon's troops and the American militia occurred on June 18, when one of Sumter's regiments tried to harass the rear of the British column and Loyalist cavalry attacked it "so vigorously that [the] Corps was totally dispersed" with considerable loss. Rawdon continued forward "without opposition; altho' the Enemy's Light Troops hoverd in our front." Sumter had failed Greene once again in this brief campaign. The South Carolinian had incorrectly guessed which route Rawdon would take to Ninety Six, and by the time he realized his error, most of his men were too far away to engage the British.[19]

Reluctant to abandon his efforts against Ninety Six without making a final effort to take the town, Greene resolved to storm the fortifications. He would not commit his entire army and risk a bloody repulse. Instead, Lee with his legion infantry and Robert Kirkwood's Delaware Continentals would attack the fort west of the spring while Lieutenant Colonel Richard Campbell of the Virginia Continentals would lead an assault party drawn from the 1st Maryland and 1st Virginia Regiments against the eastern earthwork. Greene hoped that "the success of a partial attempt to make a Lodgment on one of the Curtains of the Star Redoubt" could be followed by a larger attack that would seize the position. The American artillery opened fire on the defenses at noon on June 18, and after a heavy bombardment the attackers surged forward. Lee and Kirkwood overwhelmed the garrison of the eastern fort, and it fled to safety in the town via the covered way. The assault on the Star Fort failed. Greene held his ground until the afternoon of the next day. By then Rawdon was not far away, and the British commander noted, "upon our approach" Greene "raised the Siege & retired across the Saluda" River.[20]

Rawdon's troops marched into Ninety Six on June 21. Learning that Greene was only sixteen miles away "in a strong position behind Bush River," the persistent Irishman "resolved to try once more to bring him to action." He marched on the night of June 22, found that Greene had fallen back another twenty-four miles, pushed the pursuit that far, and discovered that Greene had withdrawn even farther. Rawdon remarked, "Our troops were by that time so overcome with fatigue, that I was obliged to halt." He returned to Ninety Six and ordered the post evacuated.[21]

Greene, who had decided to march to Charlotte, changed direction when he received word that the British had abandoned Ninety Six. Riding ahead of his troops, he examined the situation and, finding that Rawdon had occupied Orangeburg, decided to attack the town when the army came up. Howard and the hard marching infantry arrived soon after, and Greene ordered them to begin the movement toward Orangeburg on July 11. The next day the army reached the town, "but we found [the British] so strong and advantageously posted that we had little hopes of succeeding" in an assault, he observed. Nor was the American army in a condition for battle. Officers and men were exhausted after their trek of over three hundred miles since leaving Ninety Six. Howard and the other regimental officers worked even harder than the troops, monitoring their soldiers' condition and insuring that they remained combat ready. Unfortunately, food was especially lacking when the army reached Orangeburg. Henry Lee described the desperate shortages that plagued the army there:

> "We had experienced in the course of the campaign want of food, and had sometimes seriously suffered from the scantiness of our supplies, rendered more pinching by their quality; but never did we suffer so severely as during the few days' halt here. ... Of meat we had literally none; for the few meager cattle brought to camp as beef would not afford more than one or two ounces per man."

Greene decided to withdraw to the High Hills of Santee, where the troops could recover from their exertions rather than undertake further operations during the worst heat of the summer.[22]

Howard and his comrades welcomed the restful interlude at what the troops called the army's "camp of repose." Lee noted the contrast with the army's previous condition, remarking that "the troops were placed in good quarters, and the heat of July rendered tolerable by the high ground, the fine air, and good water of the selected camp. Disease began to abate, our wounded to recover, and the army to rise in bodily strength." There was also a sufficient stock of grain in the surrounding countryside to feed the men properly.[23]

Nevertheless, the army was not on holiday. Greene insisted that his officers maintain strict discipline at all times. Howard supervised a range of daily activities: assigning men to guard duty, drilling and parading his regiment, and insuring that the grounds of the camp, clothing, and weapons were kept clean and "in the best order." He regularly checked the condition of his men in the hospital, insuring that there were no shirkers in his unit. A key element of enforcing discipline involved holding courts martial to try soldiers accused of breaches of duty, and Howard presided over several such courts during the army's time in camp. For example, on August 5, Howard and his fellow officers sentenced Joden Roziers of the North Carolina Continentals to death for desertion, "bearing Arms against the United States," and "Passing thro' Camp with a fictitious Name." In a more personal case for the young Marylander, the court also pronounced the death sentence for Sergeant John Radley of Howard's own regiment. Radley was found guilty of "Expressing himself in a Disaffected manner" and making "Disrespectful" comments about his commanding officer, "frequently saying in presence of the Soldiers" that Howard "would never endeavor to injure the Enemy." Howard must have been affronted by Radley's slurs, but his character would not have allowed such considerations to influence his judgment in the case. He knew that he had done everything in his power to defeat the British army, and longed for the opportunity to do so again.[24]

Before Howard and the Americans could once more engage the British, the royal cause had suffered a serious loss. Lord Rawdon, probably the most capable British officer in South Carolina, was forced to give up his command. Although he was two

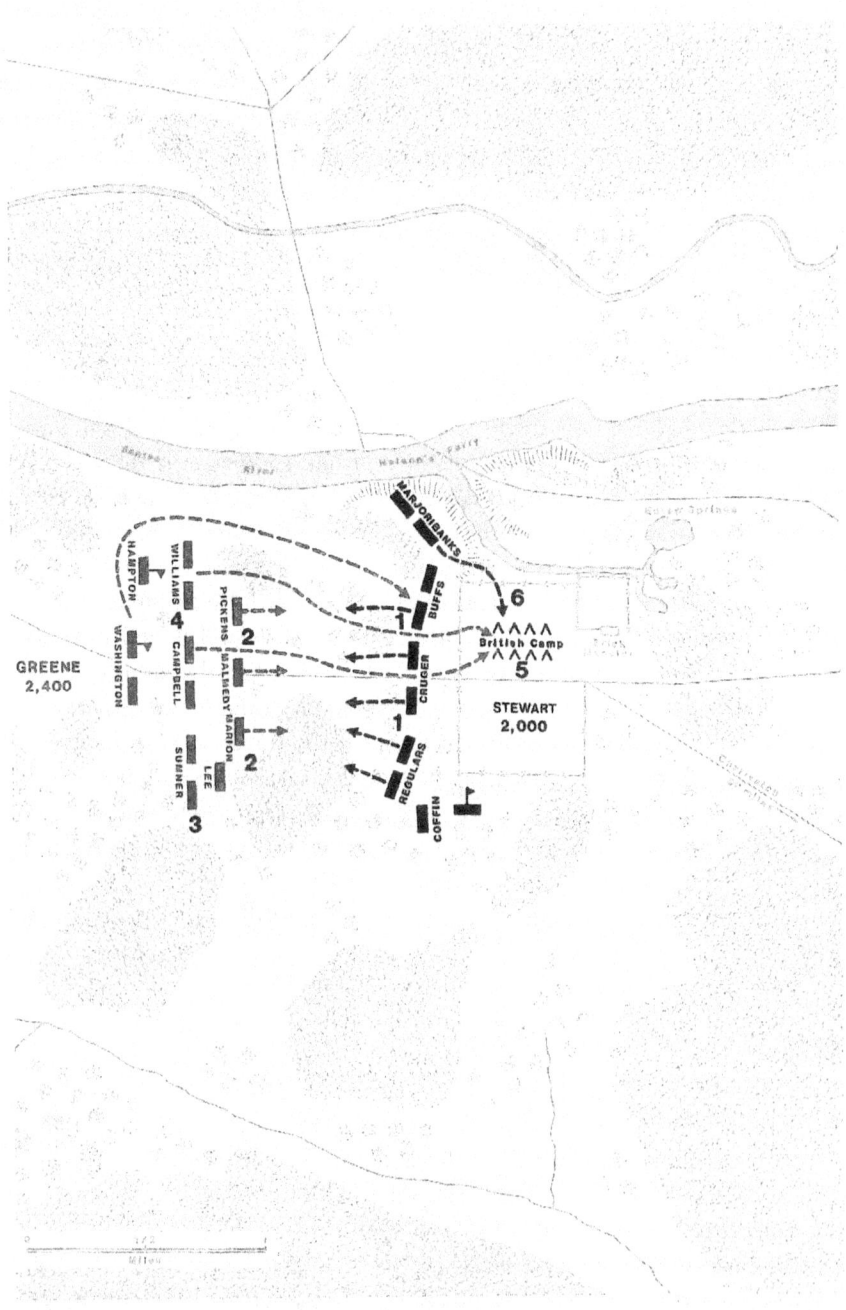

years younger than Howard, the Irish nobleman's strength had been sapped by the brutal southern heat and rigors of the campaign. In early June, a doctor told Rawdon that he "could not outlive the Summer in this Climate." Although he admitted that "I am by no means now in a state of health fit to undertake the business upon which I am going," Rawdon's sense of duty motivated him to lead the relief expedition to Ninety Six. The campaign took a further toll on him, and he sailed for England in August.[25]

The Battle of Eutaw Springs

Rawdon's replacement as field commander of the British forces in South Carolina was Scottish Lieutenant Colonel Alexander Stewart, who had arrived in Charleston with the three regiments of reinforcements on June 3. Since he had not served previously in the War for Independence, Stewart was an unknown quantity to the Americans. His British comrades, who knew him better, held him in low regard. Rawdon declared that Stewart "has too high an opinion of himself," while Major James Wemyss, assigned to staff duties in Charleston, portrayed him as "a brave officer, rather of indolent habits, and a little too fond of the bottle." Stewart's abilities would soon be put to the test, as Greene was preparing to leave the High Hills of Santee and strike another blow at the enemy.[26]

During August, numerous reinforcements had either arrived at Greene's camp or assembled nearby, prepared to cooperate with the Continental Army. They included two Continental regiments from North Carolina plus 150 militia from that state, 550 South Carolina militia under proven leaders Francis Marion and Andrew Pickens, and another 150 state troops under Lieutenant Colonel William Henderson. Their presence swelled the American ranks to more than 2,400 men. For several weeks, Greene had hoped to increase in strength, complaining that had it not been for his army's weakness, "Mr Stewart should not have lain so long quiet." Now, he believed his numbers were sufficient to challenge the British army. On August 22nd, he ordered his officers to prepare the men to march the next day. He did not announce his intentions, but privately informed George Washington that he planned "to make an attack on the enemy."[27]

Since Stewart's force was at McCord's Ferry near the point where the Congaree and Wateree rivers meet to form the Santee, Greene had to take a roundabout route, going all the way to Camden to cross the Wateree and then southwest to cross the Congaree. The long march finally brought the Americans to McCord's Ferry in early September, but by that time Stewart had fallen back to Eutaw Springs on the Santee. The Americans pushed forward and reached Burdell's Tavern, about seven miles from Stewart's camp at the Roche Plantation, on September 7th. Greene issued orders for his troops to march early the next morning to attack the British.[28]

Stewart had no idea that the Americans were so close. "Notwithstanding every exertion being made to gain intelligence of the enemy's situation, they rendered it impossible by waylaying the bypaths and passes through the different swamps," he reported. Thus, with not even an inkling of the threat he faced, at dawn on September 8 the British commander sent out parties totaling about three hundred men to gather sweet potatoes from nearby plantations to feed his men. The foragers took their muskets but only four rounds of ammunition each. Their departure reduced Stewart's force to just 1,400 men fit for duty according to a field return prepared that day. At 6 a.m., after the foraging parties had left, two American deserters came into the British lines. They informed Stewart of Greene's position and claimed that the American army consisted of four thousand men and four pieces of artillery. Although he was skeptical of their report, Stewart prudently dispatched Major John Coffin with 50 cavalry and 140 light infantry to scout the road that led from Burdell's Tavern to the British camp.[29]

By the time Coffin set out, Greene's troops were already on the road. The leading units had left camp at 4 a.m., with Lee's legion in front, followed by Henderson's South Carolina state troops and the North Carolina militia under a French officer, the Marquis de Malmedy. The two Maryland regiments were assigned to the tail end of the column, so Howard and his men had to stand in ranks in the predawn darkness, impatiently waiting for the other troops to proceed.[30]

After marching about three miles, Greene's vanguard met Coffin's detachment. Thinking that the Americans were "a party of Militia," Coffin's Loyalist cavalrymen charged. Lee and Henderson greeted them with a heavy fire. When the Loyalists halted, the legion infantry counterattacked. Coffin broke off the battle and rushed back to camp to inform Stewart that the Continental Army was approaching. The sound of musket fire attracted the attention of the British foraging parties, who had dispersed into small groups. They made their way back to the road, only to stumble into the American column. Fighting broke out between the foragers and Greene's marching troops. Sergeant William Seymour of the Delaware Continentals described one such encounter, writing that "we fell in with a foraging party of sixty men, loaded with potatoes, most of whom we either killed, wounded, or captured." Overall, about half of the British foragers managed to escape death or capture, but they were cut off from the rest of their army and did not rejoin their units until after the battle.[31]

Meanwhile, Coffin brought Stewart the news that Greene's army was advancing. The British commander "determined to fight them, as from their numerous cavalry a retreat seemed to me to be attended with dangerous consequences." Drums sounded throughout the camp, and the British soldiers formed for action. In an unusual move for a professional British officer, Stewart ordered Loyalist John Harris Cruger, who had directed the defense of Ninety Six, to take command of the army's front line. While protocol might have dictated against giving such an important responsibility to a Loyalist officer, events would soon show that Stewart had acted wisely when he gave Cruger that assignment.[32]

Cruger hurriedly deployed his regiments. The flank battalion, composed of the light infantry and grenadier companies drawn from each of Stewart's regiments, took post on the right. Its commander, Major John Marjoribanks, placed his men behind the sloping bank of Eutaw Creek, where thick scrub oak at the top of the bank screened them from view. Their position was in advance of, and at almost a right angle to the rest of the British line. Next to the flank battalion, the 3rd Regiment, nicknamed the "Buffs," faced west and formed their battle line. The 63rd Regiment stood to the Buffs' left, followed by the 64th and Cruger's own unit, the 1st Battalion of DeLancey's Brigade. The Provincial Light Infantry, comprised mostly of South Carolina Loyalists, held the extreme left of the line. Two three-pounder cannon near the road supported the British right, and two six-pounders were placed on the left. Stewart assigned some Loyalist militia to guard his wagon train, and kept three small infantry units, the New York and New Jersey Volunteers and a detachment of the 84th Regiment, in reserve along with Coffin's cavalry. However, when Greene's army reached the field and began forming to attack, Stewart realized that the American line extended a considerable distance to the south beyond his own line, and ordered all of the reserve infantry forward. Cruger posted them on the left to match Greene's deployment.[33]

Greene was also busy positioning his troops, using the same alignment he had employed at Guilford Courthouse: militia in the first line and Continentals in the second. On the Americans' far left stood the South Carolina state cavalry under Colonel Wade Hampton, then the state infantry under Henderson and Andrew Pickens's militia. Malmedy's North Carolina militia held the center, with Francis Marion's brigade to their right. Lee's legion anchored the right flank. The second line consisted of the two Maryland Continental regiments, commanded by Colonel Otho Williams, on the left, Lieutenant Colonel Richard Campbell's pair of Virginia Continental regiments in the center, and General Jethro Sumner's two regiments of North Carolina Continentals on the right. Two three-pounders were positioned in the road where they dueled with the British light cannon; the Americans' more powerful six-pounders were with the Continental infantry in the second line. Greene held Captain Robert Kirkwood's company of Delaware Continental infantrymen and William Washington's cavalry in reserve.[34]

Cruger ordered each unit commander to send some troops forward to form a skirmish line in front of the main British position. While the armies moved into position, the opposing skirmish lines exchanged fire, and Greene stated that "the Enemies advanced parties were soon driven in." A brief lull followed and then, at about 9 a.m., the Rhode Islander gave his first line the order to attack.[35]

The North and South Carolinians surged forward through open pine forest and up a gentle slope toward the British veterans posted on the crest of a low ridge. As the Americans came within musket range of the enemy, British officers shouted orders to fire. A hail of lead balls staggered the attackers. They halted and returned fire. Both sides delivered volleys as fast as the men could reload. The militia, who usually did not perform well in this kind of fighting, stood their ground: "The militia fought with a degree of spirit and firmness that reflects the highest honor upon this class of Soldiers," Greene observed. Determined as they were, however, these citizen-soldiers eventually found the British fire more than they could stand. The North Carolinians in the center broke first, and Greene rushed Sumner's North Carolina Continentals to fill the gap in the line. Shortly afterward, raked by fire from the Buffs in their front and Marjoribank's battalion on their flank that wounded their commander, Lieutenant Colonel Henderson, the South Carolina state infantry began to fall back in confusion before Hampton rallied them.[36]

The fighting continued with "redoubled fury." Greene could not help but praise the steadfast British troops, asserting that their "spirit" was equal to that of the Americans, and adding that "they really fought worthy of a better cause." Their toughness eventually began to tell. Sumner's North Carolina Continentals "were all new Levies, and had been under discipline but little more than a month." Now, in the heat of battle, they held their ground "with a degree of obstinacy that would do honor to the best of veterans." That description applied even more accurately to their opponents, whose persistence the valiant North Carolina recruits could not overcome. Their ranks thinned by casualties, Sumner's troops began to fall back. Elated with this apparent success, the British troops on the left launched a spontaneous charge. Stewart, having given no order to counterattack, attributed their actions to "some unknown mistake."[37]

Pouring through the gap in the American center, the British outflanked both Marion and Pickens, who were forced to retreat. Greene remained unperturbed; he saw the British advance not as a potential disaster for his army, but as an opportunity. He ordered the Virginia and Maryland Continentals to charge and sweep the British from the field with their bayonets. Howard, who had been watching the battle unfold from astride his horse in the second line, relayed the order to his men and led the cheering 2nd Maryland forward.[38]

The surprise blow shattered the British army. Greene described the Continentals' "brisk charge with trailed arms, through a heavy cannonade and a shower of musket balls. Nothing could exceed the gallantry and firmness of both officers and soldiers upon this occasion—they preserved their order, and pushed on with such unshaken resolution, that they mowed down all before them." The Maryland Continentals never hesitated, even though the British troops in their front had not joined the counterattack and were still well posted. Howard, sword in hand, accompanied his men until they were almost bayonet-to-bayonet with the enemy. Some officers battled one another with swords, before the British, seeing the units to their left falling back, began to waver. Howard and the commander of the 1st Maryland, Major Henry Hardman, ordered their men to fire, and the point-blank fusillade sent the British reeling. Farther south, the Virginians who had halted forty yards from the still-charging British, blasted them with a musket volley, and then resumed their advance. As the British line crumbled, the infantry of Lee's legion "wheeled and poured a destructive enfilading fire" into the enemy's left flank. "The Enemy were routed in all quarters," Greene declared. Shouting with triumph, the Continentals pursued the fleeing British across the field. Complete victory seemed to be within the Americans' grasp.[39]

Greene's attack, however, rapidly lost momentum. Stewart had instructed Major Henry Sheridan of the New York Volunteers that if the army had to retreat, the Loyalist officer should occupy the two-story, brick Roche house behind the British right and "check the enemy should they attempt to pass it." Sheridan did so, and received valuable assistance from Marjoribanks and the flank battalion. When the British retreat left his troops isolated, Marjoribanks ordered his men to face left, file alongside the creek under cover of its banks, and take a new position. Some of his troops remained in the shelter of the creek bed, while others occupied the fenced garden between the brick house and Eutaw Creek, linking their line with Sheridan's. These were the only organized British troops on the field other than Coffin's cavalry. The Loyalist militia had fled, and Stewart and Cruger were frantically trying to rally their broken regiments.[40]

The Marylanders on the American left were checked, as Stewart had hoped by a "galling and destructive fire" from the windows of the brick house, and if they attempted to rush the structure, Marjoribanks's troops would be able to fire into their flank as well. Howard must have found the situation eerily similar to that at Germantown, Pennsylvania, four years earlier. There the British had unhinged George Washington's attack by staunchly defending a stone house, and now it appeared that the king's troops might once again be saved from defeat by taking refuge in a similar building. Greene, as his friend Henry Knox had done at Germantown, decided to bring up artillery to blast the British out of the house. He had his own pair of six-pounder cannons available along with the two that the British had abandoned. Howard directed his men as they exchanged fire with the enemy, probably wondering if Greene's bombardment would be any more successful than Knox's had been. If Howard reminded his superiors of what had transpired at Germantown, and urged them to try a different plan, neither he nor they ever mentioned it later.[41]

No matter how strong the resistance from the brick house, its defenders would be surrounded if the rest of Greene's troops continued their advance and drove Stewart's other units, which were reorganizing east of the camp, from the field. Unfortunately, to reach the ground where the British officers were working to reorganize their forces meant that the American troops would have to pass through the British camp, which proved to be an insurmountable obstacle.

American officers claimed after the battle that the troops who entered the camp, including the Virginia Continentals and later, Marion's brigade, sent by Greene as a reinforcement, were seduced by the bounty they found among the tents and lost all order and discipline. That could not have been true. Had the camp abounded with "liquors and refreshments," Stewart would not have had to send three hundred men to gather sweet potatoes. Greene reported that the night after the battle, American scouts saw Stewart destroy his army's supply of rum, which had been in the wagons, not the camp. In all probability, the camp itself effectively halted the American advance in that area. Troops reaching the camp deployed in line of battle would have had to break ranks and move in single or double file between the tents, picking their way around stakes and ropes. Emerging in a trickle on the opposite side, they would have been easy targets for the sharpshooters in the brick house. One American participant in the battle asserted that "no cover" from the fire of the building's defenders "was anywhere to be found except among the tents," or behind one of the house's outbuildings. These circumstances, along with the confusion in the Virginia regiments that resulted from the fatal shooting of their commander, Lieutenant Colonel Campbell, caused the advance through the camp to falter.[42]

Once again Greene saw victory slipping away from him. His artillerists had placed their guns so close to the Roche house that they were in easy musket range of the defenders. As soon as they began blasting the house with six-pound iron balls, they "drew all the fire from the windows upon" themselves. Despite their danger, the crews continued to bombard the building. "Never were pieces better served," Greene noted, but the British in the house "soon killed or disabled nearly the whole" of the gun crews.[43]

John Eager Howard was also severely wounded in the fighting at the brick house— "shot down with a broken collar bone"—while directing his troops in the attack on the building. Two lieutenants in his regiment were killed alongside him at about the same time. Despite the severity and pain of his injury, Howard "could not be prevailed on to leave the Feild ... for many Hours," wrote Doctor Richard Pindell, who treated the wound in the midst of the battle.[44]

The valor of Howard and his soldiers notwithstanding, Greene knew that he had to bring the battle to a favorable conclusion quickly and decided to commit his last reserves. He ordered the cavalry of Lee's legion to advance past the camp on the American right in the hope that this would break the deadlock there, and sent instructions to William Washington's Continental Light Dragoons and Robert Kirkwood's company of Delaware Continentals to attack Marjoribank's battalion on the American left. Both assaults miscarried. The legion cavalry went into action without Lee, who took his infantry across the field to assist in the attack on the Roche house. Coffin saw the threat posed by the enemy horsemen and he immediately counterattacked with his own cavalry, driving back the legion. On the opposite flank, Washington, perhaps seduced by dreams of striking the decisive blow on his own, sent his mounted troops racing forward without waiting for Kirkwood's infantry. Reaching the impenetrable thicket that shielded the British flank battalion, the cavalrymen discharged their pistols and carbines to little effect. Unable to reach the defenders with their sabers, Washington and his soldiers rode back and forth in front of the British position, seeking an opening that would allow them to penetrate the brush. Marjoribanks's men shot them down at close range. The fire killed Washington's horse, trapping him beneath it. His surviving troops fled. A British soldier emerged from the brush and pinned Washington with his bayonet, inflicting a minor wound. Washington was taken prisoner. Kirkwood reached the scene a little later and engaged Marjoribanks, but could make no impression on the larger British force. That night, Washington's command could muster only thirty unwounded men; the regiment was later disbanded.[45]

With the failure of Greene's final attacks, the initiative shifted to the British. Marjoribanks and Sheridan sent their men sallying from their positions, seized the four pieces of artillery (two of Greene's and the two British cannons that the Americans had captured earlier), and rolled them back to a secure position alongside the brick house. Stewart and Cruger used the time gained when the American offensive stalled to reorganize their troops. Now, watching this success on their right and Coffin's repulse of the legion cavalry on their left, Stewart led the rest of the army forward and drove the Americans from the camp. Marjoribanks joined the assault, "made a rapid move to their left and attacked the enemy in flank, upon which they gave way in all quarters," Stewart wrote. Greene, his troops exhausted from four hours of battle, low on ammunition, and out of tactical options, ordered a retreat back to Burdell's Tavern.[46]

Howard, along with Lieutenant Colonel William Henderson, was taken to the house of Thomas Jones. Dr. William Read, who was summoned to treat them, turned his attention first to Henderson, who was "in a deplorable condition." When Read had finished with Henderson, Howard asked if the doctor would tend to his injury. "Yes, certainly," Read replied, and asked his name. Discovering that it was Howard, Read declared that he "well knew his celebrity," and set to work on his wound. According to one account, when the doctor examined the damage to Howard's left shoulder, he found it more severe than expected, and instructed the soldier assisting him "to watch closely during the night lest the wound should bleed again, as the patient would die in that case, if not immediately attended to." Howard was said to have overheard and stayed awake all night to monitor the wound himself.[47]

Many other wounded men were also awaiting treatment that night. Casualties at the Battle of Eutaw Springs were high. Howard noted that "nearly one-half my men were killed or wounded, and I had seven officers out of twelve disabled—four killed and three severely wounded." Reports of American casualties varied. Otho Williams listed Continental losses as 114 killed and 262 wounded, and 408 altogether, implying that a further 32 men were missing. Robert Kirkwood recorded different figures for the Continentals in his journal, along with 85 casualties among the South Carolina state troops and militia and 45 in the North Carolina militia. Kirkwood's record of militia casualties, when added to Williams's tally of Continental losses (probably the most accurate count) shows that Greene lost a total of 538 men. The Americans also lost both of their six-pounder cannon but managed to carry off one of the British three-pounders.[48]

Stewart's losses were even more severe in proportion to his army's strength. Of the troops who had actually participated in the battle, 85 were killed, 351 wounded, and 257 were missing. Most of them were captured when the British line collapsed in the face of the Continentals' attack. Some 150 men from the foraging parties had also been lost, the majority taken prisoner, bringing total British casualties to about 686 out of the 1,700 in Stewart's command. With his force so badly weakened, Stewart could not risk remaining so far from Charleston. He spent the next two days removing his wounded, burying the dead, and destroying surplus equipment. Then he withdrew to Monck's Corner. Except for a few raiding parties, no major British force would again venture into the interior of South Carolina. Greene had once again suffered a tactical defeat, only to emerge with a strategic victory.[49]

Greene did not realize the full impact of the battle for sometime, and he worried that Stewart might make another foray. If the British advanced, he did not want them to capture Howard or any other officers, who were then in a "flying hospital" at McCord's Ferry. He ordered Doctor James Browne to move them to a more secure place. Browne informed Greene that Howard and Henderson were still together and wished to remain so. Both men promised Browne that "they will keep prepared to move upon the earliest Notice," but asked Greene's permission "to stay a little longer where they are as a few days may make a great Alteration in their favor." The ordeal caused by their wounds and recovery had forged a strong bond between the two officers.[50]

Six weeks after the battle, many people did not know that Howard's wound was mending; reports still circulated that he was killed at Eutaw Springs. These inaccurate accounts must have caused great distress for his family. Eventually they received the good news that Howard was alive, and his brother James journeyed to South Carolina to help him on the trip home.

One problem that the Howard brothers did not need to worry about was the British army in Virginia. On October 19, 1781, Lord Cornwallis surrendered his army to a combined French and American force led by George Washington and the Comte de Rochambeau, which marked the end of major military operations in the United States and insuring that American independence had been won.[51]

John Eager Howard and his brother left the army's camp in the High Hills of Santee in mid-November, 1781. The recovering young officer carried letters for many of his friends and fellow officers, including one from Nathanael Greene that testified to the Marylander's valuable service. Greene told the correspondant:

> "This will be handed to you by Colonel Howard, as good an officer as the world affords. "He has great ability and the best disposition to promote the service. My own obligations to him are great—the public's still more so. He

deserves a statue of gold no less than the Roman and Grecian heroes."[52]

By December 21st, Howard was back in Maryland, where Greene had put him in charge of recruiting troops for a new Continental unit, the 5th Maryland Regiment. Howard was to command the unit when its ranks were filled. He had not yet fully recovered from his wound, and spent time convalescing at the home of his childhood friend, Doctor Thomas Cradock. During that time Howard also began a correspondence with Miss Peggy Chew, daughter of the family that owned the stone house in Germantown, Pennsylvania, on the field where he had fought earlier in the war. In March 1782, he informed Greene that he had "recovered from his wounds," although one of Howard's sons later wrote that the injury Howard had suffered at Eutaw Springs "kept him in ill health for several years," and that "he never entirely recovered." Diligent as always, Howard actively pursued his recruiting duties until the war officially ended, even though few people saw the need to enlist in light of the inactive military situation. On December 23rd, 1783, Howard may have been present when George Washington appeared before the Continental Congress in Annapolis to return his commission as commander-in-chief of the American army. Artist John Trumbull, in his painting of the event, depicted Howard standing to Washington's right with other Maryland officers, which included Otho Williams and William Smallwood. Washington was America's hero, but his triumph would not have been possible without the assistance of capable subordinates like John Eager Howard.[53]

---

1   Thomas Sumter to Greene, May 11, 1781, Francis Marion to Greene, May 12, 1781, in Conrad, ed., *Papers of Greene*, 8:244, 246 (quotation); John W. Gordon, *South Carolina and the American Revolution: A Battlefield History* (Columbia: University of South Carolina Press, 2003), 151-52; Lee, *Memoirs*, 347; Rawdon to Cornwallis, May 24, 1781, Cornwallis Papers, PRO 30/11/6, 106 (quotation).
2   Greene to Henry Lee, May 13, 1781, in Conrad, ed., *Papers of Greene*, 8:249 (quotation); Gordon, *South Carolina and the Revolution*, 152-53.
3   Rawdon to Cornwallis, May 24, 1781, Cornwallis Papers, PRO 30/11/6, 106.
4   Rawdon to Cornwallis, May 24, 1781, Cornwallis Papers, PRO 30/11/6, 106.
5   Lee, *Memoirs*, 352.
6   Gordon, *South Carolina and the Revolution*, 158; Pancake, *This Destructive War*, 210.
7   Rawdon to Cornwallis, Cornwallis Papers, PRO 30/11/6, 106.
8   Lee, *Memoirs*, 344; Pancake, *This Destructive War*, 209-10; Rawdon to Cornwallis, June 4, 1781, Cornwallis Papers, PRO 30/11/6, 174 (quotation).
9   Greene to Henry Lee, May 22, 1781, in Conrad, ed., *Papers of Greene*, 8:291-92 (quotation); Pancake, *This Destructive War*, 210-11.
10   Pancake, *This Destructive War*, 210; Gordon, *South Carolina and the Revolution*, 156; Robert D. Bass, *Ninety Six: The Struggle for the South Carolina Back Country* (Lexington, SC: Sandlapper, 1978), 389.
11   Greene to Lee, May 29, 1781, Otho Williams to John Harris Cruger, June 3, 1781, Cruger to Williams, June 3, 1781, in Conrad, ed., *Papers of Greene*, 8:326 (quotation), 339, 340; Bass, *Ninety Six*, 387, 389; Pancake, *This Destructive War*, 210; Steuart, *History of the Maryland Line*, 12.
12   Bass, *Ninety Six*, 395; Rawdon to Cornwallis, June 5, 1781, Cornwallis Papers, PRO 30/11/6, 174 (quotation); Pancake, *This Destructive War*, 212.
13   Sumter to Greene, June 7, 1781, Greene to Marion, June 10, 1781, in Conrad, ed., *Papers of Greene*, 8:360, 374.

14 Bass, *Ninety Six*, 397-98.
15 Bass, *Ninety Six*, 398; Pancake, *This Destructive War*, 192, 213.
16 Bass, *Ninety Six*, 398; Pancake, *This Destructive War*, 213.
17 Greene to Abner Nash, June 12, 1781, Greene to Sumter, June 12, 1781 and June 13, 1781, in Conrad, ed., *Papers of Greene*, 8:381 (quotation), 382 (quotation), 385 (quotation).
18 Sumter to Greene, June 13, 1781, Greene to William Washington, June 14, 1781, Greene to Sumter, June 15, 1781, and June 18, 1781, in Conrad, ed., *Papers of Greene*, 8:388 (quotation), 389, 390 (quotation), 404 (quotation).
19 Rawdon to Cornwallis, Aug. 2, 1781, Cornwallis Papers, PRO 30/11/6, 347 (quotations); Pancake, *This Destructive War*, 212-13, 214.
20 Greene to Samuel Huntington, June 20, 1781, in Conrad, ed., *Papers of Greene*, 8:421 (quotation); Pancake, *This Destructive War*, 213-14; Rawdon to Cornwallis, Aug. 2, 1781, Cornwallis Papers, PRO 30/11/6, 347 (quotation).
21 Rawdon to Cornwallis, Aug. 2, 1781, Cornwallis Papers, PRO 30/11/6, 347.
22 Greene to Thomas McKean, July 17, 1781, in Conrad, ed., *Papers of Greene*, 9:28-29 (quotation); Pancake, *This Destructive War*, 214-15; Lee, *Memoirs*, 386 (quotation).
23 Lee, *Memoirs*, 393.
24 General Greene's Orders, July 18, 1781, and Aug. 5, 1781, in Conrad, ed., *Papers of Greene*, 9:34 (quotation), 131 (quotation).
25 Pancake, *This Destructive War*, 193 (quotation), 215-16; Rawdon to Cornwallis, June 7, 1781, Cornwallis Papers, PRO 30/11/6, 194 (quotation).
26 Rawdon to Cornwallis, June 7, 1781, Cornwallis Papers, PRO 30/11/6, 194 (quotation); James Wemyss, *Sketches of the characters of the General Staff officers and Heads of Departments of the British Army that served in America during the revolutionary war, (the Northern army excepted) with some remarks connected therewith. By a Field officer who served the whole of that war*, in Thomas Sumter Papers, Lyman C. Draper Manuscript Collection, 17VV, 202, microfilm, David Library of the American Revolution, Washington Crossing, PA (quotation).
27 Pancake, *This Destructive War*, 216-17; General Greene's Orders, Aug. 22, 1781, Greene to Henry Lee, Aug. 22, 1781, and Greene to George Washington, Aug. 26, 1781, in Conrad, ed., *Papers of Greene*, 9:222, 223 (quotation), 258 (quotation).
28 Pancake, *This Destructive War*, 217; Greene to Thomas McKean, Sept. 11, 1781, in Conrad, ed., *Papers of Greene*, 9:328.
29 Alexander Stewart to Cornwallis, Sept. 9, 1781, in K. G. Davies, ed., *Documents of the American Revolution*, Vol. 20 (Dublin: Irish University Press, 1979), 227-28 (quotations); Return of the Rooting Party sent out by Lt. Col. Steward, Sept. 8, 1781, and Return of the Army under Lt. Col. Stewart, Sept. 8, 1781, Colonial Office Transcripts, Library of Congress, Washington, DC.
30 Greene to McKean, Sept. 11, 1781, in Conrad, ed., *Papers of Greene*, 9:328, 329; Seymour, *Journal*, 31.
31 Greene to McKean, Sept. 11, 1781, in Conrad, ed., *Papers of Greene*, 9:329 (quotation); Seymour, *Journal*, 31 (quotation); Return of the Rooting Party, Sept. 8, 1781.
32 Stewart to Cornwallis, Sept. 9, 1781, in Davies, ed., *Documents of the Revolution*, 20:227 (quotation), 228.
33 Stewart to Cornwallis, Sept. 9, 1781, in Davies, ed., *Documents of the Revolution*, 20:228; Stewart to Cornwallis, Sept. 26, 1781, Cornwallis Papers, PRO 30/11/6, 399; Lee, *Memoirs*, 467-68.
34 Greene to McKean, Sept. 11, 1781, in Conrad, ed., *Papers of Greene*, 9:328-29.
35 Greene to McKean, Sept. 11, 1781, in Conrad, ed., *Papers of Greene*, 9:329 (quotation); Pancake, *This Destructive War*, 219.
36 Greene to McKean, Sept. 11, 1781, in Conrad, ed., *Papers of Greene*, 9:329 (quotation); Pancake, *This Destructive War*, 219; "Battle of Eutaw. Account furnished by Co. Otho Williams, with additions by Cols. W. Hampton, Polk, Howard and Watt," in Robert W. Gibbes, *Documentary History of the American Revolution, Consisting of Letters and Papers relating to the Contest for Liberty Chiefly in South Carolina*, Vol. 3 (New York: D. Appleton & Co., 1857), 148.
37 "Battle of Eutaw," in Gibbes, *Documentary History*, 3:148 (quotation), 149; Greene to McKean, Sept. 11, 1781, in Conrad, ed., *Papers of Greene*, 9:329 (quotations); Stewart to Cornwallis, Sept. 9, 1781, in Davies, ed., *Documents of the Revolution*, 20:228 (quotation).
38 "Battle of Eutaw," in Gibbes, *Documentary History*, 3: 149-50.
39 Greene to McKean, Sept. 11, 1781, in Conrad, ed., *Papers of Greene*, 9:331 (quotation); "Battle of Eutaw," in Gibbes, ed., *Documentary History*, 3:150-51 (quotation).

40 Stewart to Cornwallis, Sept. 9, 1781, in Davies, ed., *Documents of the Revolution*, 20:228 (quotation); Stewart to Cornwallis, Sept. 26, 1781, Cornwallis Papers, PRO 30/11/6, 399.
41 "Battle of Eutaw," in Gibbes, *Documentary History*, 3:152, 153 (quotation); Greene to McKean, Sept. 11, 1781, in Conrad, ed., *Papers of Greene*, 9:331.
42 "Battle of Eutaw," in Gibbes, *Documentary History*, 3:153-154 (quotation); Pancake, *This Destructive War*, 220 (quotation); Greene to McKean, Sept. 11, 1781, in Conrad, ed., *Papers of Greene*, 9:332.
43 "Battle of Eutaw," in Gibbes, *Documentary History*, 3:155 (quotation); Greene to McKean, Sept. 11, 1781, in Conrad, ed., *Papers of Greene*, 9:331 (quotation).
44 "Reminiscences of Dr. William Read," in Gibbes, *Documentary History*, 2:282 (quotation); "A Militant Surgeon of the Revolution: Some Letters of Richard Pindell, M.D.," *Maryland Historical Magazine*, Vol. 18, No. 4 (Dec. 1923), 319 (quotation).
45 "Battle of Eutaw," in Gibbes, *Documentary History*, 3:152, 154-55; Morrill, *Southern Campaigns*, 168; Stewart to Cornwallis, Sept. 9, 1781, in Davies, *Documents of the Revolution*, 20:228; Stewart to Cornwallis, Sept. 26, 1781, Cornwallis Papers, PRO 30/11/6, 399; Account of John Chaney in John C. Dann, ed., *The Revolution Remembered: Eyewitness Accounts of the War for Independence* (Chicago: University of Chicago Press, 1980), 232.
46 Stewart to Cornwallis, Sept. 9, 1781, in Davies, ed., *Documents of the Revolution*, 20:228 (quotation); Greene to McKean, Sept. 11, 1781, in Conrad, ed., *Papers of Greene*, 9:332.
47 "Reminiscences of Dr. Read," in Gibbes, *Documentary History*, 2:281-82; Elizabeth Read, "John Eager Howard, Colonel of the Second Maryland Regiment," *Magazine of American History*, Vol. 7, No. 4, Oct. 1881, 280 (quotation).
48 Scharf, *History of Maryland*, 427 (quotation); Kirkwood, "Journal," 24; "State of the Continental Troops," in Gibbes, ed., *Documentary History*, 3:144; Greene to McKean, Sept. 11, 1781, in Conrad, ed., *Papers of Greene*, 9:332.
49 Return of Killed, Wounded, and Missing at Eutaw Springs, in Tarleton, *History of the Campaigns*, 513; Return of the Rooting Party, Sept. 8, 1781, Colonial Office Transcripts; Stewart to Cornwallis, Sept. 26, 1781, Cornwallis Papers, PRO 30/11/6, 399; Pancake, *This Destructive War*, 220-21.
50 Dr. James Browne to Greene, Sept. 27, 1781, in Conrad, ed., *Papers of Greene*, 9:402.
51 Pancake, *This Destructive War*, 229-30.
52 *Otho Williams to Elie Williams, Nov. 10, 1781, Otho Holland Williams Papers; Greene to unknown recipient, Nov. 14, 1781, in Conrad, ed., Papers of Greene, 9:571-72 (quotation).*
53 Greene to unknown recipient, Nov. 14, 1781, and Howard to Greene, March 26, 1782,in Conrad, ed., *Papers of Greene*, 9:572, 10:541 (quotation); Allen, *Garrison Church*, 155; Unknown son of John Eager Howard to Mr. Walsh, Jr., Dec. 30, 1830, Howard Papers (quotation); Laura Rice, *Maryland History in Prints* (Baltimore: Maryland Historical Society, 2002), 22.

CHAPTER NINE
POLITICIAN AND BUSINESSMAN

John Eager Howard returned home to Maryland at the age of thirty with a reputation as one of the Revolution's genuine heroes, an asset that would provide him with many opportunities after the war. Freed from his military responsibilities, Howard focused his attention on managing his long-neglected real estate holdings. While establishing himself as one of Baltimore's most successful businessmen, he also found time for friendship, marriage, and service to his city and state in a variety of political offices.

As early as 1780, Howard had large land holdings north and west of Baltimore surveyed and subdivided into lots that he could sell or lease. In 1782, his recruiting duties left him with free time to devote personal attention to his properties, and asked the Maryland legislature for permission to lay out lots, streets, lanes, and alleys on some of his land and to incorporate that area into Baltimore. The legislature declared that Howard's proposal "would tend greatly to the advantage of the said town" and approved his request, stipulating that he pay for the work and that it be subject to the approval of Baltimore's commissioners.[1]

Howard's land holdings were perfectly situated to capitalize on the expansion of Baltimore. Maryland's largest city had grown steadily throughout the war and served as a major export outlet for grain produced on inland farms. As Baltimore grew, so did the value of Howard's real estate. He managed his business affairs astutely and developed his unimproved land into a network of lots, homes, and businesses. These activities provided him with substantial income through rents and periodic sales. He prudently invested much of the proceeds in bank notes and the stock of solid companies, carefully avoiding potential risks.

At the war's end, Howard welcomed home an old friend, Otho Holland Williams. The two enjoyed pleasant times together in the years after the war, although it is likely that the more gregarious Williams instigated most of their social activities. In April 1784 Williams remarked that Howard was "as politely good natured and as unintelligible ... as ever" while the two former officers spent time in activities such as "a clamorous conversation in a congress of belles and beaux," attended an "elegant party of pleasure," and "joined a more beautiful and more agreeable party of ladies" after a ride through Baltimore and the surrounding countryside in Howard's carriage.[2]

Williams met Mary Smith of Baltimore on one of these social occasions, and they married in October 1785. Despite the change this made in their relationship, Howard and Williams remained close, loaning each other money, purchasing items for one another, and assisting each other in various ways. For example, Howard asked Williams to manage the repairs to his house in Bath, Virginia, and showed his frugality by requesting that Williams minimize expenses by doing "as little as necessary." Later, Howard helped Williams purchase land that included an orchard.[3]

Like his friend, Howard had also been pursuing a romantic interest. In April 1787, Williams observed that "Howard is courting in Philadelphia." The object of

Howard's affection was Margaret Oswald Chew, known as "Peggy." They had met at some point during the war. As early as 1781, Howard's friend Doctor Thomas Cradock was writing to Peggy on behalf of Howard while the latter recovered from his wound. Peggy's previous suitor was the famous Major John Andre, a British officer who had served as an aide to General William Howe during the occupation of Philadelphia. Peggy's father, Benjamin Chew, was a prominent Loyalist. Teenaged Peggy had welcomed the attentions of the dashing Andre, who escorted her to balls and wrote poems dedicated to her. If the two managed to remain in contact after the British evacuated Philadelphia in June 1778, their relationship certainly came to an end when the army hanged Andre in October 1780 for his role as a spy valued in Benedict Arnold's treason. Nevertheless, Peggy enjoyed teasing Howard with comments about Andre's gallantry and charm; on one occasion, she "remarked that 'Major Andre' was a most witty and cultivated gentleman," provoking Howard to respond that Andre "was a ------- spy … nothing but a ------- spy!"[4]

Thirty-four-year-old John Eager Howard and twenty-six-year-old Peggy Chew were married at Christ Church in Philadelphia on May 18, 1787. Four days later, the bride's parents hosted a dinner at their Philadelphia residence at which George Washington was a guest. Very likely some of the discussion between Washington, Howard, and Benjamin Chew turned to their shared connection with the Battle of Germantown. Chew owned the stone house, Cliveden, where Howard and Washington had fought a decade earlier.[5]

Shortly after their marriage, Howard brought Peggy to her new estate, Belvidere, an elegant mansion that he was building on a three-hundred-acre tract north of Baltimore known as "Howard's Park." When completed in 1794, Belvidere consisted of three wings, each the size of a large house, connected by colonnades. Howard had begun work on the structure in 1786, and was closely involved in its design and construction, at times becoming "so much engaged with my buildings that it is impossible to leave home." The mansion hosted many visitors from the elite of Maryland society, including Howard's former military comrades Otho Williams, Mordecai Gist, William Smallwood, and Samuel Smith, as well as Charles Carroll and Samuel Chase, who had both signed the Declaration of Independence. Howard also extended his hospitality to the Episcopal bishops of Maryland and other members of the clergy. Peggy earned a reputation as an excellent hostess and was praised as "a lady of much animation of character and genial manners."[6]

From all appearances, the Howards enjoyed their lives at Belvidere and had a very successful marriage. Peggy called her husband "the Colonel," but in her correspondence referred to him as her "Lord and slave" and her "good squire." Her taciturn husband often called his wife "Peggy" in the early years of their marriage, although as time passed he usually referred to her as "Mrs. Howard" or simply "my wife." His choice of words reflected eighteenth-century formality rather than any lack of affection. The Howards clearly enjoyed a loving relationship and their family was central to their lives. Between 1788 and 1806 the couple had nine children, eight of whom lived to adulthood.[7]

Howard took a particular interest in his children's education. He financed travel and schooling in Europe for his sons, and at home he introduced them to the world of business. He tried to instill his own frugality in his children, writing of one of his sons employed in the family business that "my plan is to give him employment to make money, and not to spend it." Howard also supervised two of his nephews, the sons of Benjamin Chew, Jr., when they attended school in Baltimore. His concern with education extended beyond his own family: as a trustee of the Garrison Forest Academy, he corresponded with a professor at Yale College in an effort to recruit the most qualified faculty members for the Maryland school, and he also helped to insure that the financing was ample to support them.[8]

In his youth, Howard had been active in the Episcopal Church, and he resumed his involvement after the war. He also encouraged his children in the development of their own faith. Howard belonged to Old St. Paul's Parish in Baltimore, was often elected to the vestry, and on three occasions served as a delegate to diocesan conventions. He was a friend of James Kemp, the Episcopal Bishop of Maryland, and during his lifetime donated land to the Episcopal, Roman Catholic, Presbyterian, and Methodist churches.[9]

Howard was also active in the Society of the Cincinnati, an organization of former Continental Army officers. He was involved in the Maryland chapter from its formation in 1783, winning election to the office of vice president in 1795 and serving in that role until he became president of the organization in 1804, a position he held until his death. Much of his effort in the Society was focused on helping needy veterans. Dr. Richard Pindell, who had dressed Howard's wound after the Battle of Eutaw Springs, wrote Howard in 1785 to thank him for the generosity. Howard sometimes contacted friends to try to find employment for former soldiers who were in "real distress." When he held public office, Howard helped many veterans obtain assistance.[10]

Given the renown he had earned as a Revolutionary war hero and his proven abilities in business, it was natural that Marylanders would turn to Howard for political leadership. His career in public service began in 1785 with his appointment as a justice of the Baltimore County Court, an office that he held for three years. He also served as a justice on Baltimore County's Orphan's Court and as a senatorial elector from the same county. Howard's first significant role in national politics came when, on December 11, 1787, the Maryland legislature chose him to "represent this state in Congress the ensuing year."[11]

When Howard took his seat in the Continental Congress, the ratification process for the new federal Constitution had already begun. Howard, like most former Continental officers, was a Federalist who favored strengthening the central government, and he ran for delegate to Maryland's Constitutional Convention. He and his three fellow Federalist candidates from Baltimore County were defeated by opponents of the Constitution; however, the Federalists prevailed at the state convention. On April 28th, 1788, Maryland became the seventh state to ratify the Constitution. At the Fourth of July parade in Philadelphia two months later, Howard received the honor of marching as one of "ten gentlemen, representing the states that have adopted the federal Constitution ... bearing distinguished flags and walking arm in arm, emblematic of Union."[12]

Even though the ratification process for the Constitution was under way, it was still the responsibility of the Continental Congress to govern the United States until a new government was formed. When thirty-five-year-old John Eager Howard arrived in New York in early 1788, he was burdened with many personal distractions. Married for less than eight months, still building his Baltimore home, and expecting his first child in a few months, Howard informed Maryland governor William Smallwood that "the situation of my private affairs will prevent my continuing long from home." Howard followed the practice of other representatives, skipping some sessions to attend to personal business as long as there were enough other members on hand to constitute a quorum. He remained in New York until the end of February, and then apparently returned home to stay with Peggy until their son, John Eager Howard, Jr., was born on June 25th. Howard went back to New York for the July congressional session but did not attend in the fall. Much of Howard's work in Congress involved military and veterans' affairs.[13]

Shortly after completing his service in the Continental Congress, Howard was elected governor of Maryland on November 21, 1788. He had to leave his still unfinished home at Belvidere and move with Peggy and his young son to Jennings House in Annapolis, the official residence of Maryland's governors. Howard served three consecutive terms as governor, the maximum allowed by the state constitution, and his terms were filled with important activities that affected both his own state and the new national government. He signed 49 bills into law in 1788, 61 in 1789, and 66 the following year. Legislation that dealt with state issues included authorizing construction of roads and bridges, providing relief for the state's poor, and even preventing "the going at large of swine, goats and geese in Elkton." Some of the bills that Howard signed dealing with federal issues included Maryland's ratification of the Bill of Rights and approval of relocating the federal capital to a location along the Potomac River. During Howard's first year in office, he and the five-member Executive Council also reviewed the results of Maryland's presidential election and appointed the electors who chose George Washington to be the first president of the United States. In March 1791, near the end of Howard's final term as governor, Washington made an official visit to Annapolis. The governor hosted a dinner for his former commanding officer at the governor's residence on March 26, followed by a ball "at which was exhibited everything which this little city contained of beauty and elegance." The next morning, Washington left for his home at Mount Vernon, Virginia, accompanied part of the way by Howard and other prominent Marylanders.[14]

Howard had proven himself to be a popular and effective governor, and as his final term neared its end, the general assembly sought to continue utilizing his abilities by electing him to the state senate on September 19, 1791. The new office allowed Howard to spend more time at home with his family, since he was only required to be in Annapolis for the legislative session in November and December each year. As a state senator, Howard focused much of his attention on issues related to education, the Maryland judiciary, and his home city of Baltimore. In 1793 he supported legislation declaring Maryland's support for President Washington's policy of neutrality in the war between France and Great Britain. During his time in the state senate, he also held various other positions, including Commissioner of the City of Baltimore, Associate Justice of Baltimore County, and presidential elector in the 1792 contest that saw Washington chosen for a second term.[15]

Although Howard accepted these civil appointments, he declined the opportunity to return to military service. In 1794, when protests in western Pennsylvania against the federal excise tax on whiskey turned violent, President Washington called out the army and state militias to suppress the "Whiskey Rebellion." Maryland was asked to provide troops, and the state government issued Howard a commission as major general in the militia to command them. Howard, however, refused the appointment, probably because he preferred to devote his time to his family and business affairs. President Washington must have been unhappy with Howard's decision, since in an assessment of the abilities of current and former officers in 1792, the president had considered Howard well qualified to serve as a brigadier general in the federal army.[16]

Washington retained a high opinion of Howard's abilities, however, and in November 1795 he asked the Marylander to join his cabinet. The president decided to move Secretary of War Timothy Pickering to the Department of State, and asked Howard to fill Pickering's former position. "I shall use no other arguments to induce your acceptance than such as candour dictates," Washington wrote. "These are, that I believe the duties of the Office will be well executed by you: that I conceive the appointment will be very agreeable to the public," and, the president added, Howard's willingness to serve "would be very agreeable" to the president himself. Washington wrote the letter on November 19, and dispatched Howard's wartime comrade, Henry Lee, to deliver it in person. Lee arrived in Baltimore three days later and after meeting with Howard, reported to the president that "I had I thought good ground this morning to conclude that he would accept your call."[17]

Before making his offer, Washington visited Howard's father-in-law, Benjamin Chew, to inquire into the prospects of Howard's acceptance. Chew spoke frankly, telling the president "that I much doubted whether [Howard] would not in common prudence think yourself obliged to decline the honor." Among the reasons Chew cited for his son-in-law's likely rejection of the post were the need for Howard to manage his property in Maryland, and the difficulty of supporting his family in Philadelphia on the small salary allotted the secretary of war. Undeterred, Washington told Chew that he would write to Howard on the matter, and he asked that their discussion be kept secret.[18]

Henry Lee changed his opinion by the afternoon of November 22nd, and had come to "fear" that Howard would not agree to serve in the cabinet. Lee was correct; that day, unaware that his father-in-law had already spoken with Washington about the position, Howard wrote to Chew explaining his decision. "The information to me was very unexpected," Howard noted, "and of course I have not had time to give the matter that consideration which its importance required, but at first view such powerful objections occur that I cannot hesitate in determining to decline it." Howard listed his reasons, including the fact that his own "buildings & other improvements take from me my money as fast as I receive it," and therefore he would have to borrow money to establish a household in Philadelphia. "A further objection arises from an apprehension that the improvements which have cost me much labour and expence will suffer greatly by my absence." Besides the financial effects, Howard added that he had just hired a tutor for his sons, and since their education was "of no small importance" to him, he did not want to move "without knowing in what other suitable manner to provide for them." Howard affirmed his high regard for Washington and his gratitude for "this mark of confidence and trust," but reiterated his refusal.[19]

Howard's reply to Washington, written on November 23rd included another reason for declining the appointment. Howard explained:

> *"This mark of your confidence has left so deep an impression on my mind that I should not hesitate to comply with your wish, could it be done without making sacrifices that I am persuaded you would not think advisable. My constitution was so much impaired during the war that for several years the effects were sensibly felt."*

Washington, though disappointed, took Howard's rejection of his offer with good grace, replying that "the reasons which you have assigned for not doing it carry conviction along with them, and must however reluctantly be submitted to."[20]

If Washington was able to dispense with Howard's services as secretary of war, Maryland's legislature continued to rely upon their state's war hero for political leadership. On November 21, 1796, the representatives elected Howard to the United States Senate to complete the few months remaining in the term of Richard Potts, who had resigned. Just over two weeks later, the legislature chose Howard to serve the next six-year term. Howard traveled to Philadelphia and was sworn in as a member of the Senate on December 27. In all likelihood, he accepted the Senate seat because the limited length of sessions allowed him to spend a considerable amount of time at home, whereas the appointment as secretary of war (that he declined at almost the same time) would have required him to spend nearly all of his time in the capital.[21]

Howard was one of 21 Federalist senators, compared to 11 Republicans. He shared the Federalists' belief in government by a meritocracy of wealthy, educated men committed to the public good, although his voting record indicated that he acted independently of his party when he believed doing so was in the best interests of the United States. A friend described him as "one of the staunch adherents to the principles of the Washington School ... he possessed largely the esteem and confidence of that eminent man, I had almost said political apostle." Howard would only serve briefly under Washington, however, as John Adams succeeded the Virginian as president on March 4, 1797.[22]

Consistent with his earlier political service, Howard was often assigned to committees dealing with military and veterans' affairs. Because of his experience with city planning in Baltimore, he also served on committees that dealt with developing the new federal capital. Unlike some of his colleagues who grasped every opportunity to regale their fellow Senators with eloquent speeches, the quiet Howard preferred to direct his efforts to solid committee work and thoughtful deliberation of issues. One of his most important assignments was to the committee charged with reviewing President Adams's recommendations for the military establishment.[23]

Military matters grew in importance as tensions escalated between the United States and France, sparked by diplomatic disputes, French naval seizures of American merchant ships, and the pro-British stance of Adams and most Federalists in regard to the Anglo-French war. Over the objections of Vice President Thomas Jefferson's Republicans, who supported France in the conflict, Adams and the Federalist-dominated Congress began preparing for war. Howard, putting patriotism ahead of party, managed to stay clear of the political fray while maintaining the confidence and respect of his fellow Senators regardless of their party affiliation. On July 3, 1798, he joined them in a unanimous vote confirming President Adams's nomination of George Washington as commander-in-chief "of all the armies raised, or to be raised, in the United States."[24]

Washington, working diligently to organize an army in the event of war, sought qualified officers to command the troops. He included Howard as one of only eight possible candidates for brigadier and major general on a list he compiled in mid-July. Once again, however, Howard proved reluctant to return to military service. By December, as recruiting proceeded very slowly and Howard continued to refuse a brigadier general's commission, a frustrated Washington wrote to Secretary of War James McHenry urging that the latter "press Colo. Howard *strongly* to come forward." Howard not only declined, but did not respond to requests to recommend others for military assignments, prompting Washington to complain to McHenry that "I am sorry that Colo Howard and General Lloyd have declined making a selection of persons for officering the eventual Army from Maryland." Howard never explained his refusal to become involved with the formation of the army; perhaps he realized that the whole situation with France had been overblown. In 1799 the United States and France signed a peace agreement and the still incomplete army was no longer needed.[25]

After passing legislation to enlarge the army, Congress had taken steps to suppress potential supporters of France within the United States, and, many Federalists hoped, to undermine Jefferson's Republicans by muzzling their opposition to Federalist policies. Together, these laws were known as the Alien and Sedition Acts. The legislation dealing with aliens (immigrants who had not yet become citizens) extended the length of residence in the United States required for citizenship from seven to fourteen years and allowed the president, in time of war or imminent foreign threat, to confine or deport any non-citizens deemed dangerous to the country. The Sedition Act was introduced by Howard's fellow senator from Maryland, James Lloyd. In a blatant assault on individual liberties guaranteed by the Bill of Rights, the Sedition Act imposed prison sentences and fines on anyone who "shall threaten any officer of the United States Government with any damage to his character, person, or property," including the "printing, writing, or speaking in a scandalous or malicious way against the government of the United States, either house of Congress, or the

President."26

John Eager Howard was absent when Congress approved the Alien Acts, but returned to the capital in time for the Senate debate on the Sedition Act. In a remarkable display of political courage, Howard was the only Federalist member of the Senate to side with the Republicans in opposing the legislation in a series of votes on July 4, 1798. He voted against making it a crime to "defame the President of the United States, or any court or judge thereof," but the Senate voted 15-8 to retain that language. Howard then voted, along with only five Republicans, to strike a clause prescribing the punishment for defaming the President or Congress as a maximum of two years' imprisonment and a fine of up to $2,000. Finally, he voted against the Sedition Act itself, and was on the losing side of the 18-6 vote. Howard refused to succumb to Federalist hysteria, and would not join the other members of his party in their stampede to trample the rights that he had fought so hard to obtain.27

At the end of 1799, Federalists and Republicans temporarily put aside their differences to mourn the death of George Washington, who had died at his Mount Vernon home on December 14. Howard attended the memorial service held in Philadelphia twelve days later, where Henry Lee proclaimed the departed general and president as "first in war, first in peace, and first in the hearts of his countrymen."28

Washington's legacy lived on, not only in the memories of people like Lee and Howard, but in the new capital city named after him. Congress convened for its first session in the District of Columbia in November, 1800. The city was still primitive, "little more than a scattering of new buildings between a forest and the Potomac and Anacostia rivers. Pennsylvania Avenue, studded with stumps and alder bushes, led from the Capitol through a morass" to the executive mansion. Inside the Capitol building, John Eager Howard was elected president *pro tem* of the Senate and pledged that he and his colleagues would work effectively with President John Adams to address important issues facing the United States.29

Howard had only a year left to work with Adams, as the temperamental president, having angered many Americans with policies such as the Alien and Sedition Acts, failed to win reelection in 1800. Thomas Jefferson succeeded him as president on March 4, 1801. Jefferson's Republicans had also done well in state and congressional elections, and now had a majority of 17-15 over the Federalists in the Senate. Howard voted consistently with his Federalist colleagues, but repeatedly backed the losing side on issues as diverse as the repeal of some internal taxes, changes to the naturalization laws, pensions for dependents of sailors and marines killed in the line of duty, and incorporation of an insurance company in Washington, D.C. He also served on a committee that reviewed the government's military appropriations request. On October 18, 1803, his service in the Senate came to an end when the Maryland legislature chose Samuel Smith, a Republican, to replace him.30

After leaving the U.S. Senate, Howard never again held elective office. He was appointed to various local positions, which included the Commissioner of the State Penitentiary in Baltimore, and he received some votes for governor in every annual election from 1806 to 1811. Some members of the state legislature suggested in 1809 that he replace Smith in the Senate, but the representatives did not act on the proposal. In 1816, with the Federalists in disarray and about to fade from American politics, some party leaders unofficially named Howard their vice-presidential candidate. He received 22 of the 34 electoral votes won by the Federalists; Robert G. Harper received 3 and Connecticut could not decide how to allocate its 9 votes.[31]

Howard expressed no regrets over the end of his political career. Instead, he devoted his efforts to managing his extensive property holdings and other investments. He described his business strategy in a letter to his brother-in-law, Benjamin Chew, a few months after he had left the Senate. "As to my own property, I inherited most of it from my ancestors who purchased it more than a century ago, and by the blessing of God it shall go to my children, not by me lessened in value, though a good deal diminished in extent by sales for the purpose of making improvements, and for expenses of different kinds." Howard invested carefully, paying particular attention to the trustworthiness of businessmen. He noted, for example, that he preferred "the Bank of Maryland because it has a proprietor of character," but disliked the president of a local bank who had "acquired such an itch for speculation that I do not think the bank safe." Howard's caution yielded good results. At the time of his death in 1827, he was collecting annual rents of $119,758 on 289 lots in Baltimore. The total value of his real estate holdings, including Belvidere, 400 lots in Baltimore, 2,092 acres in three Maryland counties, and property in Bath, Virginia, amounted to $1,084,745.[32]

Although he sought to profit from his business enterprises, Howard was generous in his gifts to the city of Baltimore and local organizations. He donated the land for the city's Washington Monument and Lexington Market, and also sold at reduced prices or gave real estate to churches on which were built St. Paul's Parish House, the Eutaw Street Methodist Church, and the Roman Catholic Basilica of the Assumption. In addition, he provided a loan and donation to finance construction of Maryland Medical College's Davidge Hall.[33]

Another organization to which Howard devoted a great deal of attention was the American Colonization Society. Created in an effort to solve the problems of slavery and racism in the United States, the Society promoted the settlement of free blacks in Africa with the goal that its work "will ultimately be the means of exterminating slavery in our country." The Society boasted such famous members as President James Monroe, future president Andrew Jackson, and congressional luminaries Henry Clay and Daniel Webster. Howard served as both a national officer and president of the Society's Maryland chapter. Although the Society did not succeed in eliminating slavery, it founded the African nation of Liberia and transported over 13,000 blacks there by 1867, many of them on a Society vessel named the *Colonel Howard*.[34]

Howard's commercial and philanthropic activities were interrupted briefly by the War of 1812, which also resulted in his split from the Federalist Party. Most Federalists opposed the war against Great Britain and blamed President James Madison for inciting the conflict. When a Federalist mob rampaged through Baltimore, Howard denounced their actions as "most abusive and mischievous and a disgrace to the federal cause." The arch-Federalists, perhaps remembering Howard's opposition to the Sedition Act, in turn declared that he "does more harm to the cause by opposing everything that is proposed by the party, than any other man in the country." Howard responded to such criticism by breaking with the Federalists. He did not return to military service during the war, but actively assisted in the defense of Baltimore as a member of the Committee of Supply and the Committee of Vigilance and Safety. His activities included raising funds and supervising projects such the construction of fortifications. After the unsuccessful British naval attack on Fort McHenry in Baltimore Harbor in September 1814, Baltimore officials named Howard one of three envoys to meet with President Madison in Washington and "respectfully communicate ... the situation of the City of Baltimore."[35]

The War of 1812 helped to revive Americans' interest in their earlier conflict with Great Britain, as did the realization that the heroes of the Revolutionary generation were passing away and their firsthand knowledge of events would go with them. Some veterans of the Revolution had begun writing their memoirs even earlier, and it was natural that they, as well as historians seeking to chronicle the War for Independence, would seek out respected participants for information. Many turned to Howard for assistance, and he was exceptionally qualified to help them. He had read the histories of the Revolution that had already been published and even more importantly, had a prodigious memory for the details of his own experience.

Howard corresponded extensively with Henry Lee while the latter wrote his memoirs. The first edition was published in 1812; Lee had graciously acknowledged in his book that "in the progress of this work ... reference was frequently had to the authority and reminiscences of Colonel Howard." Howard later assisted Henry Lee, Jr., in preparing a revised edition of his father's memoirs. He also provided information to John Marshall for a biography of George Washington, to William Johnson for a biography of Nathanael Greene, and to Alexander Garden for his history of the Revolution. Howard took his contributions to these volumes very seriously, and he disliked it when the various authors, feuding over inconsistencies in each other's work, invoked his authority to support their positions. He also objected when Henry Lee, Jr., rewrote his words. When Howard brought one such instance to Lee's attention, Lee defended his right "to select such facts of your observation as appear to suit me." Despite these problems, Howard's accounts of crucial events, including the battles of Cowpens, Guilford Courthouse, and Hobkirk's Hill, proved to be invaluable resources to the historians of his own era as well as to later students of the Revolution.[36]

While engaged in making his contribution to the history of the Revolution, Howard and his wife suffered a series of personal tragedies. In May 1821 their eldest daughter, Juliana Howard McHenry, died, and seven months later, one of their young grandsons passed away. These losses were followed by another devastating loss in the autumn of 1822. John McHenry, the husband of recently deceased Juliana, contracted "a high bilious fever" while at Mercersburg, Pennsylvania. Learning that his brother-in-law was ill, John Eager Howard, Jr., rushed to Mercersburg to care for him. Soon after reaching the epidemic-wracked town, Howard, Jr., also contracted the disease, and both men died. The loss of his eldest son and namesake cracked Howard's usual steely resolve. It was perhaps the only time in his adult life that Howard "allowed any mortal to be acquainted with his feelings." He confessed that his son's death caused him "the utmost grief."[37]

Less than two years later, John Eager Howard experienced another great personal loss when his wife Peggy Chew Howard died at Belvidere. She was sixty-three years old. Although he grieved at the loss of his beloved wife and companion of thirty-seven years, Howard bore her death stoically. One of Howard's nephews wrote a few days after Peggy's death, "The Col. evinces the strongest evidence of a majestic strength of mind, with which I think he is remarkably gifted.... The Col. is perfectly composed with all the philosophy of silent & inexpressible, unmurmuring grief."[38]

Perhaps to distract himself from his tragic loss, in the following months Howard became deeply involved in preparations to welcome another Revolutionary hero, the Marquis de Lafayette, to Baltimore. As president of the Maryland chapter of the Society of the Cincinnati, Howard wrote to the marquis and invited him to meet with its Baltimore members. Lafayette accepted and, accompanied by Secretary of State John Quincy Adams, arrived in the city on September 30. Howard was among the Maryland dignitaries who greeted Lafayette at Fort McHenry, and gave a brief speech welcoming him. Lafayette responded to Howard's remarks with praise for the Maryland Continentals' Revolutionary service. "It has been the lot of the Maryland Line to acquire glory in instances of bad as well as good fortune, and to whom can I better speak of the glory of that Line than in addressing Col. Howard?" the marquis asked. Lafayette stayed in Baltimore until October 11, attending a variety of events in his honor, and departed with two silver medals that Howard had presented to him.[39]

Such events, along with business affairs, occupied Howard's time as a widower. After the deaths of Thomas Jefferson and John Adams on July 4th, 1826, Howard and two of Maryland's other renowned Revolutionary leaders, Charles Carroll and Samuel Smith, were assigned prominent roles in Baltimore's commemoration of the two deceased founders. Several months later, Howard invited a group of local businessmen to Belvidere for a dinner at which Evan Thomas, recently returned from England, described the new railroads operating there. Howard believed that the new technology would bring great benefits to the United States, and after bringing together these potential investors, became a member of the committee that worked to get state approval for a railroad. The Maryland legislature granted a charter to what would become one of America's most famous and important railroads, the Baltimore & Ohio, on April 29th, 1827.[40]

Howard's activities to develop the Baltimore & Ohio Railroad would be his last important contribution to his city, state, and country. By the spring of 1826, he could sense that his health was failing. "I shall be 74 on Sunday next and can not expect to remain much longer," he wrote on May 29th. His decline became obvious and a serious concern to his family early in 1827. On February 17th, Howard's son George noted ominously that his father "has an inflammation of his lungs; he has been very much depleted by frequent bleeding" – the standard medical treatment of that time – and "although he may be sustained and raised from his weak state, yet I think at his advanced age ... that the chances of recovery are unfavorable."[41]

The old warrior fought back and ten days later was noticeably on the mend. "He is so much stronger, that he has twice left his bed for half an hour, and enjoyed the luxury of an arm chair, which must be great after a confinement to bed of a fortnight," his son Charles wrote. Howard eventually resumed something of a normal routine during the summer and early fall. He went horseback riding on October 3rd and caught a chill. Charles summoned a doctor the next day, and after an administration of medicine brought no result, the doctor resorted to bleeding. Howard was bled twice on October 5 and again the next day. A second doctor was called, and he approved of the treatment that had been administered. The bleeding did not work, and Howard's condition worsened. He suffered from a severe cough and "a good deal of pain" in his right lung, leading his family to conclude on October 8 that he would not recover. They reviewed his will with him, and requested that an Anglican priest bring him communion. Beyond that, they could do nothing except watch by Howard's sickbed. At about 7 p.m. on October 12th, 1827, John Eager Howard, who had survived the storm of battle on so many fields, quietly passed away at his home.[42]

---

1   Session Laws, 1782, Apr. 25-1782, Jun. 15, in Alexander Contee Hanson, ed., *Laws of Maryland, made since 1763, consisting of acts of Assembly under the proprietary government, resolves of convention, the Declaration of rights, the constitution and form of government, the Articles of confederation, and, acts of Assembly since the revolution* (Annapolis, MD: Frederick Green, 1787), Vol. 203, 305.
2   Otho Williams to Philip Thomas, March 12, 1784 (quotations), April 27, 1784 (quotation) April 12, 1786 (quotation), Williams Papers, MHS (quotation).
3   Introduction to the Williams Papers; John Eager Howard to Williams, July 1, 1787 (quotation), April 15, 1788, Williams Papers.
4   Allen, *Garrison Church*, 155; Williams to Philip Thomas, April 4, 1787, Williams Papers (quotation); Burton Alva Konkle, *Benjamin Chew, 1722-1810: Head of the Pennsylvania Judiciary System under Colony and Commonwealth* (Philadelphia: University of Pennsylvania Press, 1932), 180, 190 (quotation); John Andre, "Andre to Peggy Chew," Howard Papers.
5   Francis B. Culver, "The Chew Family," *Maryland Historical Magazine*, Vol. 30, No. 2, June, 1935, 169; George Washington, Diary, May 22, 1787, Library of Congress.
6   Elizabeth Read, "Howards of Maryland," 240; Cary Howard, "John Eager Howard," 313; Howard to Benjamin Chew, Jr., July 27, 1793, Sept. 3, 1793, Sept. 5, 1793 (quotation), Chew Family Papers, Historical Society of Pennsylvania, Philadelphia; Scharf, *Chronicles of Baltimore*, 240-42 (quotation); Howard to unnamed wine merchant, 1795, Howard Papers.
7   Read, "Howards of Maryland," 243; for John Eager Howard's references to his wife, see for example Howard to Benjamin Chew, Jr., July 27 and Oct. 15, 1793, March 29, July 25, 1795, Aug. 23, 1800, Sept. 22, 1810, April 29, 1813, Chew Family Papers; information on the Howard children appears in Bill and Martha Reamy, eds., *Records of St. Paul's Parish* (Westminster, MD: Family Line Publications, 1988); Rieman Steuart, "Roll of the Society of the Cincinnati in Maryland," in *History of the Maryland Line*; Edward C. Papenfuse, Alan F. Day, David W. Jordan, and Gregory A. Stiverson, *A Biographical Dictionary of the Maryland Legislature, 1635-1789*, Vol. 1 (Baltimore: The Johns Hopkins University Press, 1979); "1820 Household Census of J. E. Howard," Bayard Papers.
8   Howard to Benjamin Chew, Jr., Oct. 30, 1810, Feb. 6, 1811 (quotation), Feb. 12, 1811, April 12, 1806, Nov. 2, 1806, Nov. 9, 1806, March 15, 1807, Benjamin Chew, Jr. Correspondence, Chew Family Papers; Howard to Benjamin Silliman, Sept. 8, 1825, Vertical File Q9700000002156, MHS.
9   Reamy, *Records of St. Paul's Parish*, 158-59; Benjamin Chew Howard, "Colonel John Eager Howard of Maryland," Society of the Cincinnati Library, Washington, DC.
10 Steuart, "Roll of the Society of the Cincinnati," in *History of the Maryland Line*, 98; Richard Pindell to Howard, Oct. 29, 1785, Bayard Papers (quotation); Howard to Williams, Dec. 11, 1786, Williams Papers (quotation); Pindell to Howard, Dec. 8, 1816 and April 5, 1817, Howard to Pindell, Jan. 20, 1817, Williams Papers.
11 "John Eager Howard (1752-1827), Governor of Maryland, 1788-1791," Archives of Maryland (Bio-

graphical Series), MSA SC 3520-692; Maryland Senate Journal, Dec. 11, 1787, MSA SC M 3185, 915 (quotation).
12 Annie Leakin Sioussat, *Old Baltimore* (New York: Macmillan, 1931), 122-23; "Order of procession, in honor of the establishment of the Constitution of the United States," in "Documents from the Continental Congress and the Constitutional Convention, 1774-1789," Library of Congress (quotation).
13 Howard to William Smallwood, Jan. 27, 1788, in Paul H. Smith, ed., *Letters of Delegates to Congress, 1774-1789* (Washington: Library of Congress, 26 vols., 1976-2000), Vol. 24, 622 (quotation); Proceedings of Congress, Feb. 14, Feb. 18, Oct. 2, 1788, in *Journals of the Continental Congress, 1774-1789* (Washington: US Government Printing Office, 34 vols., 1904-1937), Vol. 34:45, 50, 578.
14 Frank F. White, Jr., "The Governors of Maryland, 1777-1970," Archives of Maryland (Biographical Series), MSA SC 3520-692; *Laws of Maryland Made and Passed at a Session of Assembly, Begun and held at the city of Annapolis, on Monday the third of November, 1788* (Annapolis: Frederick Green, [c. 1789]), (quotation, pages are not numbered); *Laws of Maryland Made and Passed at a Session of Assembly ... 1789* (Annapolis: Frederick Green, [c. 1790]); *Laws of Maryland Made and Passed at a Session of Assembly ... 1790* (Annapolis: Frederick Green [c. 1791]); Aubrey C. Land, ed., *Journal and Correspondence of the Council of Maryland, 1784-1789* (Baltimore: Maryland Historical Society, 1970), Vol. 1, xix, Vol. 71, 320-21; Donald Jackson and Dorothy Twohig, eds., *The Diaries of George Washington*, Vol. 6 (Charlottesville: University Press of Virginia, 1979), 100-03 (quotation).
15 Papenfuse, et al, eds., *Biographical Dictionary of the Maryland Legislature*, 1:467; *Votes and Proceedings of the Senate of the State of Maryland, November Session, 1793*, 7, 9; *Votes and Proceedings of the Senate of the State of Maryland, November Session, 1792*, 1158, 1197; *Votes and Proceedings of the Senate of the State of Maryland, November Session, 1795*, 4, 1346; *Votes and Proceedings of the Senate of the State of Maryland, November Session, 1794*, 14; *Votes and Proceedings of the Senate of the State of Maryland, November Session, 1796*, 1367; *Votes and Proceedings of the Senate of the State of Maryland, November Session, 1791*, 18, Maryland State Archives, Annapolis; Land, ed., *Journal and Correspondence of the Council of Maryland*, 72:276, 305; "John Eager Howard," Archives of Maryland (Biographical Series); Senate Journal (Session Laws 1793), Archives of Maryland, Vol. 645, 98.
16 Archives of Maryland, Early State Records, MSA SC M 3167, 311; Scharf, *Chronicles of Baltimore*, 272; George Washington, "Opinion of the General Officers," March 9, 1792, Washington Papers.
17 Washington to Howard, Nov. 19, 1795, (quotation); Henry Lee to Washington, Nov. 22, 1795, (quotation), Washington Papers.
18 Benjamin Chew to Howard, [Nov. 1795], Bayard Papers.
19 Lee to Washington, Nov. 22, 1795, Washington Papers (quotation); Howard to Benjamin Chew, Nov. 22, 1795, Bayard Papers (quotations).
20 Howard to Washington, Nov. 23, 1795 (quotations); Washington to Howard, Nov. 30, 1795 (quotation), Washington Papers.
21 Archives of Maryland, Senate Journal, Vol. 105, 9, 20; "Journal of the Senate of the United States," Dec. 27, 1796, Library of Congress.
22 "Journal of the Senate," March 4, 1797; Benjamin Chew to Benjamin Chew Howard, Sept. 28, 1833, Bayard Papers (quotation).
23 "Journal of the Senate," Jan. 13, 1797, Feb. 9, 1797, May 29, 1797.
24 David McCullough, *John Adams* (New York: Simon and Schuster, 2001), 484-85, 499; "Journal of the Senate," May 29, 1797, July 3, 1798 (quotation); *A Memoir of the Late Col. John Eager Howard reprinted from the Baltimore Gazette of Monday, October 15th, 1827* (Baltimore: Kelly, Hedian, & Piet, 1863).
25 Washington to Alexander Hamilton, July 14, 1798; Washington to James McHenry, Dec. 14, 1798 (quotation) and July 7, 1799 (quotation); Page Smith, *John Adams* (Garden City, NY: Doubleday & Co., 1962), Vol. 2, 1010, 1063.
26 Smith, *John Adams*, 2:975.
27 "Journal of the Senate," July 4, 1798.
28 "Journal of the Senate," Dec. 26, 1799, Dec. 27, 1799.
29 Samuel Eliot Morison, *The Oxford History of the American People* (New York: Oxford University Press, 1965), 360 (quotation); "Journal of the Senate," Nov. 21, 1800, Nov. 25, 1800.
30 "Journal of the Senate," March 31, April 3, April 26, April 29, 1802, Feb. 25, Feb. 28, Oct. 18, 1803.
31 "John Eager Howard," Archives of Maryland (Biographical Series); White, "Governors of Maryland," 317-18; *Votes and Proceedings of the House of Delegates of the State of Maryland, June Session, 1809*, 515, Maryland State Archives; Robert Ernst, *Rufus King: American Federalist* (Chapel Hill: University of North Carolina Press, 1968), 351-52.

32 Howard to Benjamin Chew, Jr., Feb. 11, 1810 (quotation), Nov. 17, 1812 (quotation), April 27, 1815 (quotation), Benjamin Chew, Jr., Correspondence, Chew Family Papers (quotation); Papenfuse, et al, *Biographical Dictionary*, 1:468. Based on the Consumer Price Index, Howard's 1827 rental income was equivalent to $2,567,824 in 2007, and his real estate holdings valued at $23,258,862. These figures represent the most conservative estimate as calculated at http://www.measuringworth.com/uscompare/, accessed June 27, 2009. If an annual price increase of 2.5% were used instead, the resulting figures would be $10 million in annual rents and property value of $90 million in 2007.
33 Benjamin Chew Howard, "Colonel John Eager Howard;" Margaret Byrnside Ballard, *A University is Born* (Union, WV: Old Hundred Union, 1965), 17.
34 Henry Noble Sherwood, "The Formation of the American Colonization Society," *Journal of Negro History*, Vol. 2, No. 3, July 1917, 225 (quotation), 228; Scharf, *Chronicles of Baltimore*, 389; *Memorial of the Semi-Centennial Anniversary of the American Colonization Society, Celebrated at Washington, January 15, 1867: With Documents Concerning Liberia* (Washington: American Colonization Society, 1867), 186, 190.
35 Howard to Benjamin Chew, Jr., Aug. 2, 1812, Benjamin Chew, Jr., Correspondence, Chew Family Papers (quotation); Mrs. Robert Goodloe Harper to Robert Goodloe Harper, March 5, 1810, Harper-Pennington Papers, Maryland Historical Society (quotation); Richard Walsh and William Lloyd Fox, eds., *Maryland: A History, 1632-1974* (Baltimore: Maryland Historical Society, 1974), 243-44; Scharf, *Chronicles of Baltimore*, 340; William D. Hoyt, Jr., ed., "Civilian Defense in Baltimore, 1814-1815: Minutes of the Committee of Vigilance and Safety," *Maryland Historical Magazine*, Vol. 39, No. 3, Sept. 1944, 300-01 (quotation).
36 Lee, *Memoirs*, 314, 362 (quotation); Henry Lee, Jr., to Howard, [1822], [1824], and undated (quotation), Howard Papers.
37 *Niles' Weekly Register*, Oct. 20, 1822; William W. Chew to Benjamin Chew, Jr., May 30, 1824 (quotation), John Eager Howard to Benjamin Chew, Jr., Oct. 20, 1822 (quotation), Benjamin Chew, Jr., Correspondence, Chew Family Papers.
38 Obituary of Mrs. John Eager Howard, *Baltimore Patriot & Mercantile Advertiser*, June 5, 1824; William W. Chew to Benjamin Chew, Jr., May 30, 1824 (quotation), Benjamin Chew, Jr., Correspondence, Chew Family Papers.
39 *Register of the Society of the Cincinnati of Maryland brought down to February 22nd, 1897* (Baltimore: Society of the Cincinnati of Maryland, 1897), 51-53; *Baltimore Patriot & Mercantile Advertiser*, Oct. 8, Oct. 9, Oct. 11, 1824; John Quincy Adams, *The Diary of John Quincy Adams, 1794-1845* (New York: Longmans, Green and Co., 1929), 330-31; Scharf, *Chronicles of Baltimore*, 411 (quotation), 412-13;
40 Hamilton Owens, *Baltimore on the Chesapeake* (Garden City, NY: Doubleday, Doran, and Co., 1941), 234-35; Charles Francis Stein, Jr., *Origin and History of Howard County, Maryland* (Baltimore: Howard County Historical Society, 1972), 111-12.
41 Howard to Benjamin Chew, Jr., May 29, 1826 (quotation), George Howard to Benjamin Chew, Jr., February 17, 1827 (quotation), Benjamin Chew, Jr., Correspondence, Chew Family Papers.
42 Charles Howard to Benjamin Chew, Jr., Feb. 27, 1827 (quotation), John Eager Howard to Benjamin Chew, Jr., May 18, 1827, James Howard to Benjamin Chew, Jr., Oct. 8, 1827 (quotation), Benjamin Chew, Jr., Correspondence, Chew Family Papers; Benjamin Chew Howard, "Memorandum Relating to the Last Illness of John E. Howard," Nov. 11, 1827, Bayard Papers.

EPILOGUE

COMMEMORATION OF A HERO

In the aftermath of John Eager Howard's death, two states commemorated his service. South Carolina was the site of many of Howard's most significant contributions to American victory in the Revolutionary War, and, just a few months after his death and burial, that state's legislature unanimously passed a resolution honoring the old soldier. "Among the master-spirits who battled for independence, we are to remember with veneration the late patriotic and venerable Colonel John Eager Howard," the legislators wrote. "His illustrious name is to be found in the history of his country's suffering and the annals of his country's triumphs. In the day of peril and of doubt ... when danger was everywhere, and when death mingled in the conflict of the warrior, Howard still clung to the fortunes of the struggling Republic. He was his country's common friend and his country owes him one common inextinguishable debt of gratitude." Therefore, the resolution asserted, "South Carolina, with whose history his name is identified, is proud to acknowledge her obligation. ... The State of South Carolina can never forget the distinguished services of the deceased." The legislature of Howard's home state of Maryland approved a similar resolution on March 15, 1828, recognizing him as "one of the most distinguished officers of the war of the revolution ... and at all times one of the most honorable and virtuous of our citizens."[1]

Memories of the Revolution burned brightly during the first seventy-five years of the Republic's existence. When the words to "Maryland, My Maryland" were written at the start of the Civil War, there was no need to explain the line in the third verse that rang out: "Remember Howard's warlike thrust," because most Marylanders in 1861 knew the stories of John Eager Howard and his decisive bayonet charge at the Battle of Cowpens. Today, most listeners are perplexed by that line, and have no knowledge of its origin. Over time, memories of individuals like Howard have gradually faded from the public memory.

A stately, equestrian statue of John Eager Howard stands on Mount Vernon Place in Baltimore as one of the few remaining reminders of his story. Situated only yards away from the Washington Monument, for which Howard donated the land, the statue was unveiled on January 16, 1904, at ceremonies that featured Daniel Gilman, President Emeritus of The Johns Hopkins University, as the speaker. Gilman recalled Howard's cool, deliberate manner in combat, and observed that "a moment's hesitation, a timid advance, a half-hearted leader might have lost everything. But Howard was quick to think, bold in action, inspiring as a leader."[2]

Despite this dramatic retelling of Howard's exploits and the impressive statue that was set in place, the once-renowned hero has faded deeper and deeper into undeserved obscurity. But his story remains compelling, and adds an important dimension to any study of the Revolution, especially in the South. John Eager Howard was an accomplished army officer, a conscientious political leader, and that rare public personage in American history who maintained an untarnished reputation throughout his life and after his death. This member of the founding generation deserves the recognition that he earned over a lifetime of service to his city, state, and nation. As the writer who composed Howard's obituary observed, "the example of such a citizen is a legacy to his country, of more worth than the precepts of an age."[3]

---

1   Rev. J. D. Bailey, *Some Heroes of the American Revolution* (Spartanburg, SC: Band & White, 1924), 43 (quotation); Archives of Maryland, Session Laws, 1827 Session, Vol. 474, 308-09 (quotation).
2   *Baltimore Sun*, Jan. 17, 1904; Daniel Coit Gilman, *The Launching of a University and Other Papers: A Sheaf of Remembrances* (New York: Dodd, Mead & Co., 1906), 381, 386 (quotation).
3   *Baltimore Gazette*, Oct. 15, 1827.

BIBLIOGRAPHY

Primary Sources – Manuscripts

Archives of Maryland. Early State Records. Maryland State Archives, Annapolis.

Bayard Family. Papers. Maryland Historical Society (hereafter MHS), Baltimore.

Chew Family. Papers. Historical Society of Pennsylvania, Philadelphia.

Continental Congress. Papers, 1774-1789. Microfilm.

Cornwallis, Charles, Earl. Papers. PRO 30/11. Microfilm

Documents from the Continental Congress and the Constitutional Convention, 1774-1789. Library of Congress, Washington, DC.

Draper, Lyman C. Manuscript Collection. Microfilm.

Genealogy – McHenry Howard. Manuscript G-5087, MHS.

Germain, Lord George. Papers. William L. Clements Library, Ann Arbor, MI.

Harper-Pennington Family. Papers. MHS.

Howard, Benjamin Chew. "Colonel John Eager Howard of Maryland." Unpublished biography. Society of the Cincinnati Library, Washington, DC.

Howard, Cornelius. Last Will and Testament. Baltimore County, MD, Register of Wills.

Journal of the Senate of the United States. Library of Congress.

Journals of the Continental Congress. Library of Congress.

Maryland House of Delegates Session Laws, 1827. Maryland State Archives.

Maryland Senate Journals. Maryland State Archives.

Revolutionary War Collection. MHS.

Lee Family. Papers. Robert E. Lee Memorial Association, Stratford Hall, VA.

Smallwood, William. Papers. MHS.

Valley Forge Muster Roll,
http://valleyforgemusterroll.org/ContinentalArmy/TheRegiments/4thMD. Accessed May 15, 2006.

Washington, George. Papers and Diary. Library of Congress.

Williams, Otho Holland. Papers. MHS.

Primary Sources – Published

Adams, John Quincy. *The Diary of John Quincy Adams, 1794-1845*. New York: Longmans, Green and Co., 1929.

Archives of Maryland. Vol. 11. Edited by William Browne. Baltimore: Maryland Historical Society, 1892. Vol. 18, Baltimore: Maryland Historical Society, 1900. Vol. 78, Baltimore: James Lucas & E. K. Deaver, 1836.

Beatty, William. "Journal of Capt. William Beatty. 1776-1781." *Maryland Historical Magazine* 3 (June 1908), 104-19.

"Civilian Defense in Baltimore, 1814-1815: Minutes of the Committee of Vigilance and Safety." Edited by William D. Hoyt, Jr. *Maryland Historical Magazine* 39 (Sept 1944):293-09.

Clinton, Henry. *The American Rebellion. Sir Henry Clinton's Narrative of His Campaigns, 1775-1782, With an Appendix of Original Documents*. Edited by William B. Willcox. New Haven: Yale University Press, 1954.

Collins, James P. *Autobiography of a Revolutionary Soldier*. Edited by John M. Roberts. Clinton, LA: Feliciana Democrat Print, 1859.

Dann, John C., editor. *The Revolution Remembered: Eyewitness Accounts of the War for Independence*. Chicago: University of Chicago Press, 1980.

Davies, K. G. editor. *Documents of the American Revolution*. Vol. 20. Dublin: Irish University Press, 1979.

Gibbes, Robert W., editor. *Documentary History of the American Revolution, Consisting of Letters and Papers relating to the Contest for Liberty Chiefly in South Carolina*. Vol. 3. New York: D. Appleton & Co., 1857.

Greene, Nathanael. *The Papers of General Nathanael Greene*. Vols. 1, 2, 6. Edited by Richard K. Showman. Vol. 7. Edited by Richard K. Showman and Dennis M. Conrad. Vols. 8, 9. Edited by Dennis M. Conrad. Chapel Hill: University of North Carolina Press, 1976-1997.

Hanson, Alexander Contee, editor. *Laws of Maryland, made since 1763, consisting of acts of Assembly under the proprietary government, resolves of convention, the Declaration of rights, the constitution and form of government, the Articles of confederation, and, acts of Assembly since the revolution*. Vol. 203. Annapolis, MD: Frederick Green, 1787.

Howard, John Eager. "Colonel John Eager Howard's Account of the Battle of Germantown." Edited by Justin Windsor. *Maryland Historical Magazine* 4 (Dec. 1909): 314-20.

Journals of the Continental Congress, 1774-1789. Washington: US Government Printing Office, 34 Vols., 1904-1937.

Kirkwood, Robert. "The Journal and Order Book of Captain Robert Kirkwood of the Delaware Regiment of the Continental Line." In *Papers of the Historical Society of Delaware*, Vol. 56. Wilmington: Historical Society of Delaware, 1910.

Land, Aubrey C., editor. *Journal and Correspondence of the Council of Maryland, 1784-1789*. Baltimore: Maryland Historical Society, 1970.

Laws of Maryland Made and Passed at a Session of Assembly, Begun and held at the city of Annapolis, on Monday the third of November, 1788. Annapolis: Frederick Green, [c. 1789]. *Laws of Maryland Made and Passed at a Session of Assembly ... 1789. Laws of Maryland Made and Passed at a Session of Assembly ... 1790*. Annapolis: Frederick Green, [c. 1789-1791].

Lee, Henry. *The Revolutionary War Memoirs of General Henry Lee*. Edited by Robert E. Lee. New York: Da Capo Press, reprint edition, 1998.

Lee, Thomas Sim. "Governor Thomas Sim Lee's Correspondence, 1779-1782." Edited by Helen Lee Peabody. *Maryland Historical Magazine* 46 (March 1955): 33-46.

O'Hara, Charles. "Letters of Charles O'Hara to the Duke of Grafton." Edited by George C. Rogers, Jr. *South Carolina Historical Magazine* 65 (July 1964): 158-80.

Pindell, Richard. "A Militant Surgeon of the Revolution: Some Letters of Richard Pindell, M. D." *Maryland Historical Magazine* 18 (Dec. 1923): 309-23.

Reamy, Bill and Martha, editors. *Records of St. Paul's Parish*. Westminster, MD: Family Line Publications, 1988.

----------. *St. Thomas's Parish Registers, 1732-1850*. Silver Spring, MD: Family Line Publications, 1987.

Saffell, W. T. R., editor. *Records of the Revolutionary War, containing the Military and Financial Correspondence of Distinguished Officers*. Philadelphia: G. G. Evans, 1858.

Smith, Paul H., editor. *Letters of Delegates to Congress, 1774-1789*. Washington: Library of Congress, 26 Vols., 1976-2000.

Seymour, William. "A Journal of the Southern Expedition, 1780-1783." In *Papers of the Historical Society of Delaware*, Vol. 15. Wilmington: Historical Society of Delaware, 1896.

Tarleton, Banastre. *A History of the Campaigns of 1780 and 1781, in the Southern Provinces of North America*. London: T. Cadell, 1787.

Votes and Proceedings of the House of Delegates of the State of Maryland, June Session, 1809. Maryland State Archives.

Votes and Proceedings of the Senate of the State of Maryland. 1791-1796. Maryland State Archives.

Washington, George. *The Diaries of George Washington*. Edited by Donald Jackson and Dorothy Twohig. Vol. 6. Charlottesville: University Press of Virginia, 1979.

Weedon, George. *Valley Forge Orderly Book of General George Weedon.* New York: The New York Times, 1972.

Young, Thomas. "Memoirs of Major Thomas Young." *The Orion* 3 (October 1843):84-105.

Newspapers and Pamphlets

Baltimore Gazette. Oct. 15, 1827.

Baltimore Patriot & Mercantile Advertiser. May-Oct., 1824.

Baltimore Sun. Jan. 17, 1904.

A Memoir of the Late Col. John Eager Howard reprinted from the Baltimore Gazette *of Monday, October 15th, 1827.* Baltimore: Kelly, Hedian, & Piet, 1863.

Memorial of the Semi-Centennial Anniversary of the American Colonization Society, Celebrated at Washington, January 15, 1867: With Documents Concerning Liberia. Washington: American Colonization Society, 1867.

Niles' Weekly Register. Oct. 20, 1822.

Register of the Society of the Cincinnati of Maryland brought down to February 22nd, 1897. Baltimore: Society of the Cincinnati of Maryland, 1897.

Secondary Sources

Alden, John Richard. *The South in the Revolution, 1763-1789.* Baton Rouge: Louisiana State University Press, 1957.

Allen, Rev. Ethan. *The Garrison Church. Sketches of the History of St. Thomas Parish, Garrison Forest, Baltimore County, Md.* Edited by the Rev. Hobart Smith. New York: J. Pott & Co., 1898.

Ammerman, David. *In the Common Cause: American Response to the Coercive Acts of 1774.* New York: Norton, 1975.

Babits, Lawrence E. *"A Devil of a Whipping": The Battle of Cowpens*. Chapel Hill: University of North Carolina Press, 1988.

Bailey, Rev. J. D. *Some Heroes of the American Revolution*. Spartanburg, SC: Band & White, 1904.

Ballard, Margaret Byrnside. *A University is Born*. Union, WV: Old Hundred Union, 1965.

Barnes, Robert. *The Greenspring Valley: Its History and Heritage. Volume 2: Genealogies*. Baltimore: Maryland Historical Society, 1978.

Bass, Robert D. *Ninety Six: The Struggle for the South Carolina Back Country*. Lexington, SC: Sandlapper, 1978.

Beirne, Francis F. *St. Paul's Parish, Baltimore: The Chronicle of the Mother Church*. Baltimore: Horn-Shafer, 1967.

----------. *The Amiable Baltimoreans*. New York: Dutton, 1951.

Bicheno, Hugh. *Rebels & Redcoats: The American Revolutionary War*. London: HarperCollins, 2003.

Bilias, George Athan, editor. *George Washington's Generals and Opponents: Their Exploits and Leadership*. New York: Da Capo Press, 1994.

Boles, John, editor. *Maryland Heritage: Five Baltimore Institutions Celebrate the American Bicentennial*. Baltimore: Maryland Historical Society, 1976.

Buchanan, John. *The Road to Guilford Courthouse: The American Revolution in the Carolinas*. New York: John Wiley & Sons, 1997.

Culver, Francis B. "The Chew Family." *Maryland Historical Magazine* 30 (June, 1935): 159-75.

Davis, Burke. *The Cowpens-Guilford Courthouse Campaign*. Philadelphia: Lippincott, 1962.

Enholm, David, David Skaggs, and W. Jeffrey Welsh. "Origins of the Southern Mind: The Parochial Sermons of Thomas Cradock of Maryland, 1744-1770." *Quarterly Journal of Speech* 73 (May 1987): 200-18.

Ernst, Robert. *Rufus King: American Federalist*. Chapel Hill: University of North Carolina Press, 1968.

Evans, Henry Ridgely. *Progenitors of the Howards of Maryland*. Baltimore: Evans, 1938.

Flexner, James Thomas. *George Washington: The Forge of Experience, 1732-1775*. Boston: Little, Brown, 1965.

Flood, Charles Bracelen. *Rise, and Fight Again: Perilous Times Along the Road to Independence*. New York: Dodd, Mead & Co., 1976.

Gilman, Daniel Coit. *The Launching of a University and Other Papers: A Sheaf of Remembrances*. New York: Dodd, Mead & Co., 1906.

Golway, Terry. *Washington's General: Nathanael Greene and the Triumph of the American Revolution*. New York: Henry Holt and Co., 2005.

Gordon, John W. *South Carolina and the American Revolution: A Battlefield History*. Columbia: University of South Carolina Press, 2003.

Greene, George Washington. *Historical View of the American Revolution*. New York: Hurd & Houghton, 1876.

----------. *The Life of Nathanael Greene, Major-General in the Army of the Revolution*. Vol. 3. New York: Hurd and Houghton, 1871.

Gunby, A. A. *Colonel John Gunby of the Maryland Line: Being Some Account of his Contribution to American Liberty*. Cincinnati, OH: R. Clarke, 1902.

Haller, Stephen E. *William Washington, Cavalryman of the Revolution*. Bowie, MD: Heritage Books, 2001.

Hanson, George A. *Old Kent: The Eastern Shore of Maryland. Notes Illustrative of the Most Ancient Records of Kent County, Maryland*. Baltimore: J. P. Des Forges, 1876.

Higginbotham, Don. *Daniel Morgan, Revolutionary Rifleman*. Chapel Hill: University of   North Carolina Press, 1961.

----------. *The War of American Independence: Military Attitudes, Policies, and Practice, 1763-1789.* New York: Macmillan, 1971.

Howard, Cary. "John Eager Howard: Patriot and Public Servant." *Maryland Historical Magazine* 62 (Sept. 1967): 300-17.

Huttenhauer, Helen G. and G. Alfred Helwig. *Baltimore County in the State and Nation.* Towson, MD: Board of Education of Baltimore County, 1957.

Jacob, John J. *A Biographical Sketch of the Life of the Late Captain Michael Cresap.* Cincinnati, OH: J. F. Uhlhorn, 1866.

"John Eager Howard (1752-1827, Governor of Maryland, 1788-1791." Archives of Maryland (Biographical Series). Maryland State Archives.

Johnson, William. *Sketches of the Life and Correspondence of Nathanael Greene, Major General of the Armies of the United States in the War of the Revolution.* 2 Vols. Charleston, SC: A. E. Miller, 1822.

Konkle, Burton Alva. *Benjamin Chew, 1722-1810: Head of the Pennsylvania Judiciary System under Colony and Commonwealth.* Philadelphia: University of Pennsylvania Press, 1932.

Konstam, Angus. *Guilford Court House 1781: Lord Cornwallis's Ruinous Victory.* Westport, CT: Praeger Publishers, 2004.

Land, Aubrey C. *Colonial Maryland: A History.* Millwood, NY: KTO Press, 1981.

Layman, Joyce. "The Cradock Tradition of Service." *History Trails* 20 (Autumn 1985): 1-4.

Mackesy, Piers. *The War for America, 1775-1783.* Lincoln: University of Nebraska Press, 1993.

McCullough, David. *John Adams.* New York: Simon and Schuster, 2001.

McGuire, Thomas J. *The Philadelphia Campaign: Germantown and the Roads to Valley Forge.* Mechanicsburg, PA: Stackpole Books, 2007.

Morison, Samuel Eliot. *The Oxford History of the American People.* New York: Oxford University Press, 1965.

Morrill, Dan L. *Southern Campaigns of the American Revolution*. Baltimore: Nautical & Aviation Publishing, 1993.

Myers, Theodorus Bailey. *One Hundred Years Ago. The Story of the Battle of Cowpens*. Charleston, SC: News & Courier, 1881.

Nelson, Paul David. *Horatio Gates: A Biography*. Baton Rouge: Lousiana State University Press, 1976.

"An Old Baltimore Mansion." Author unknown. *Appleton's Journal* 12 (Dec. 26, 1874): 801-03.

Owens, Hamilton. *Baltimore on the Chesapeake*. Garden City, NY: Doubleday, Doran and Co., 1941.

Pancake, John S. *This Destructive War: The British Campaign in the Carolinas, 1780-1782*. University: University of Alabama Press, 1985.

Papenfuse, Edward C., Alan F. Day, David W. Jordan, and Gregory A. Stiverson. *A Biographical Dictionary of the Maryland Legislature, 1635-1789*. Vol. 1. (Baltimore: The Johns Hopkins University Press, 1979.

Peckham, Howard H. *The War for Independence: A Military History*. Chicago: University of Chicago Press, 1958.

Peden, Henry C. *Revolutionary War Patriots of Baltimore Town and Baltimore County, 1775-1783*. Silver Spring, MD: Family Line Publications, 1988.

Piecuch, Jim. *The Battle of Camden: A Documentary History*. Charleston, SC: The History Press, 2006.

----------. *Three Peoples, One King: Loyalists, Indians, and Slaves in the Revolutionary South, 1775-1782*. Columbia: University of South Carolina Press, 2008.

Read, Elizabeth. "The Howards of Maryland." *Magazine of American History* 3 (April 1879): 239-49.

----------. "John Eager Howard, Colonel of the Second Maryland Regiment." *Magazine of American History* 7 (Oct. 1881): 276-82.

Rice, Laura. *Maryland History in Prints*. Baltimore: Maryland Historical Society, 2002

Royster, Charles. *A Revolutionary People at War: The Continental Army and American Character, 1775-1783*. New York: W. W. Norton, 1979.

Scharf, Thomas J. *The Chronicles of Baltimore. Being a Complete History of Baltimore Town and Baltimore City from the Earliest Time to the Present Day*. Baltimore: Turnbull Brothers, 1874.

Schaun, George and Virginia. *Everyday Life in Colonial Maryland*. Lanham: Maryland Historical Press, 1996.

Sherwood, Henry Noble. "The Formation of the American Colonization Society." *Journal of Negro History* 2 (July 1917): 209-28.

Sioussat, Annie Leakin. *Old Baltimore*. New York: Macmillan, 1931.

Smith, Page. *John Adams*. 2 Vols. Garden City, NY: Doubleday, 1962

Smith, Samuel S. *The Battle of Monmouth*. Trenton: New Jersey Historical Commission, 1975.

Stein, Charles Francis, Jr. *Origin and History of Howard County, Maryland*. Baltimore: Howard County Historical Society, 1972.

Steuart, Rieman. *A History of the Maryland Line in the Revolutionary War, 1775-1783*. Baltimore: Society of the Cincinnati of Maryland, 1969.

Stevens, John Austin. "The Southern Campaign, 1780: Gates at Camden." *Magazine of American History* 5 (Oct. 1880): 241-320.

Symonds, Craig L. *A Battlefield Atlas of the American Revolution*. [Annapolis, MD]: Nautical & Aviation Publishing Co., 1986.

Thomas, Dawn F. *The Greenspring Valley: Its History and Heritage. Volume One: A History*. Baltimore: Maryland Historical Society, 1978.

Treacy, M. F. *Prelude to Yorktown: The Southern Campaign of Nathanael Greene, 1780-1781*. Chapel Hill: University of North Carolina Press, 1963.

Walsh, Richard, and William Lloyd Fox, editors. *Maryland: A History, 1632-1974*. Baltimore: Maryland Historical Society, 1974.

White, Frank F., Jr. "The Governors of Maryland, 1777-1970." Archives of Maryland (Biographical Series). Maryland State Archives.

Wright, Robert K., Jr. *The Continental Army*. Washington, DC: US Army Center of Military History, 2000.

INDEX

Adams, John, 138, 139, 140, 143
Adams, John Quincy, 7, 143
Alien and Sedition Acts, 139-40
American Colonization Society, 141
Anderson, Capt. Richard, 64
Anderson, Thomas, 85
Andre, Maj. John, 134
Armand, Col. Charles, 39
Armstrong, Gen. John, 17
Arnold, Gen. Benedict, 134
Augusta, Georgia, American capture of, 116
Balfour, Lt. Col. Nisbet, 100, 114, 115
Beall, Gen. Rezin, 12
Beatty, Capt. William, 23, 104, 105, 106
Belvidere (Howard estate), 7, 134, 136
Bennington, Battle of, 22
Boston Tea Party, 9
Brandywine, Battle of, 16-17
Brooklyn Heights, Battle of, 12-13
Browne, Dr. James, 128
Bryan, Col. Samuel, 40, 41
Buford, Col. Abraham, 32
Burgoyne, Gen. John, 22
Burr, Aaron, 8
Butler, Gen. John, 86
Camden, South Carolina, 35, 36, 37, 49, 95, 99, 100
  Battle of, 39-43, 47, 59, 61, 86
  British evacuation of, 109
Campbell, Lt. Col. Richard, 102, 118, 123, 126
Campbell, Col. William, 85, 86, 87, 88, 92
Carrington, Lt. Col. Edward, 52, 73, 77
Carroll, Charles,, 134, 143
Caswell, Gen. Richard, 35, 36, 37, 39, 40-41
Charleston, South Carolina, 2
  British capture of, 31-32
Chase, Samuel, 134
Cherokee Indians, 31, 33, 44
Chew, Benjamin, Jr., 7, 135

Chew, Benjamin, Sr., 20, 134, 137
Chitty, Capt. C. K., 58
Clarke, Col. Elijah, 116
Clinton, Gen. Sir Henry, 24-25, 31, 32, 55, 99, 101
Coffin, Maj. John, 102, 103, 105, 122, 123, 125, 126, 127
Collins, James, 60, 61
Continental Congress, 10, 11, 14, 17, 25, 32, 36, 43-44, 47, 50, 70, 129, 135, 136
Cornwallis, Gen. Charles, Earl, 16, 32, 36-37, 43, 44, 45, 48, 49, 52, 54, 55-57, 61, 65, 69, 70, 71-72, 73-75, 76, 77-78, 79, 81-82, 83, 84, 85, 94, 99-100, 106, 128
  at Battle of Camden, 39-42
  at Battle of Guilford Courthouse, 87-93
Cowpens, Battle of, 4, 61-65, 69-70, 86
Cradock, John, 9, 12
Cradock, Rev. Thomas, 8
Cradock, Thomas, Jr., 9, 129, 134
Craig, Maj. James, 94
Creek Indians, 31, 33
Cruger, Lt. Col. John Harris, 115, 116, 117, 122-23, 125, 127
Davidson, Gen. William, 49, 54, 73-74
Davie, Col. William R., 43, 52
De Buy, Maj., 92
Declaration of Independence, 10
Dixon, Col. Henry, 40
Dorsey, Capt. Daniel, 19, 21
Duffey, Capt.-Lt. Patrick, 22-23
Duncanson, Capt., 64
Eaton, Gen. Thomas, 86, 88
Eutaw Springs, Battle of, 122-28
Ferguson, Maj. Patrick, 44-45, 49, 54
Fleury, Marquis de, 24
flying camp, 11-12, 13-14
Ford, Lt. Col. Benjamin, 26, 102, 104, 105
Fort Granby, 113-114
Fort Motte, 108, 113

161

INDEX

Fort Washington, 13
Fort Watson, 99, 108, 116
Fox, Charles James, 93
Gates, Gen. Horatio, 22, 35-36, 44, 45, 47-49, 50-51, 95
  at Battle of Camden, 39-43
Germain, Lord George, 31
Germantown, Battle of, 1-2, 17-22, 125
Giles, Maj. Edward, 69
Gilman, Daniel, 147
Gist, Gen. Mordecai, 9, 18, 21, 32, 44, 134
  at Battle of Camden, 39, 41, 42, 43
Gray, Col. Robert, 48
Green, Col. John, 92
Greene, Gen. Nathanael, 3, 6, 13, 14, 18, 54, 55, 56-58, 65, 69, 72-73, 74, 75, 76-77, 78, 79, 81, 83, 84, 94-95, 99, 100-01, 106-09, 113, 114, 119, 121, 122, 129
  at Battle of Germantown, 20-21
  takes command in South, 50-52
  at Battle of Guilford Courthouse, 85-93
  at Battle of Hobkirk's Hill, 102-05
  at Siege of Ninety Six, 115-18
  at Battle of Eutaw Springs, 123-28
Guilford Courthouse, Battle of, 85-93, 105, 107
Gunby, Col. John, 43, 86, 87, 90-91, 93, 106, 107-08
  at Battle of Hobkirk's Hill, 102, 104, 105
Hall, Col. Josias Carvil, 12, 14, 15, 19, 26
Hamilton, Alexander, 8
Hammond, Col. Samuel, 62
Hampton, Col. Wade, 123, 124
Hardman, Maj. Henry, 124
Harrison, Col. Charles, 106
Hawes, Lt. Col. Samuel, 102, 104
Hazen, Col. Moses, 18, 19, 20
Henderson, Lt. Col. William, 121, 122, 123, 124, 127, 128
Hill, Col. William, 58
Hobkirk's Hill, Battle of, 101-05
Howard, Charles, 144
Howard, Cornelius, 15-16
Howard, Cornelius Jr., 9
Howard, George, 143

Howard, James, 128
Howard, John Beale, 9
Howard, John Eager, 1, 3-4, 5, 6, 7, 8, 15, 16, 17, 23, 24, 25, 26, 27, 35, 36, 37, 44, 45, 48, 50, 51, 52, 54, 56, 58-59, 60, 70-71, 73, 74, 75-76, 77, 78, 79, 81, 84-85, 95, 99, 106-07, 109, 113, 114, 118, 119, 128, 129, 133-37, 141-44, 147-48
  joins Revolutionary movement, 9-10
  in New York campaign, 12, 13, 14
  at Battle of Germantown, 18-22
  sent to the South, 32-34
  at Battle of Camden, 39, 41-43
  at Battle of Cowpens, 61-65
  at Battle of Guilford Courthouse, 86-93
  at Battle of Hobkirk's Hill, 102-04
  at Siege of Ninety Six, 115, 116, 117
  at Battle of Eutaw Springs, 122, 124-27
  U.S. Senator, 138-40
Howard, John Eager, Jr., 136, 142
Howard, Margaret (Peggy) Chew, 129, 134, 136, 143
Howard, Ruth Eager, 16
Howard, Violetta, 12
Howe, Gen. Sir William, 11, 12, 13, 14, 15, 16, 17, 18, 19, 21, 22, 24, 134
Huger, Gen. Isaac, 72-73, 74, 86, 90, 92, 102, 106
Hyde, Lt. Col. William, 12
Jacob, John J., 42, 43
Jefferson, Thomas, 70, 139, 140, 143
Kalb, Gen. Baron Johann de, 1, 2, 32, 35, 95
  at Battle of Camden, 39-42
Kemp, Bishop James, 135
Kings Mountain, Battle of, 44-45, 49, 54, 55
Kirkwood, Capt. Robert, 43, 50, 86, 88, 89, 90, 100, 101, 102, 105, 118, 123, 126, 127
Knox, Gen. Henry, 6, 20, 125
Kosciuszko, Col. Tadeusz, 52, 115
Lafayette, Marquis de, 1, 6, 32, 143
Lawson, Gen. Robert, 86, 89
Lee, Gen. Charles, 13, 14, 25

Lee, Lt. Col. Henry, 4, 8, 15, 34, 42, 58, 73, 75, 76, 77, 78-79, 81, 83-84, 85, 94, 99, 107, 108, 113-14, 116, 118, 119, 137, 140, 142
  at Battle of Guilford Courthouse, 86-88, 92, 93
  at Battle of Eutaw Springs, 122, 123, 125, 126
Leslie, Gen. Alexander, 55, 57, 71
  at Battle of Guilford Courthouse, 87-89, 92
Lexington and Concord, Battles of, 9, 11
Lincoln, Gen. Benjamin, 1, 32, 36
Lloyd, James, 139
Loyalists, 31, 34, 36, 40, 43, 44-45, 48, 50, 54, 57, 60, 61, 73, 79, 82-84, 94, 100, 102, 108-09, 114, 115, 117, 123, 125
Lux, George, 24
Lynch, Col. Charles, 86, 88, 89
Madison, James, 141, 142
Maham, Col. Hezekiah, 116
Malmedy, Marquis de, 122, 123
Marbury, Capt. Joseph, 75
Marion, Gen. Francis, 4, 32, 37, 99, 101, 108, 113, 114, 121, 123, 124, 125
Marjoribanks, Maj. John, 123, 124, 125, 126, 127
Martin, Gov. Josiah, 82
Maxwell, Maj. Andrew, 113
McArthur, Maj. Archibald, 62, 63, 65
McHenry, James, 139
McHenry, John, 142
McHenry, Juliana Howard, 142
McLeod, Lt. John, 91
McLure, John, 9
Monmouth, Battle of, 25
Morgan, Gen. Daniel, 4, 22, 47-48, 49, 50, 52, 54-61, 69, 70-71, 72, 73, 74, 75-76, 78, 86, 95
  at Battle of Cowpens, 61-65
Motte, Rebecca, 113
Musgrave, Col. Thomas, 20
Nash, Gov. Abner, 83
New York Campaign, 11-13
Ninety Six, Siege of, 114-18
Norwood, Capt. Edward, 25

O'Hara, Gen. Charles, 73, 74
  at Battle of Guilford Courthouse, 87, 90, 91, 93
Oldham, Capt. Edward, 83
Philadelphia
  British capture of, 17
  British evacuation of, 24-25
Phillips, Gen William, 72, 99
Pickens, Col. Andrew, 54, 59, 60, 70, 71, 83-84, 85, 116, 121, 123, 124
Pickering, Timothy, 20, 137
Pinckney, Maj. Thomas, 37, 40
Pindell, Dr. Richard, 126, 135
Polk, Col. Thomas, 51, 52
Princeton, Battle of, 15
Putnam, Gen. Israel, 12
Pyle, Dr. John, 83-84
Radley, Sgt. John, 119
Rawdon, Lt. Col. Francis, Lord, 36-37, 49, 99, 100, 101-02, 107, 108-09, 113, 114-15, 116, 117-18, 119, 121
  at Battle of Camden, 40, 41
  at Battle of Hobkirk's Hill, 102-05
Read, Col. James, 102
Read, Dr. William, 127
Rochambeau, Comte de, 128
Rugeley, Henry, 37, 50
Rutledge, Gov. John, 57
St. Clair, Gen. Arthr, 27
Saratoga, Battle of, 22, 24, 35, 47
Savannah, Georgia, operations at, 31
Senf, Col. John Christian, 37, 40
Seymour, Sgt. William, 78, 100, 103, 122
Sheridan, Maj. Henry, 125, 127
Singleton, Capt. Anthony, 88
Slaves, 31, 102, 115, 116
Smallwood, Gen. William, 11, 12, 13, 17, 18, 21, 24, 26, 27, 32, 43-44, 51-52, 129, 134, 136
  at Battle of Camden, 39, 40, 41, 42
Smith, Mary, 133
Smith, Lt. Col. Samuel, 19, 26, 134, 140, 143
Society of the Cincinnati, 135
Southern Theater, conditions, 33-35

Stamp Act, 8, 10
Stedman, Charles, 82
Stephens, Gen. Adam, 21
Steuben, Gen. Baron Friedrich von, 3, 23-24, 31
Stevens, Gen. Edward, 37, 39, 40, 72, 86, 89
Stewart, Lt. Col. Alexander, 121-22, 123, 124, 125, 126, 127-28
Stone, Col. John Hawkins, 18
Stuart, Lt. Col. James, 90, 91, 93
Sullivan, Gen. John, 18-19, 20, 21
Sumner, Gen. Jethro, 123, 124
Sumter, Gen. Thomas, 4, 32, 36, 37, 43, 49, 57-58, 95100, 101, 107, 113, 117-18
Tarleton, Lt. Col. Banastre, 43, 55, 56, 57, 58, 59, 69, 71, 74, 75, 78, 82-83, 84, 85, 94
  at Battle of Camden, 39, 41
  at Battle of Cowpens, 60-65
  at Battle of Guilford Courthouse, 87, 90, 91, 92
Thomas, Evan, 143
Townshend Acts, 9
Tramell, Capt. Dennis, 58
Trenton, Battle of, 15
Triplett, Maj. Francis, 72
Wallace, Capt. Andrew, 62
War of 1812, 141-42

Washington, Gen. George, 1, 2-3, 5, 6, 11, 12, 13, 14, 15, 16, 17, 18, 20, 21, 22, 23, 24, 25, 27, 31, 32, 35, 36, 47, 48, 50, 70, 128, 129, 134, 136, 137, 138, 139, 140
Washington, Lt. Col. William, 48, 49, 50, 52, 54, 55, 58, 59, 69, 70, 73, 76, 77, 84, 85, 101, 106, 107, 117
  at Battle of Cowpens, 61-62, 64
  at Battle of Guilford Courthouse, 86, 91-92, 93
  at Battle of Hobkirk's Hill, 102-05
  at Battle of Eutaw Springs, 123, 126-27
Waters, Col. Thomas, 55
Watson, Lt. Col. John, 101, 108
Wayne, Gen. Anthony, 18, 19, 20-21, 47
Webster, Lt. Col. James, 85
  at Battle of Camden, 39, 40, 41
  at Battle of Guilford Courthouse, 87-90, 92, 93
Wemyss, Maj. James, 121
Whiskey Rebellion, 137
White Plains, Battle of, 13
Williams, Col. Otho Holland, 26, 34, 35, 36, 37, 40, 42, 43, 44, 45, 69, 75, 76, 77, 78, 84-85, 86, 102, 105, 107, 116, 123, 127, 129, 133, 134
Wilmington, North Carolina, 94
Woodford, Gen. William, 47
Young, Thomas, 58, 59-60, 61, 62

www.ingramcontent.com/pod-product-compliance
Lightning Source LLC
Chambersburg PA
CBHW072134160426
43197CB00012B/2104